CONTENTS

Introduction To A New Puppy

Owning a puppy is a wonderful experience if you are prepared to love and care for your pet, but please never take this decision lightly. Be realistic, and ask honest, personal questions. If it goes wrong, there will be heartbreak ahead for you and your puppy. *What Puppy?* offers useful information to help prospective owners think about what having a puppy involves, and advises on how to choose the right puppy for them, their family, and their circumstances.

Why do you want a puppy?

Humans choose dogs as friends and companions because they offer unconditional love. Dogs ask only for companionship, exercise, and food. They come in all shapes, sizes, and coat types: small, medium, large, and giant-sized, smooth- or long-coated. And they have so many individual attributes that it is difficult to decide which puppy will suit you. So it is important to be clear before buying one: Why do you want a dog?

- As companion or playmate?
- As a guard dog?
- For exercise and improving your health?
- For enjoying shows, competitions, or walking companionship?
- Fulfilment of a childhood wish?
- Need for a working dog?
- To get out and about socially?

What kind of puppy do you want?

The choice of a puppy should focus on which breed or variety suits your lifestyle. With so many pedigree breeds, designer dog crosses, and mixed breeds available, careful selection to match your circumstances is essential. Some breeds need more walking, for others

training is paramount, and some need time-consuming grooming and involvement in activities. Puppies demand lots of time and attention during the first two years of their life for housetraining, obedience training, socializing and grooming so that they become well-behaved members of the community and not a walking liability.

Think about:

- How much time do you have?
- Would your puppy be home alone?
- Is there enough space?
- Time and frequency needed for daily exercise?
- Is there a yard or open space nearby?
- Cost of food and equipping a home for an adult dog
- How much time is there for grooming and training?
- Will your puppy have a home for life?

If you cannot contemplate positive answers to these questions, please ask yourself:

Should I really have a puppy?

What kind of puppy will suit your circumstances?

If you decide that you can commit to a puppy for life, think what your main considerations are when choosing a puppy to join your family. The table on page 5 may help you to decide what dog would best suit your lifestyle.

Can puppy come on vacation?

Puppies cannot go into kennels under six months old, so you will have to take the puppy with you, providing you are not traveling abroad. Or you'll have to ask someone to look after him. Older puppies can be left in boarding kennels but need current inoculations. You can use house sitters, but that will probably be more expensive than kennels.

POINTS TO BE CONSIDERED WHEN SELECTING YOUR PUPPY

Pedigree Dog
- Size and nature will be apparent
- Health may need more attention
- Breed features are known
- Characteristics are predictable
- Knowledgeable breeders are involved
- Increased costs

Designer or Mixed-Breed Dog
- Unknown origin or two combined breeds
- Usually healthy (but not always)
- Individual features appear on dog
- Character may be difficult to determine
- Limited background information
- May or may not be within budget

Large Dog
- Will need plenty of space
- Will need plenty of exercise
- Higher fencing may be essential
- Unsuitable for changing circumstances
- May have dominant natural behaviors
- Less likely to cause trips or falls
- Food costly and storage more problematic
- More 'poo' to pick up and dispose of

Small Dog
- Less space needed
- Exercise level comparable to size
- Limited or average containment needed
- Will be easier if circumstances change
- More manageable natural behaviors
- May not suit active family life
- Economical to feed
- Less 'poo' to pick up and dispose of

Male Dog
- May be stronger or more dominant
- May seek female company
- Marks own territory
- More inclined to guard the home

Female Dog
- Some breeds may be more submissive with children
- Season occurs at regular intervals
- Urine burns the grass
- Possibly less territorial

Long Coat
- Long grooming sessions often needed
- Skill may be needed for trimming
- More effort to bath the dog
- More dirt brought into home
- May need cleaning after toileting

Short Coat
- Only occasional brushing needed
- Occasional bathing only
- Cleaner with respect to dirt in the home
- May shed more copiously than long coat

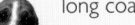

● *Dogs come in all shapes and sizes, and suit a lot of different purposes. With so many available, it can be difficult to choose.*

Selecting Your Puppy

Most breed standards tell you what you can expect from specific breeds. Generally, every puppy has potential to be a good or a bad puppy, but the outcome depends very much on how the puppy was bred, socialized, and trained; how the owner raises him; and any other environmental influences.

Buying from a reputable pedigree dog breeder

Never buy from puppy mill breeders. Their puppies are not always purebred, and many are raised in poor surroundings or suffer poor health. Good breeders explain their breed to new owners and provide advice on care, feeding, health matters, socializing, training, and grooming. Owners should not be left alone to learn about caring for their puppy. These are key points you want to cover when choosing a breeder or a puppy from a good kennel.

- The breeder gives advice on the breed, health matters, and preparing to take your puppy home.
- The litter looks happy, healthy, well fed, clean, and wormed.
- Appropriate paperwork is available for the puppy.
- Puppies are well socialized.
- Dams, and possibly sires, are available to inspect.
- Puppies' living area is light, airy, and clean.
- Puppies are leaving their birth home for their owners.
- Puppies bought for a specific reason, e.g. showing, are suitable for that purpose.

Choosing a designer breed

Remember, designer breeds are "cross breeds" not pedigrees, and have no registration papers. Some designer breeds are available from trustworthy breeders, some are not. Many designer breeds are advertised as being healthier than their parent breeds, but this is not always the case. For instance, research shows that the incidence of eye problems in Labradoodles is higher than in the parent breeds. Ask breeders for evidence that they have checked this, and ask to see health certificates for both parents. Non-shedding coats are determined by genetic inheritance and the generation level that is reached after first crosses, so check how many puppies bred previously have actually been non-shedding.

Choosing an older or rescue dog

There are many sources for buying rescue dogs. Reputable charities often deal with rehoming and may check owners' homes to ensure that puppies only go to appropriate long-term homes. Retired breeding dogs, Greyhounds, and abandoned dogs and puppies are often available, but they may have no history, so get to know their temperament before making a decision. It is important to know the dog's estimated age, and about any problems that may appear later, or potential health problems that may cause increased costs.

BREED TYPES AND THEIR TRAITS

Breed group	Family suitability	Natural behavior
SPORTING e.g. Retrievers, Setters, Spaniels	Good temperaments, calmer demeanor, often easier to train, child friendly, some need plenty of exercise, enjoy family life. Most popular breed group.	Hunting, training, good companions, take part in many canine activities.
HOUNDS e.g. Dachshund, Elkhound	Various sizes, friendly, some gentle breeds suitable for most families.	Natural scenting or sight abilities, fast runners, and need plenty of exercise.
HERDING e.g. Border Collie, Sheltie	Sheep-herding breeds, many types of coat and temperaments, highly trainable, ideal for competitions.	More in touch with natural behaviors.
TERRIER e.g. Airedale, Soft-coated Wheaten	Intelligent, devoted and loyal, mostly good with children, small and medium sizes to choose from.	Enjoy digging, need training in short sharp bursts, can challenge dynamics if two family terriers disagree.
TOY e.g. Chihuahua, Pekingese, Pug	Small breeds need less walking, more suited to small homes and apartments. Not all ideal as family pets.	Home-loving. Some long coats need time spent on grooming.
NON-SPORTING e.g. Poodle	Variety of sizes available, good family dogs, loyal.	Larger breeds need more space, some may be more difficult to train.
WORKING e.g. Bernese Mountain Dog	Larger sizes available, intelligent, highly trainable so ideal if you want a dog to train for canine activities.	Often have a natural instinct for herding and alerting, vary in reactivity, not all suitable for families.
DESIGNER BREED e.g. Labradoodle, Cockapoo	Often have best of both breeds, mixed breed groups can unite advantages of character from one with coat of the other.	May not be as healthy as the parent breeds, some unpredictability in size, temperament, and character.
MIXED BREED DOG	Mixed parentage, but a dog's looks give clues to its nature, often pretty colors, healthier, puppies and adults available.	Rescue homes may know the background; if not, you pick by what you can see: looks, size, behavior.

Bringing Your Puppy Home

When you collect your puppy, the breeder should provide:

Pedigree registration documents All pedigree puppies have them, unless breeders have specific reasons why they do not, which they should tell you. You need the documents to change registered ownership with the appropriate Kennel Club.

Contract of sale, receipt for payment Conditions of purchase should be clearly stated, and should show how much you paid to make the puppy legally yours.

Puppy nutrition sheet Diet sheets should be provided before collecting the puppy to enable new owners to stock up with the right foods. Some breeders provide several days of food to ensure the puppy has enough of the same provisions, in case some foods are difficult to obtain.

Puppy pack/guidance notes Notes should be provided that advise about socializing, training, food, grooming, and exercising your puppy for at least the first few months. Some breeders may provide books to help, too.

Preparing your home for your puppy

- Select a suitable quiet site that is easily cleaned as a place for puppy's bed.
- Put away anything a puppy could chew, including electrical cords.
- Use gates to prevent access to "off-limit" areas.
- Store cleaning products safely and securely out of the way.
- Make sure you yard is well fenced.
- Register with a local veterinary practice.

Essential items of equipment

Dog beds Cardboard boxes initially. There are various sizes, types, and styles of bed from which to choose: pillow beds, orthopedic beds, mats, or crates. Be wary of shredding and ingesting stuffing.

Blankets Probably available from around the home or thrift shops, but they must be washable, and several are needed to manage during puppy's early days at home. Do not leave puppies unsupervised with blankets or anything that could be potentially ingested.

Towels Old towels for wiping a wet puppy are ideal, as they run and splash around in anything interesting they find.

Pet carrier (*above*) Use to bring your puppy home. Make sure it is the right size and line it with newspaper and a blanket for the journey.

Pen Useful for containing puppies, particularly until housetraining is accomplished.

Water and food bowls At least one of each is needed. Water must always be available; the food bowl needs washing between meals.

Newspaper or pee pads For lining pens or putting in front of beds in case of any accidents.

Food Check out local sources of puppy food before bringing the puppy home, as some are cheaper to order for direct delivery, or may be regularly available at

● *Puppies learn to walk best when attached to a light leash. It should be long enough for owners to hold comfortably. Collars should be checked frequently for fit.*

a local source in smaller quantities if storage space at home is difficult.

Collar Small puppy collars are useful for puppy to wear as soon as he arrives home. Puppy will be so busy getting to know his new home, he will not have time to wonder what is around his neck.

Leash and harness Puppy leashes can be bought along with the collar. Harnesses may be purchased later so you can bring your puppy with you to find a suitable fit.

Coat Some breeds are sensitive to the cold, so consider purchasing a coat for cooler weather.

Grooming kit Some breeds benefit from particular brushes and combs suitable for their type of coat, but small puppies may need softer brushes than adults. Take advice from the breeder on what is best. Soft children's toothbrushes, nail clippers, and dog shampoos can be found at pet stores or supermarkets.

Poo bags, shovel, and paper towels For cleaning up after your puppy when you take him outside—available from local stores or supermarkets.

Choosing toys

A variety of toys in different shapes and sizes are ideal, but try to choose something suitable for the natural behaviors of your puppy's breed. Terriers, for instance, enjoy shaking rope toys; working breeds like to run after balls; Retrievers appreciate dumb-bell shapes to retrieve.

● *This 9-week-old puppy enjoys shaking rope toys as they appeal to his natural behaviors.*

Rope toy

Remember when you buy or make toys:
- No sharp edges to damage soft mouths.
- Try to choose "indestructible" toys and avoid things like decorative bells and tassels that can be detached and swallowed.
- Balls should be large enough not to present any risk of swallowing.
- Make sure to remove staples from old boxes.
- Never give plastic bottles as playthings—puppies can break them into shards.
- Children's toys are unsuitable for puppies to play with and should be avoided.

Food To Keep Your Puppy Healthy

Puppy foods are designed and compounded by licensed canine nutritionists. They analyze all aspects of the various meats, grains, vitamins, minerals, and other supplements available. They use only regulated, safe products that contain the correct amounts of protein, fat, carbohydrate, and fiber. This is done with the end product being a total, balanced puppy food. All that's needed is the bag, can, or plastic package that keeps your pup in prime health, one that gives him the energy he needs, and is palatable in the bargain. Ample fresh drinking water at all times is a must.

● Feeding is an ideal time to teach a puppy good manners, but never tease a puppy with his food.

A balanced diet contains:

Protein For maintenance, growth, and regulating metabolism.

Carbohydrate Converts to glucose for energy metabolism.

Fat Essential fatty acids maintain skin and coat, and provide energy.

Minerals and vitamins For bone formation, development, and good blood chemistry.

Fiber To support digestive function.

Don't let price govern your choice of a puppy food. Look for the analysis of components used, the percentage of water, protein, fat, and carbohydrate in the product. Check the digestibility of each component. Ask another pet parent or a veterinarian what they feed.

Choosing from the options available

Ideally, puppies should remain on the same diet for at least two weeks, while they settle into their new home. Once settled, owners can change the diet to one of their choice, but this must be done carefully and gradually over a period of days:

- 3/4 of old food, 1/4 of new food for 3–4 days
- 1/2 of old food, 1/2 of new food for 3–4 days
- 1/4 of old food, 3/4 of new food for 3–4 days
- All new food

If a puppy refuses his food, alter your feeding regime. If you are feeding scraps—stop that practice. Never feed scraps! If feeding in the kitchen or at dinner time, change the time and place. If feeding dry food, try moistening the kibble with warm water and let it set a few minutes before offering it to your puppy. If still refused, try moistening the kibble with a bit of warm broth or bullion. If he still ignores the food, take his temperature, check his mouth for foreign objects, loose teeth, or inflamed gums. If the pup's temperature is above 103 degrees, call your veterinarian.

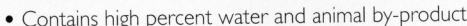

WHAT CHOICES ARE AVAILABLE?

Wet food	Canned	• Contains high percent water and animal by-products • Often is mixed with kibble for acceptability • May contain allergens that are unidentifiable • Cheap brands may contain indigestible products • May upset digestive tract • Canned food may spoil unless refrigerated • If left on floor, will attract insects

	Semi soft moist packs	• Products usually smell and taste like meat • May cause excessive water consumption • Expensive to feed to larger breeds
	Frozen	• Contains animal by-products of questionable quality • Not meant to be total nutrition • Difficult to ascertain necessary vegetable ingredients • Packaging creates problems in freezer • Product is bulky and difficult to handle

Dried food	Kibble	• Generic products are questionable quality • Premium products are usually better accepted • Do not always accept package-feeding directions • Dry food may be fed free-choice • Many brand names available • Fed alone or with canned food • Buyer gets what he pays for • Cheap kibble produces bulky feces • Handling is convenient for owner

Natural/Mixed diets	Raw meat, vegetables, and small raw bones	• Knowledge of canine nutrition is needed • Knowledge of puppy nutrition is mandatory • Too much or too little protein is dangerous • Knowledge of needed vitamins and minerals • Bones in any form shouldn't be allowed • Quality of meats vary from source to source • Cooking and mixing is messy and time-consuming • Enthusiasts believe it can reduce allergies and digestive problems

Looking After Your Puppy's Health

Puppies need regular health checks, particularly as they grow. Different checks are needed either daily, weekly, monthly, or yearly.

DAILY CHECKS

Eye cleaning Some puppies have "goo" in their eyes after sleeping; remove this daily with a damp cotton ball to prevent infections. Continual runny eyes can indicate infection, allergy, or a dietary problem and need veterinary treatment.

Summer/winter checks Check between the toes for grass seeds or stones in summer and ice particles in winter. Also check for seasonal parasites, broken nails, or hardened lumps of mud stuck in the hair between the toes.

Handling experience Regular handling of a puppy encourages socialization. Different breeds may need more handling, but this develops a puppy's understanding and acceptance of being handled from a young age. It also helps if puppies are used to being handled when they visit the veterinarian for health checks or treatment, and they are more likely to accept grooming, training, or other necessary attention as they mature.

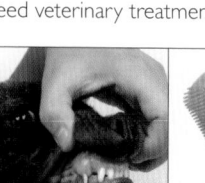

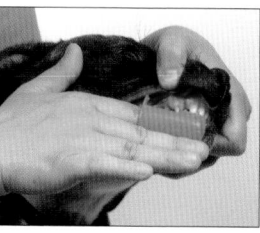

Teeth cleaning Chews and bones help to keep teeth clean, but brushing teeth *(above)* twice a week with a toothbrush and dog toothpaste is beneficial. Teeth should look clean with no tartar build-up, and gums should be pink and healthy-looking. Check for biscuit pieces or bone segments stuck in the gums. Good diet, teeth cleaning, and some common sense used regularly, along with the provision of rawhide bones and chews, will prevent costly veterinary treatment and keep puppies healthy.

Encourage your puppy to sit for handling.

Paw pad condition Pads can easily be injured—cuts may become infected and need cleaning. Dipping the paw in warm, salty water or an antiseptic cleansing wash will prevent infections and may avoid a trip to the veterinarian.

● *All puppies should be well handled before they go to their new home, and should enjoy this contact. If they are nervous, encourage them by gentle stroking and giving a small treat.*

WEEKLY CHECKS

Lumps and bumps Check for knots in puppy's coats to prevent moist dermatitis. Dried mud may cause lameness if left between the toes.

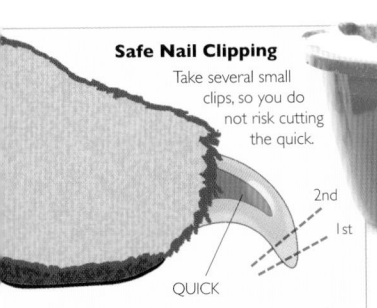

Safe Nail Clipping

Take several small clips, so you do not risk cutting the quick.

2nd
1st

QUICK

If cut, the quick will bleed profusely. Blood flow can be stopped with styptic powder.

● *Bathe small puppies in the sink or a bowl, larger puppies can go in the bath.*

Nail cutting Check the pup's toenails. If any reach the floor, then a nail trim is necessary. With a pair of sharp canine nail trimmers, snip off the tips of the nails and dewclaws. Keep your cut well behind the "quick," which contains blood vessels and nerves. The quick is easily identified in white toes, but difficult to see in black nails. Start cutting just the very sharp point of a nail and work back toward the foot. If the pup yips, don't panic, check the nail for a drop of blood and if any is found, apply digital pressure until bleeding stops. If no blood is seen, continue the nail trim. If bleeding continues, apply a styptic stick or styptic powder to the nail and hold there for a minute.

Ear cleaning Clean ears regularly, particularly on dogs with long floppy ears or long coats where hair grows in the ear canal.

MONTHLY CHECKS

Bathing Grooming your puppy is a must and a bath is an excellent way to learn more about your pup's personality. After you've combed and brushed him, place him in a large sink or tub. Put several inches of warm, soapy water in the tub and boost him in. After sudsing him up, drain the water and rinse him with lots of warm, clean water. Bathe him only when necessary. Use a dog shampoo without insecticides unless needed for parasites (fleas or lice).

Gender checks In a male puppy, check to assure that both testicles have descended into the scrotum. In either a male or female puppy, check the navel area to see if there is an umbilical hernia. That surgical problem will appear as a soft bulbous swelling. Perform these checks monthly. If anything appears abnormal, consult your veterinarian.

Feces and urine checks A puppy's fecal excretion should be soft but not runny. It should be a mid-brown color, without foreign material, mucus, or blood. A veterinarian will check the pups for most worms under a microscope. Tapeworms are visible and look like tiny grains of rice sticking to the anal hair. No puppy should be given worm medication except if known to be harboring that parasite. A veterinarian may administer the medication or dispense it for home administration. Urine color should be a light yellow and should be passed without effort many times a day.

Puppy's Health *continued*

YEARLY CHECKS

Inoculations A puppy's passive immunity decreases soon after he stops nursing. At this point, the pup is at risk for several serious diseases. To prevent those diseases, your puppy should receive vaccinations at approximately seven weeks of age. Your veterinarian will advise you which diseases are prevalent in your area. Booster vaccinations are advised at three weeks after the initial inoculations, and another booster is given at one year of age. Rabies is a fatal disease that can be transmitted by infected mammals such as bats, foxes, coyotes, raccoons, and many others. Like other mammals, humans are susceptible to rabies and without immediate treatment—they die. All states have laws to protect us and our pets. A rabies vaccination is required when he is three months old.

Puppies travelling interstate need:
- Health Certificate signed by licensed veterinarian
- Rabies vaccination certification by licensed veterinarian
- Adequate traveling means (air, car)
- Bottled water and bowl
- Supply of usual food

Veterinary health checks Dogs should be examined by your veterinarian annually. This exam should check your pet's heart and lungs, eyes, ears, teeth, feet and nails, skin and coat. Your pet's diet should be discussed, a fecal sample should be taken for parasites, and your veterinarian might administer a blood test to ascertain heartworm presence. Your veterinarian should also discuss your pet's weight, tick and flea control, and general condition.

LIFETIME CHECKS

Your puppy should be professionally examined for hereditary diseases at various times of life according to age, weight, and breed. Some diseases occur in very young puppies, others are found in older pets. Some of those diseases can be identified by typical symptoms occurring in your puppy, and others are found in older dogs by specific examinations, such as X-rays. Hereditary diseases of internal organs may be discovered by specific blood tests and symptoms. DNA sampling of many breeds is now underway by the AKC to advise breeders of possible carriers of inherited diseases. The results of those samples are important to eliminate genetic problems in the breed.

Neutering

Spaying (neutering) a female puppy is safe and effective at three months of age. Castration of a male puppy may be done at a similar age. These irreversible surgeries will dramatically reduce some serious reproductive disease of intact females and males, and will control mating urges and actions in both. They do not affect trainability of your pup or its protective instincts; obesity is caused only by overfeeding.

Worming

All puppies do not have worms! Your veterinarian can perform a simple, inexpensive, microscopic test on a sample of the puppy's stool that will diagnose most testinal parasites; tapeworm segments can be seen ith the naked eye. Medicine to kill the worms is oisonous. To administer parasite treatments of any kind n a routine basis is obviously unnecessary and can e dangerous!

● *Puppies biting around the base of the tail need to be checked for fleas.*

● *Gentle petting encourages puppies to wait while you do daily checks.*

Both ticks and fleas can be controlled most effectively by medicine that is applied to the infested puppy's skin once a month. Lice can be controlled with dips or sprays. Some medications may also control other parasites.

Grooming

All dogs need grooming at least weekly, and often more frequently. Grooming puppies encourages them to accept handling for physical examination and visits to the veterinarian, and also helps them to bond with owners. Puppies learn that their owner is "boss," because they learn to behave while standing on a table. Some breeds need grooming daily; others with increased frequency when they are shedding copiously and dead hair needs to be removed. Some have low- or non-shedding coats that mat and tangle if dead hair is not brushed out. Dogs with ears that flop down over their ear canals should have them cleaned and wiped weekly to prevent ear infections, and any smell from the ear should be investigated. Some breeds may need to be seen by a professional groomer, which can be costly, but many breeders are willing to show you how to do this yourself.

Fleas, ticks, and lice

leas are tiny biting insects that exist everywhere. heir saliva is allergenic and causes the puppy to cratch. Fleas live part time on the host, fall to the arpet, lay eggs that hatch, and their life cycle continues. dult female ticks bury their heads in the pup's skin and uck blood. She falls to the ground and lays thousands f eggs.

Ticks may harbor and transmit serious human diseases, such as Lyme disease, tick fever, and tick aralysis.

Lice live on a puppy's skin permanently. They also eed on host's blood and can be easily found as "nits" attached to the pup's hair.

Puppy Growth and Development

Dogs exhibit more variations in height and weight than any other animal. Puppies can be as small as Chihuahuas at 6–8.5 in (16–20 cm) in height and 1–6.5 lb (0.5–3 kg) in weight or as big as a Great Dane at 30–34 in (76–86 cm) and 100–120 lb (45–54 kg). Larger breeds take much longer than toy breeds to grow to adulthood, but the principles behind their growth and development differ very little. In larger breeds, however, nutrition is even more important because diet can greatly influence bone growth and structure over the longer period of development. Bone disease can result if their diet does not have the correct nutritional balance.

● *This Great Dane needs more time to grow than small dogs like this Chihuahua, and he ha[s] different nutritional needs to achieve his lofty height.*

The right diet

Owners bear a weighty responsibility to choose the correct balanced diet to suit the size of their dog. Specific nutritional components of diets are crucial, and owners should seek advice from the breeder on what to feed their puppy for at least the first six months of life. There are plenty of nutritional dog foods available, which owners can try, but do observe your puppy

carefully to make sure he is putting on the right amount of weight and bone growth and is developing normally. Calcium, for example, is critically important for healthy bone growth and development, because bone stores calcium. Some foods are provided specifically to addre[ss] this requirement in certain breeds of dog, but they ma[y] not suit all breeds. A dog given too much calcium in hi[s] diet may even develop deformed bone and joints, because growth rate becomes uneven, while too little calcium and phosphorus may cause weak, deformed bones. Energy levels are affected too, depending on the breed's size and level of activity. Medium and large breeds fed too much energy-rich food may suffer obesity and skeletal problems as a consequence.

The graph on page 17 will help you to estimate th[e] projected pattern of growth for your type of dog, but i[t] should not be taken as an exact measure. Consult you[r] veterinarian when choosing the best diet for your pup.

| 1 day | 10 days | 4 weeks | 6 weeks | 9 weeks | 14 weeks | 5 months | 24 months |

Body Weights of Growing Dogs of Different Breeds

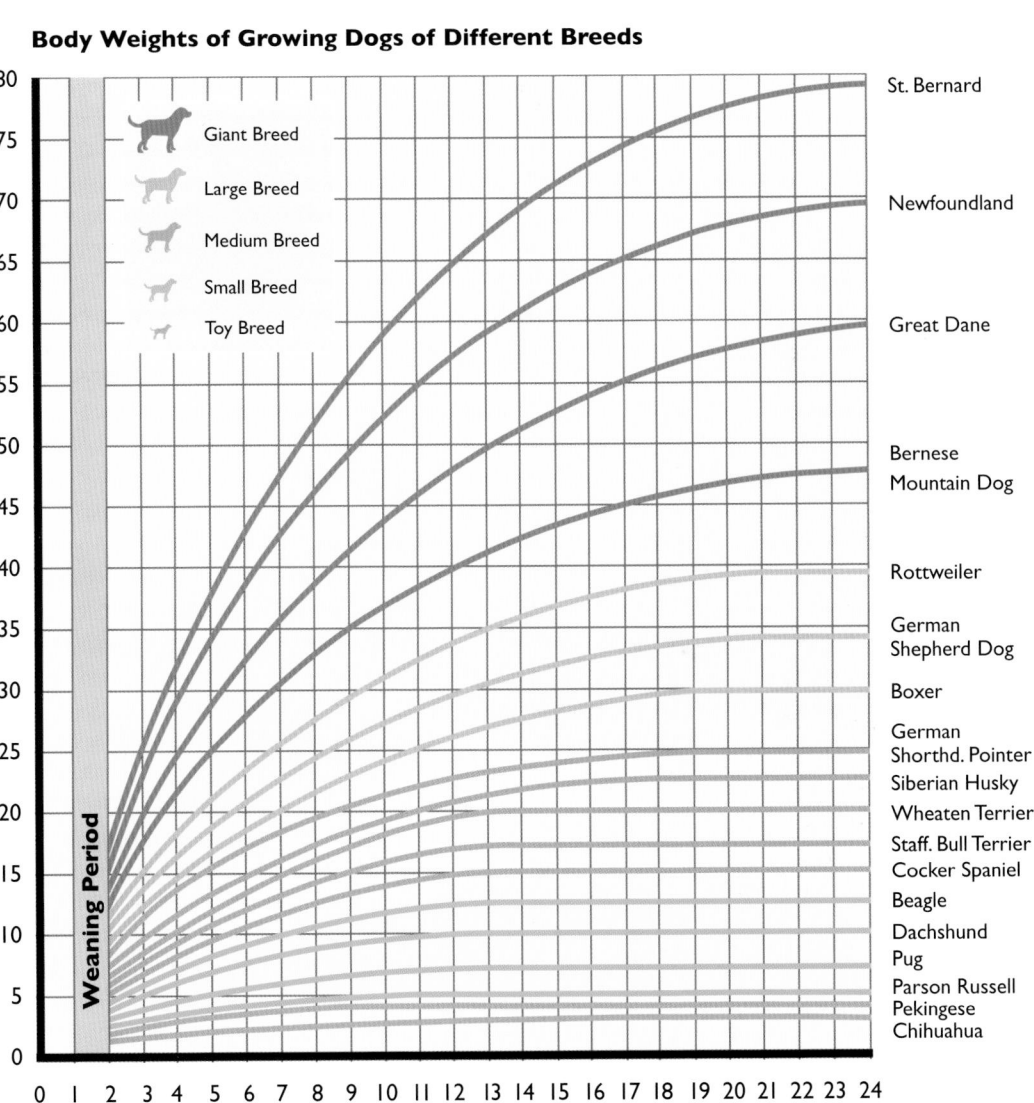

Giant Breed

Large Breed

Medium Breed

Small Breed

Toy Breed

Weaning Period

St. Bernard

Newfoundland

Great Dane

Bernese Mountain Dog

Rottweiler

German Shepherd Dog

Boxer

German Shorthd. Pointer
Siberian Husky
Wheaten Terrier
Staff. Bull Terrier
Cocker Spaniel
Beagle
Dachshund
Pug
Parson Russell
Pekingese
Chihuahua

Age (Months)

Keeping Puppy Fit and Trim

Obesity can be a real problem for your puppy if you overfeed him, or give the wrong kind of diet, because most fat cells are laid down during puppies' critical growth phase. It is best to control this problem by not allowing it to start in the first place. Approximately 25 percent of dogs are known to be overweight, and they suffer the consequences of poor health, which may well include costly treatments at the veterinarian. Obese puppies are more likely to suffer from joint problems, a reduced quality of life, and shorter lifespan, all of which can be avoided by selecting a sensible diet. Some breeds are particularly prone to problems if they are long-backed because of the double whammy of the strain on their spinal joints from carrying the extra weight, and the consequent lack of exercise. All dogs are at risk of obesity, but breeds that are particularly susceptible are Cairn Terriers, Dachshunds, Cavalier King Charles Spaniels, Beagles, Basset Hounds, Labradors, and Rottweilers.

Just like humans, puppies will avoid all sorts of problems if they are maintained to enjoy a healthy lifestyle.

Maintaining your puppy's weight

It is important to check your puppy's weight regularly to prevent him from becoming too thin or too fat. A healthy dog has bright eyes, a healthy "bloom" on his coat, and a skeleton covered in the right amount of flesh. If this is not the case, owners should:

- Make sure quantities of the diet are correct.
- Increase or reduce the essential fat components of the diet.
- Provide more exercise or more play sessions.
- Offer more toys for stimulation.
- Avoid giving too many treats.
- Avoid overfeeding your puppy during his crucial growing phase.

Growing up healthy

Most owners expect their puppy to grow up healthy, and if they are feeding correctly, exercising carefully, training appropriately, spending the right amount of time playing, grooming, and providing love and attention, then all should be well. However, there may be occasions when a puppy fails to thrive, and owners may be left wondering what they have done wrong. The table on page 19 gives ideas of how your puppy should look and behave if he is in good health.

● *The healthy Pug (left) is a good example of how to care for a puppy's health by not overindulging him with too much food.*

HEALTHY PUPPY CHARACTERISTICS

What to look at	What you should find
Eyes	Clean, bright inquisitive eyes with no evidence of dullness, no "goo," crusts, or infection in the corners.
Nose	Cold nose, with a moist feel.
Mouth	Clean, pink healthy-looking gums with clean white teeth and sweet-smelling breath.
Ears	Clean ears with no evidence of dirt or wax and no smell.
Skin and coat	Slightly pink skin in light-colored dogs with healthy hair growth. Coat and skin look clean with no crusty skin and with a healthy "bloom."
Paws	Trimmed nails, hard pads without roughness, clean between the toes.
Rear end	Clean around the anus with no dried feces, trim off some hair/fur if there is a deposit. Feces are mid-brown in color (depends on food), slightly moist, with no mucus or blood present.
Appetite	Puppy is hungry and eager to eat his dinner without hesitation.
General appearance	Growth and development is keeping apace with breed expectations.
Mental responses	Puppy is interested and stimulated by everything going on around him. Curious and investigative, eager to explore.
Activity levels	Puppy is running around full of life, bright and alert, and ready to do anything.

● *Your puppy should exhibit energy, and be inquisitive and mischievous if he is in a healthy condition. A puppy that is listless, sleeping a lot, and not enjoying exercise needs to be checked by a veterinarian.*

Learning About The World

Different dog breeds exhibit behaviors that are natural to their breed because our ancestors bred them for those traits—sporting dogs retrieve for hunting, working dogs guard property, and terriers dig to hunt prey. Consequently, you can expect dogs from particular groups to display behaviors that are associated with those characteristics. You should try to take advantage of these natural behaviors when socializing and training your puppy. **Socialization** refers to the process of getting your puppy accustomed to the presence of other people and animals around him, while **habituation** refers to the process of getting him used to other places and unfamiliar objects in different environments.

● Rewarding good behavior helps puppies to learn manners.

around their home and accept a repertoi of different household events. They have some idea of personal space in relation toys, going potty, and where to sleep ar eat, but they need time to get used to this routine in their new home.

There may be other pets in the new household that they need to be introduced to so tha they grow up accepting their position in the family order. Basic training can start at this time; it involves learning how to behave with other people or other pets in the family, becoming familiar with the daily routine, learning to come when called, to sit for treats, accepting who is in charge, and not to bite anyone wit their sharp little teeth. Socialization as the puppy becomes more adventurous should address their nee to learn from experience and understand how to behave at home and in the community.

Socialization

Most breeders will have started this process before a puppy leaves for his new home, as socialization starts at birth and progresses through to six months. While socialization is important from early days, new owners must spend time following a process of socialization continuously to produce a confident, well-behaved dog. Most 8-week-old puppies are ready to move on to new challenges; they are familiar with everyday noises

Habituation

Backyards are usually the first place in which puppies learn about their environment, and they also learn where they can go and where they cannot. Outside the yard, habituation training must include traveling in a car, visiting the veterinarian, or going to a groomer—these are all different environments that a puppy must become familiar with. Providing new stimuli is essent while your puppy is becoming familiar with you an your home to prevent him from becoming nervo or fear-aggressive when he goes elsewhere. A puppy cannot go out until immunizations are complete, but yc

● Introduced early, puppies and kittens learn about each other in the right way and will respect one another's company.

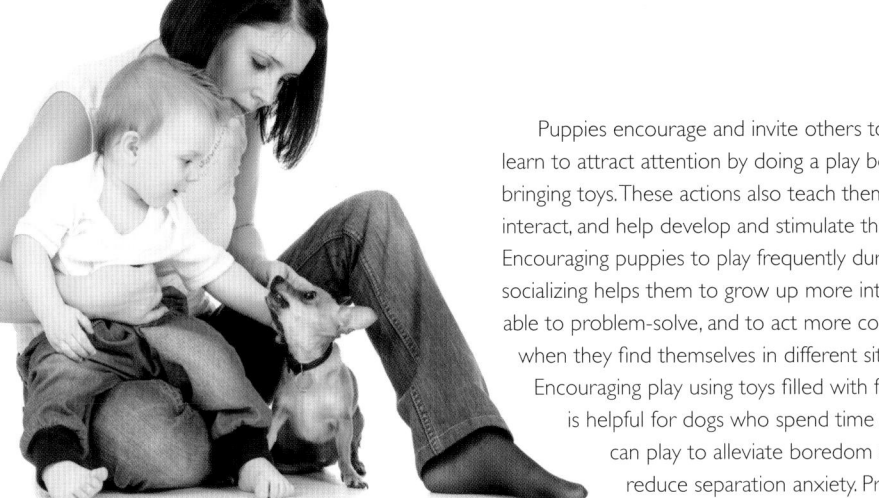

Puppies encourage and invite others to play, and learn to attract attention by doing a play bow, or by bringing toys. These actions also teach them how to interact, and help develop and stimulate their minds. Encouraging puppies to play frequently during socializing helps them to grow up more intelligent, able to problem-solve, and to act more confidently when they find themselves in different situations. Encouraging play using toys filled with food treats is helpful for dogs who spend time alone; they can play to alleviate boredom and to reduce separation anxiety. Providing toys can also direct a puppy's natural destructive urges onto items that can be easily and cheaply replaced.

When given plenty of stimulation through play, dogs develop quick and active minds. Using play in sequences

can carry him down the road to see the world outside the backyard, or visit a neighbor's yard to explore. However, while doing this, make sure that you prevent the puppy from doing things that you do not want him to do, i.e. climbing on furniture or going upstairs. This is all valuable early training.

Play

Play is important for puppies, starting at around two and half weeks. Puppies learn their life skills in play, and owners can take advantage of playtime to teach control of natural behaviors and desirable social skills before bad habits form. Barking puppies may seem cute, but it is not so cute when it happens continuously for attention as the puppy grows. Problem behaviors may occur, but if corrected early, they can be stopped. Play biting is an example. Through play biting with their littermates, puppies learn how and when to inhibit their biting response, but owners must correct this consistently for the puppy to understand that it is unacceptable to play bite humans.

● *Playing is good for learning, but make sure only toys are used!*

to elicit a response, and giving treats to reward good behavior, helps them understand how to behave to earn a reward. Stimulus-response training or clicker training uses similar methods, so the basics learned through play help to prepare puppies for more formal training later on.

Training Your Puppy

Training should focus on four specific aspects of a puppy's life: his physical well-being, emotional state, intelligence, and social confidence. To develop satisfactorily, puppies need to be habituated to different places, to learn how to socialize with different people and other animals, and to learn by association how to respond in particular ways to various situations. The basis of training comes from practicing behaviors that reinforce actions you want to encourage. Puppies learn by consequences: behaving one way gets a reward, behaving in another way results in a gruff "**No.**" In time, they are conditioned to learn this association of positive reinforcement for good behavior.

Two methods of learning are often used for training:

Clicker training Puppies learn the exact moment that a desired behavior occurs because it is "marked" by the sound of a clicker, which is followed by a reward such as a treat. This is called positive reinforcement, and the puppy learns by association. For example, if a dog jumps up and is told to get down on four paws, the owner should click the moment he does so. In this way, the puppy registers the desired behavior. Clickers are ideal for close-work training, but are not so effective for distance work.

Lure and reward Food treats are used as reinforcement and held close to the puppy's nose. Desired responses

● *Lure and reward training demonstrating the movement for 'Sit'. The puppy follows the treat and drops into a sitting position.*

can be stimulated by movement of the treat. For example, by passing a treat backward over the puppy's head while saying "Sit," the puppy can be encouraged to move into a Sit position from a Stand. He automatically sits, thus earning the reward. With patience, puppies can be lured into sequences of movement, which is the beginning of training tricks.

Training for canine activities

Well-trained dogs are a joy to be with. Owners who persevere with training may find that keeping dogs is so engrossing that they enjoy getting involved in canine activities such as agility, obedience, flyball, sledding, and so on. However, this depends on the dog's physical makeup, the natural behaviors typical of the breed, and how much time owners are prepared to spend on achieving success. Owners must be single-minded, patient, confident, and committed to regular practice. Some breeds need very sensitive training (gentle voice, calm and quiet, but determined), while others may need slightly firmer treatment to ensure success (stronger voice and tone, more assertive handling). Harsh methods (shouting, scolding, smacking) should never be used with any dog. They are always counter-productive and harm your relationship with your dog.

Exercise

All dogs need exercise, but different breeds need varying amounts. Most breeders give advice on this, but generally, puppies need to start with gentle walking, which should gradually build up to two short walks daily. When old enough, one good walk daily should satisfy an adult, bearing in mind his size, energy levels, and the amount of mental stimulation needed. By exercising correctly, your puppy's health improves, his mind is stimulated, and emotional equilibrium is maintained. Exercise also facilitates bonding through play, hunting behaviors, and social meetings with other people and their dogs.

As a guide (when fully grown):

Small dogs need two short walks daily of around half an hour each.

Medium dogs need around an hour once a day.

Large breeds may need up to two hours (or more) of running and galloping, plus extra time for play.

Lifestyles:

Apartment dogs may need a short trot down the road every two to three hours, plus a longer walk to satisfy their size and energy requirements.

Dogs with small yards may need two good hour-long runs as they will not be able to get as much exercise by playing around outside.

Large dogs with big yards can burn off a lot of energy and may be happy with less, but they will often accept as much exercise as they can get.

Using this book

● *A lot of breed information can be found online.*

This book provides useful information for prospective owners to help them choose the right breed for their lifestyle. It does not offer details on breed standards, and owners who want to show puppies for a specific purpose should consult Kennel Club standards or experts on those breeds. Readers should bear in mind that the descriptions of individual breeds refer to typical specimens, but the impact of breeding, environmental influences, socialization, quality of training, plus the health of the puppy's forebears may mean that individual dogs differ from these norms.

Anyone purchasing a puppy should research their chosen breed very carefully and make sure that they buy from reputable breeders or sources. Where breeds are identified as being **Good with children** in the Character Traits box, the entry assumes that the dog has been introduced to, and socialized with, children properly. The table entry for **Ease of training** marks some breeds as Poor, but this trait can be positively influenced by dedicated training and the handling ability of individual owners. It is a general guideline, not an immutable fact. This guide aims to provide insight into the basics of a breed and identifies the raw material that lies within each puppy. Ultimately, it is up to individual owners to guide and support their dog in the best way possible to develop his own unique potential.

Small dogs

Small dogs, from the dainty Chihuahua to little Spaniels, are easier to keep in smaller homes or apartments. They still have a lot of energy, intelligence, and personality, but they need less food and exercise to keep them satisfied. They also make good watchdogs. Some are not particularly suitable as family dogs unless trained well, but chosen carefully, owners will find much to love in these small breeds.

Chihuahua

Originating in South America, this sacred dog of the ancient Mexicans was pictured on ancient Toltec pyramids, and is said to have died alongside Aztec rulers to guide their souls to heaven and expiate their sins. The first modern specimens were found around 1850 in the Mexican state of Chihuahua and bred in the U.S. Smallest of the toy breeds, the Chihuahua is lively and playful, and loves affection and company. Graceful and compact with a saucy expression, he is alert and highly intelligent. Possessive of his owner, he loves being the center of attention. Ideal in a small apartment, he enjoys daily walking and mental stimulation. Available in smooth and long coats, in a variety of attractive colors, he can sometimes be used as a fashion accessory because his small size will fit in handbags. Popularity brings with it a need to purchase from a reputable breeder who pays attention to health and temperament.

Color choices?

Color combinations and markings vary from solid to marked or splashed. Usual colors are fawn/brown, brindle fawn/brown, silver fawn, silver gray, white, cream, chocolate, black and tan, and black. Merle (a marbled color effect) is not allowed because there may be health problems.

How much grooming?

Both coats are manageable. Long coats take two years to grow so regular grooming is essential; a gentle daily brush to remove tangles is best. Smooth coats need grooming to brush out dead hair.

Do they make good pets?

Their small size makes them suitable for most family homes. Better with older children, they are not suitable for small children as their size makes them vulnerable. They enjoy being the center of attention and like being part of small groups, but often attach themselves to individual members of the family.

● These delicate dogs are very compact and make delightful companions for owners with smaller homes.

What home suits them?

This breed can live in apartments, or small homes with yards, in the suburbs or in the country. Loving homes providing companionship, regular daily walks, and play, with plenty to do makes for a happy little dog.

What type of owner?

Chihuahuas are unsuitable for working owners, because they need a lot of attention and stimulation. Their possessive nature means that owners must give, and accept, plenty of affection. Suitable for the housebound, they exercise through play or the occasional walk, although they also enjoy outdoor pursuits with an active family.

How much exercise and stimulation?

They are accepting of limited exercise, but they also enjoy walking. Indoors, Chihuahuas exercise by playing with each other or their owner. Stimulation is good, because their minds are active.

Friendly with other pets?

This breed can appear reserved with other pets unless socialized as a puppy. Generally, however, they prefer their own kind for company.

Is puppy training easy?

Chihuahuas are not easily trained, but they can learn the basics quite early on. A firm, consistent approach with gentle training techniques is preferable. Some are slow to become housetrained, but patience pays dividends.

Personality Traits	Poor	Average	Good	Excellent
Attitude toward other dogs		●		
Quietness	●			
Behavior at home			●	
Watchdog ability			●	
Good with children		●		
Ease of training		●		
Obedience to owner		●		

Time to maturity: 2 years
Male height: 6–8.5 in (15–22 cm)
Female height: 6–8.5 in (15–22 cm)
Weight: 1–6.5 lb (0.5–3 kg)
Average lifespan: 10–18 years

Special puppy care?

Keep them warm, as puppies are sensitive to cold. Puppy eyes need attention and cleaning, and daily grooming is needed especially for longer coats. Owners should be careful with the puppy's head during the first six months as some have an open molera (a gap in the bones) on top of the skull (similar to the fontanelle of human babies). Although low maintenance to feed, puppies need careful feeding at every growth stage.

Possible health problems?

Mostly healthy little dogs, they can suffer from slipping knee caps, epilepsy, and heart problems. Due to their small size and sometimes picky eating habits, they may experience low blood sugar levels. Potential owners should buy from breeders with healthy stock who provide reports of any health checks.

What can we do together?

Chihuahua's are ideal as companion dogs, and quite popular for showing. Some enjoy long walks and mini agility.

Don't forget!

The Chihuahua's size can make them vulnerable to bad handling or being stepped on. Buy from a reputable breeder. Sometimes called teacup, pocket size, tiny toy, miniature, or standard sizes, these names only increase their value and are not associated with the breed.

Small dogs

● Smooth coat Chihuahuas have coats that are velvety to the touch. These puppies are about 10 weeks old.

Pekingese
Other names: Lion Dog, Chinese Spaniel, Pelchie Dog

The Pekingese is one of the oldest dog breeds. Pekingese were the royal dogs of China because they resembled the Chinese Guardian Lion statues that traditionally were placed in front of palaces and temples. They led highly privileged lives in the Imperial Court during the Tang Dynasty. The first five Pekingese came to Britain following the storming of the Imperial Summer Palace by British troops in 1860, and their offspring arrived in the U.S. not long after this. Pekingese are beautiful dogs with a superior manner and great personality, and they are completely devoted to their owners. Good mannered and dignified, they can be playful and sporty, but they dislike being left out and can be stubborn. An imperious, but calm and good-natured companion dog, their health has been affected by breeders exaggerating certain features, such as the short, flat face. Coat care may prove difficult for busy modern families.

Color choices?

Available colors are red, gold, sable, cream, white, black, black and tan, and occasionally blue or slate gray, but all Pekingese must have a black muzzle, nose, and lips. Albinos are unacceptable and may have health problems.

How much grooming?

Their double coat of long, straight, coarse hair over thick, soft fur can shed a lot. Most Pekingese enjoy grooming, which must go right down to the skin using a pin brush and comb. The neck mane and the profuse feathering behind the ears, under the armpits, legs, and tail need extra attention to prevent matting. Face folds need wiping daily, and bathing regularly is needed to maintain clean healthy coats. Pet owners may prefer a short clip for convenience, but even then regular brushing is still needed.

Do they make good pets?

Pekingese are good mannered and

● *This noble dog has royal bearing.*

make excellent pets. They tend to attach themselves to one person, but they still appreciate being in a family. Better with older children, they do not always tolerate young children.

What home suits them?

Pekingese suit most locations, and adapt well to apartment living. They enjoy homes with yards, and they like to explore undergrowth.

What type of owner?

Strong-willed and independent, Pekingese become very attached to their owner, who must return devotion, share a sense of humor, and treat them with the respect their superiority deserves. Owners need plenty of time for companionship, and must accept that even as puppies, coats need plenty of grooming.

How much exercise and stimulation?

Pekingese tolerate very little exercise because of breathing difficulties and short legs. They are not athletic, so they enjoy short daily strolls at a slow pace for constitutional purposes. Walking in hot weather is inadvisable because of overheating and breathing problems. Puppies gain the most stimulation from spending time with their owner.

Friendly with other pets?

Rarely aggressive, Pekingese fit in better with other pets when socialized early. Puppies may indulge in boisterous play, but care is needed to prevent injury to their prominent eyes.

Personality Traits	Poor	Average	Good	Excellent
Attitude toward other dogs				
Quietness				
Behavior at home				
Watchdog ability				
Good with children				
Ease of training				
Obedience to owner				

Time to maturity: 2 years
Male height: 6–9 in (15–23 cm)
Female height: 6–9 in (15–23 cm)
Weight: 6–12 lb (2.75–5.5 kg)
Average lifespan: 12–14 years

Is puppy training easy?

Pekingese are positive and self-opinionated and expect owners to train them only in "appropriate" skills. Handlers must be firm but gentle in training and can expect intelligent and willing responses from a quick learner.

Special puppy care?

Puppy coat care is essential to prepare for an adult life involving plenty of grooming. Care is needed to prevent injury to young dogs by rough handling, particularly with their prominent eyes, long backs, and short legs.

Possible health problems?

Pekingese are prone to breathing problems, overheating, heart, eye (tear gland infections and injuries), back problems, and patella luxation (dislocating kneecaps). The folds on the face can become infected if not cleaned regularly. Puppy heart

problems are usually successfully treated if detected early.

What can we do together?

Mainly a companion dog, Pekingese enjoy showing, and sometimes may be successful in competitive obedience (if not too energetic).

Don't forget!

Pick up Pekingese carefully, supporting them front and back in the arms, so you do not hurt their backs.

Small dogs

● Cute and cuddly, and just 8 weeks old.

Brussels Griffon
Other names: Griffon Bruxellois, Petit Brabançon, Griffon Belge

This bearded, gnome-like, and charmingly self-important little dog originated in the city of Brussels and developed from local street dogs. His personality and skills found favor in stables as a small terrier ideal for hunting vermin. In the late 19th century, Belgian coachmen became fond of the Griffon, and they were soon accompanying traveling nobility as fearless little guard dogs. Queen Marie Henriette became a breeder of Griffons, and increased their popularity worldwide. The Griffon's facial expression and whiskers endow him with monkey-like features which together with a loving, playful nature make for an entertaining companion. There are two distinct varieties—the wire-coated and the smooth-coated (Petit Brabançon). Griffons have virtually no vices, and are intelligent, obedient, and easily managed and cared for. They can sometimes be shy, but are usually fearless watchdogs, affectionate companions, and ideal for apartment living.

Color choices?
Accepted colors are clear red, black, or black and rich tan. The Griffon Belge is noted for its mixed red and black hair combination, which is accepted in Europe and the U.S., but not in the U.K.

How much grooming?
A Griffon's wiry coat needs grooming with a firm brush and comb most days, and hand-stripping every two to three months to keep the coat looking good. Smooth-coated Griffons need brushing once a week using a hound glove. Their large eyes and the wrinkle above the nose needs cleaning daily, during which you should also check for lacerations that may cause infection.

Do they make good pets?
These little dogs tend to form a particularly strong bond with their owners, and are especially suitable for single or older people. They may not appreciate boisterous small children, but their tough and sturdy physique, together with a

● *The Griffon has an elfin, quizzical expression. He has a great personality.*

delightful even temper, make them ideal pets for sensible families.

What home suits them?
Ideal for apartment dwellers because of their size and easy care, they enjoy spending time at home cuddling up with their owner rather than going for a walk, although they still need exercise and stimulation. Their home matters little—they just need an owner who returns their affection. Griffons are vulnerable to overheating, and need a cool place in the shade to rest in hot weather.

What type of owner?
Griffons are not suitable for owners with small children because they can be jealous and demanding, and appreciate a quiet home life. A sensible owner willing to spend time on grooming and training without pampering their Griffon is best.

How much exercise and stimulation?
Griffons do enjoy long country walks, but also don't mind not going far. Mostly they need plenty of mental stimulation through a lot of play and training.

Friendly with other pets?
Having originated as ratters, forming friendships with small household pets may be risky, but if well socialized from early puppy days, they usually do well with other cats and dogs.

Is puppy training easy?
Griffons can be emotionally sensitive, stubborn, willful, and

Personality Traits	Poor	Average	Good	Excellent
Attitude toward other dogs				
Quietness				
Behavior at home				
Watchdog ability				
Good with children				
Ease of training				
Obedience to owner				

Time to maturity: 2 years
Male height: 7–8 in (18–20 cm)
Female height: 7–8 in (18–20 cm)
Weight: 5–11 lb (2.3–5 kg)
Average lifespan: 10–15 years

● *Bearded and gnome-like, these 8-week-old Griffon puppies have loads of charm, and their big, trusting eyes and jaunty look is most appealing.*

Possible health problems?

Healthy and long-lived, Griffons can suffer from cleft palates (usually found post birthing), glaucoma and cataracts, patella luxation (dislocating kneecaps), heart murmurs, and syringomyelia, a serious condition when fluid-filled cavities develop within the spinal cord.

Small dogs

What can we do together?

Despite their some-times stubborn per-sonality, Griffons can do well at obedience and agility. Generally though, they just enjoy being companion pets.

...easily bored, but while they are challenging to train, they learn quickly. With positive reward-based training, which includes some fun activities, they can excel at agility or obedience trials.

Special puppy care?

Griffon puppies enjoy playing, but be careful with their eyes, as they are easily injured. Overheating is a problem, so puppies must be well protected from the heat of the sun.

Don't forget!

Never play roughly with Griffon puppies as they can be sensitive, and always encourage your puppy to lie down in the shade and give him plenty of cool (not ice cold) water on a very hot day.

Yorkshire Terrier

The Yorkie came from a mixed terrier background, and was bred for catching rats in the Yorkshire cotton mills. He rose to popularity in Victorian times to become an aristocratic lady's companion, reaching exalted heights when he became popular in fashionable Hollywood circles. Although small, he is always busy, bustling, lively, and full of importance. Not a lapdog, he has a true terrier spirit, and is brave, dominant, and strong-willed. Yorkies have a courageous personality, but they must be guided through puppyhood, because without proper training and socializing, they can be aggressive toward larger dogs. Coat care is a must if he has been chosen to show, as he needs plenty of grooming to maintain his fine silky coat fit for the show ring. There is a noticeable difference between a Yorkie bought for showing and one bought as a pet, both in size and coat.

Color choices?

There are usually four color combinations: blue and tan, blue and gold, black and tan, black and gold. Other colors are not acceptable and may carry health problems. Puppies are generally black with tan points, changing to dark steel blue several months later. Hair on the head, chest, and lower legs should be rich bright tan, until the coat matures at around three years old. A white star marking is sometimes found on the chest.

How much grooming?

The long silky hair of show dogs is not seen on pets because it needs special care to prevent damage. Most owners trim the coat short and brush out tangles. The fringe over the eyes is tied back in a bow or trimmed neatly over the forehead. The coat is hypoallergenic because very little hair is shed, so it needs regular brushing.

Do they make good pets?

Yorkies prefer older children and make great family pets, but are

● The gleaming coat of the Yorkie takes a lot of brushing to keep it looking good, and takes a long time to mature.

particularly good companions for adults, because they are very loyal and loving. They are not suitable around toddlers or children who tease, and may snap if provoked.

What home suits them?

Yorkies enjoy pampered indoor life in a house or apartment, in the city, suburbs, or country. Needing very little space, they adapt to most homes quite well.

What type of owner?

This breed demands regular attention and is very loving, appreciating owners with plenty of time who are devoted to their every need. Great fun when trained well, they enjoy being active and taking part in family life.

How much exercise and stimulation?

Puppies need short walks daily. As a sporting dog, they enjoy being out and about, so adults need a reasonable daily walk. Yorkies also enjoy hunting down rabbit holes or taking on the challenge of a bigger dog. Strict training may be necessary if he gets up to mischief!

Friendly with other pets?

Very amenable to other pets, particularly cats, if well socialized and raised with them. Bearing in mind the Yorkie ratting ancestry, small family pets such as mice, rats, and hamsters may be at risk.

Personality Traits	Poor	Average	Good	Excellent
Attitude toward other dogs				
Quietness				
Behavior at home				
Watchdog ability				
Good with children				
Ease of training				
Obedience to owner				

Time to maturity: The coat can take up to 3 years to mature
Male height: 7–10 in (18–25 cm)
Female height: 7–10 in (18–25 cm)
Weight: Up to 10 lb (4.5 kg)
Average lifespan: 12–17 years

Is puppy training easy?

His dominant personality means he may bark at anything, and needs strict handling to behave as a companion dog. Intelligent and quick to learn, he can be distracted. High energy levels and enthusiasm mean he can be stubborn.

Special puppy care?

The puppy coat needs daily grooming from early on because it does not shed naturally. Training starts early with short walks to socialize him with other animals.

Possible health problems?

Although usually quite healthy, Yorkies can suffer from dislocating elbows or knees, Legg-Perthes disease of the hip joint, cataracts, epilepsy, and heart problems. Choose breeders who check for health problems.

● *From workmans' ratters to noble ladies' companions, Yorkies are a popular choice for a family pet. This one is 6 months old.*

What can we do together?

Show dog and companion dog, and with their boundless energy and enthusiasm, Yorkies may excel at mini agility.

Don't forget!

Yorkies can get bored easily so provide a lot of toys that keep his mind active if he needs to be left alone for short periods.

Small dogs

Dachshund

Other names: Teckel, Dackel, German Badgerhound

These charming little dogs are thought to have originated in various parts of the world, their pictures appearing in Egyptian temples, while clay models have been found in Peru, Mexico, and other countries. More recently they have been linked to Germany, where a small short-legged dog was needed to hunt in confined forest areas. The meaning of the breed's name is "badger dog"—the Standard Dachshund will hunt and burrow underground for badgers and other lar animals such as foxes, while the Miniature will hunt rabbits. When hunting, this breed tend to rely on scent for trailing the prey, hence they are considere hounds rather than terriers. Dachshunds are availab in three types of coat—smooth, long, and wire-haired—and there is also a Miniature version availa The breed has a great personality, full of character can be very active; they make goo family pets, although they can b quite willful and headstrong.

Color choices?

The smooth and long-haired Dachshunds are red, black and tan, chocolate and tan, cream, dapple (merle), brindle and piebald (white on a base color). Wire-haired Dachshunds are found in most colors. Some have a small white patch on the chest.

How much grooming?

Smooth-hairs are very easy to care for, needing only a good brush twice weekly. Long-hairs need daily grooming with a brush and comb. Wire-hairs are hand stripped from being puppies to achieve the correct wire texture. The choice of a wire-hair puppy benefits from expert advice: smoother coat (not fluffy coat) puppies usually develop the best adult wire-hair texture.

Do they make good pets?

Dachshunds make devoted, loyal, and friendly pets, but occasionally they can be aggressive. They are courageous little dogs and very protective of their family. Their

● *Dachshunds are low slung, with short legs and loose skin. They were bred to hunt prey underground in deep holes.*

general demeanor and high intelligence make them excellent companions. Some show jealousy and if teased as youngsters may nip, but generally they are amenable to well-behaved children.

What home suits them?

The Dachshund's size makes him ideal for modern living in the city, suburbs, or country, and he is suit-able for apartment living provided he gets adequate exercise.

What type of owner?

Loving and full of personality even as puppies, they can be fei and stubborn. They need a strong-minded owner who will not allow them to develop bad habits, as we as a caring owner who understand their need for entertainment.

How much exercise and stimulation?

As puppies they enjoy walks of gradually increasing length, the regular exercise helping to preven back problems from developing. They enjoy playing and jumping around, but be careful with boisterous games because their long back is vulnerable to injury.

Friendly with other pets?

Very easygoing and sociable with other animals, but they do have a hunting instinct, so early socialization is needed to live in harmony. They usually enjoy the companionship of another dog in the household.

Personality Traits	Poor	Average	Good	Excellent
Attitude toward other dogs	■	■		
Quietness	■	■	■	
Behavior at home	■	■		
Watchdog ability	■	■	■	■
Good with children	■	■	■	
Ease of training	■	■		
Obedience to owner	■	■	■	

Time to maturity: 2.5 years
Male height: 8–10 in (20–25 cm)
Female height: 8–10 in (20–25 cm)
Weight: 15–28 lb (7–13 kg)
Average lifespan: 12–13 years

s puppy training easy?

Training is easier if the owner is firm and more determined than they are. Highly intelligent, smart, and strong-willed, they take advantage if owners are not firm with training. Reward-based training with a positive and consistent approach is best. Bored and untrained puppies may become destructive.

Special puppy care?

Puppies should not go on long walks too early, play too roughly, or become obese from too many treats in training because they risk back problems later in adult life. Puppies are prone to separation anxiety or chewing if left alone too long. Some are difficult to housetrain, so more patience than usual is needed in this regard.

Possible health problems?

Obesity and back problems caused by slipped discs are prominent. Also, elbow dysplasia, patella luxation (dislocating kneecaps), epilepsy, cataracts, and progressive retinal atrophy can occur. Blue, fawn, and cream colors may suffer from alopecia (hair loss).

● *Despite their charm, these 7-week-old puppies could grow up to be very mischievous.*

What can we do together?

They are great walking companion dogs when adult, and very good watchdogs.

Small dogs

Don't forget!

Be careful when carrying them, and don't let children play too roughly with them to avoid back injury.

Maltese

Other names: Maltese Lion Dog, Cokie

For many centuries the Maltese, which as its name suggests, came from the island of Malta, has wooed the hearts of ladies as a faithful companion and "comforter." It is one of the oldest of European Toy breeds, and was mentioned by Aristotle and other ancient classical authors. To keep the breed small, it is said that they were dosed with alcohol and kenneled in boxes. Their introduction to England came during the reign of Henry VII, and they were greatly fancied by the Elizabethan nobility. They made a formal debut in the 1860s when showing first started in England, closely followed by recognition in the United States in 1877. The long, soft and silky coat makes this a beautiful dog that is suitably complemented by his gentle, sweet nature and happy disposition. He is the ultimate in lapdogs, loving cuddles at home but also actively enjoying being out and about when walking with his owner.

Color choices?

Always snow white with a black button nose. Some have a slight lemon coloring that is still accepted for showing.

How much grooming?

Beautiful dogs with long silky coats and no undercoat, they demand a lot of attention to keep them looking good. Most pet owners keep a "puppy trim" even for adults, but they still need grooming daily. If kept long, owners should use a pin brush. The long hair on the head should be tied up to keep it out of the eyes. The coat sheds very little, although it mats and tangles as it is hair, not fur, and is suitable for people with allergies.

Do they make good pets?

These little dogs are most suited to families with older children who enjoy playing without being rough. They can be demanding and dependent on their owner, but are equally loving and good tempered with sensible families. Persistent barking can be a problem.

● *This sumptuous coat is beautiful but not very practical for pet owners.*

What home suits them?

Happy with city, suburban, or country life, and ideal for apartments, they do well with plenty of company. They enjoy walking, but the longer the coat, the more dirt they pick up, and more grooming will be needed.

What type of owner?

Cuddly companion dogs and comforters, they really appreciate owners who keep them close, as they will suffer separation anxiety if left alone too long. They can be very lively and exuberant puppies, so play and owner companionship with plenty of attention is important to them, although they can become dependent if an owner is not firm, becoming quite spoiled if overindulged.

How much exercise and stimulation?

Maltese enjoy good walks with the stimulation of a good snuffle in the grass, but a long coat may be a disadvantage. Mental stimulus is a must.

Friendly with other pets?

Provided they have been well socialized and raised with other pets, Maltese enjoy the company of other pets. They do have a hunting instinct, so friendships with small household pets should be limited. Their small size and playful nature may place them at risk of injury around the house.

Is puppy training easy?

Maltese prefer gentle training, and are eager to learn and please their trainer. Often hard to housetrain, they have a habit of barking that needs to be addressed early before it becomes an annoying habit.

Personality Traits	Poor	Average	Good	Excellent
Attitude toward other dogs				
Quietness				
Behavior at home				
Watchdog ability				
Good with children				
Ease of training				
Obedience to owner				

Time to maturity: 2 years
Male height: 8–10 in (20–25 cm)
Female height: 8–10 in (20–25 cm)
Weight: 4–6 lb (1.8–2.7 kg)
Average lifespan: 14 years

Special puppy care?

If the coat is left long, puppies need to get used to a lot of grooming to remove knots and tangles, and also to allow eye cleansing to avoid eye problems.

Possible health problems?

Generally very healthy, Maltese can suffer from problems such as patella luxation (dislocating kneecaps), hypoglycemia, teeth and gum weakness, and liver problems. Eye infections can develop and cause tear staining which marks the coat around the eyes.

Small dogs

What can we do together?

Long walks are enjoyed, despite his small size, and surprisingly, they do well in competitive obedience and agility.

Don't forget!

Maltese can become noisy barkers if left alone, so start to train them early to prevent the onset of separation anxiety.

● *Cuddly and affectionate, these attractive puppies make delightful pets.*

Japanese Chin

Other names: Japanese Spaniel, Chin Chin

This stylish little aristocrat's roots stretch back to the Imperial Japanese courts around the 8th century A.D., following their presentation there by Korean nobility, although even earlier records come from China where they were featured on oriental pottery. A devoted Japanese emperor even declared them an object of worship. Subsequently, Chins appeared in the West after trade opened up in the mid-19th century. They caused so much interest that dog-napping became common. Queen Victoria took an interest in breeding them, and eventually they found their way to New York and the show ring in 1882. This affectionate, entertaining little dog has a great sense of humor and is very well mannered around his family. Seldom found far from his owner, to whom he will be devoted, he rarely barks and makes an ideal apartment dog. The Chin is an excellent companion pet, but firm training is essential to prevent him from becoming spoiled.

Color choices?

Usually white with symmetrical black or red markings, with shades of red in varying intensity from deep red to lemon and brindle, and never tri-colored. A white blaze on the head and face is particularly special.

How much grooming?

The long, profuse, single coat, without curls or waves, sheds like human hair. A brush and comb daily will keep it clean and neat, with careful grooming needed under the ears, on the legs and skirt, and along the curved plumed tail. Chins have no coat odor, so they need only occasional bathing. Skin folds and eyes need regular attention, and moisture pockets in folds need wiping to prevent fungal infection.

Do they make good pets?

Chins are lively, alert, affectionate, gentle, well-mannered, and devoted to their owners—from whom they demand love and attention. They can be wary of strangers and may meet any advance with a snarl, but careful early socializing should prevent this.

● *Japanese Chins are affectionate, lively companions, and rarely forget a friend.*

What home suits them?

Ideal as clean apartment pets, Chins suit city, suburbia, or country life provided that they spend time with their owners. Regular daily walks, playtime, and plenty of owner contact are their main requirements.

What type of owner?

Chins are very devoted, preferring owners who understand their need for emotional well-being and who devote time to loving them as lapdogs. This breed suits non-working owners best, as they do not enjoy being left alone for long.

How much exercise and stimulation?

Chins are relatively tough, energetic dogs, so exercise is good, but not necessarily for mile after mile. Not the brightest of dogs, but they enjoy learning because of their eagerness to please.

Friendly with other pets?

Chins are regarded as quite cat-like in nature but without the predatory streak, and they are usually friendly with other household pets. Larger dogs in the household may appear overbearing to Chins, but if they are gentle, there should be no problem.

Is puppy training easy?

Chins love to please their owner, and will enjoy learning, but not all tasks will be achieved successfully. Early puppy training and socialization encourages a more emotionally balanced puppy.

Personality Traits	Poor	Average	Good	Excellent
Attitude toward other dogs		▪		
Quietness			▪	
Behavior at home			▪	
Watchdog ability	▪			
Good with children		▪		
Ease of training		▪		
Obedience to owner		▪		

Time to maturity: 18 months
Male height: 8–11 in (20–28 cm)
Female height: 8–11 in (20–28 cm)
Weight: 4–7 lb (1.8–3.2 kg)
Average lifespan: 12–14 years

Special puppy care?

Puppies need to be checked for signs of hypoglycemia (low blood sugar levels), such as tremors, listlessness, and a staggering gait. This can persist if puppies mature as low-weight adults. Care is needed regarding puppy diet because of the risk of allergies as they grow.

Possible health problems?

A Chin's short face and muzzle can cause breathing difficulties and heart problems, and for the same reason they can suffer from overheating. Other problems are patella luxation (dislocating kneecaps), seasonal allergies, and damage to the slightly bulging eyes from scratching or ulceration. Puppies can also suffer from hypoglycemia. Diet is important because of their sensitivity to corn.

What can we do together?

Typically, a Chin is a very calm pet that was bred as a lapdog for companionship. They love to be loved and owners will not fail to be entertained by a performance of the "Chin-spin"—rapid circles performed upright on hind legs and pawing with the front feet, while singing their "wooo" noise. They are great companions for the loving owner.

Don't forget!

Check that your puppy is being provided with the correct diet, and watch for signs of hypoglycemia and overheating.

Small dogs

● Ancestors of the Chin were very aristocratic, so Chins became quite used to being carried around in the sleeves of Oriental ladies' kimonos. This puppy is around 9 weeks old.

Papillon
Other names: Butterfly Dog, Continental Toy Spaniel, Squirrel Spaniel

Well known in European royal courts in the early 15th century, this dainty dog was often depicted in early Renaissance paintings as a drop-eared Spaniel variety, known as a "Phalène." Favored by nobility as devoted lapdogs, they are thought to originate from Italy or Spain, and became popular because of their sweet temper, playful ways, and dainty appearance. Modern Papillons have pricked ears, and the name

Papillon, meaning "butterfly" in French, was chosen because the distinctive face markings, with its blaze of white, and the upstanding fringed ears resembled a butterfly. Although slender and dainty, the Papillon is relatively hardy, always ready for a game, but equally happy to be quiet and calm. They have an appealing personality and make energetic playmates for children. The Papillon's silky coat keeps them warm in winter and cool in summer, and generally they are healthy and long-lived little dogs if cared for properly.

Color choices?
Usually white with a blaze on the face, and symmetrical body markings in any color except liver. Tri-colors are available, with black markings and tan spots. Distinctive coat markings are important only for show puppies.

How much grooming?
Caring for a Papillon's abundant, fine, and silky coat is easier if it is brushed for a few minutes daily and if tangles are removed by combing them out gently. Trimming the hair on the paws, with regular attention to nails, and bathing monthly is also recommended.

Do they make good pets?
Papillons are happy, friendly, adventurous dogs. They are good-natured with children, and, if socialized early, also with strangers and other pets. Active owners with sensible, older children are best because although these are energetic dogs, they are small and dainty enough to be vulnerable to injury if not treated carefully.

● *Papillons have distinctive facial markings and large "butterfly wing" ears.*

What home suits them?
Provided that they accompany their owner all the time, they adapt beautifully to most homes, whether a city apartment or a suburban home with a yard. Potential escape holes and low fences need special attention because they can squeeze through gaps and also jump well.

What type of owner?
Mainly companion dogs, Papillons need owners who will give them plenty of attention and not leave them home alone. They are energetic, so active owners who

enjoy walking are particularly suitable. Papillons prefer kind, gentle owners or families who are sensitive to their needs, and who bring out their charming and endearing personality.

How much exercise and stimulation?
Much of this breed's exercise comes through play, but walking regularly is necessary to provide socialization and to prevent behavioral problems. Unlike other toy breeds, Papillons enjoy long walks and agility is an ideal activity for them. They are intelligent, but need gentle, consistent training to master obedience tasks.

Friendly with other pets?
Early socialization is recommended, but they are rarely aggressive and if handled carefully, should pose no risk to other pets. Papillons are bossy and possessive, sometimes forgetting their small size around larger dogs. Keep this tendency in check through training and proper introductions. Breeders often

Personality Traits	Poor	Average	Good	Excellent
Attitude toward other dogs				
Quietness				
Behavior at home				
Watchdog ability				
Good with children				
Ease of training				
Obedience to owner				

Time to maturity: 2 years
Male height: 8–11 in (20–28 cm)
Female height: 8–11 in (20–28 cm)
Weight: 9–10 lb (4–4.5 kg)
Average lifespan: 13–14 years

recommend keeping two Papillons together as they play with and exercise one another.

Is puppy training easy?

Papillons are considered one of the easiest toy breeds to train because they want to please. They are reasonably intelligent and do well in agility, but owners should not expect too much. They need gentle, regular training to succeed.

Special puppy care?

Papillons are unsuitable for rough and tumble lives, especially when puppies, and owners should give a little extra care in those early years. Puppies can be possessive about food and toys and will benefit from firm handling in this respect. Papillons, especially puppies, are sensitive to cold, and should not be allowed to stay outside for long periods, or remain wet and cold after walks.

Small dogs

Possible health problems?

Papillons are quite hardy, but they can suffer from luxating patellas (dislocating kneecaps), eye problems, and allergies.

What can we do together?

Papillons have been successful in obedience, agility, and tracking, but their main pleasure is in spending quality time as a companion dog.

Don't forget!

Papillons will not appreciate being cold and wet. Always buy from a reputable breeder.

● *These 10-week-old cuddly puppies will make delightful family pets if their owner is patient, kind, and firm in training.*

Pomeranian
Other names: Pomeranian Loulou, Dwarf Spitz

This ball of fluff is the smallest of the spitz breeds; it is named after Pomerania, an old Prussian province in Central Europe. With a deep thick coat, bright eyes, and bushy tail, they are descended from larger forebears who were sled dogs in Iceland and Lapland. Favored by Queen Victoria, she bred and showed them, and is said to have reduced the original height by 50 percent. They have become one of America's most popular toy dogs since their debut in 1890. This tiny dog may look like a fluffy decorative plaything, but they need plenty of time for proper grooming. With a huge personality for such a small dog, they are outgoing, bossy, very loyal, and protective. Pomeranians are active and take an interest in everything around them, making them an intriguing pet with great character. They can be one of the more expensive toy dogs to buy.

Color choices?

Pomeranians come in a wide color choice that includes white, cream, orange, orange sable, wolf sable, red, brown, beaver, blue, black, and parti-colors—black and tan, brown and tan, spotted, and brindle. Evidence shows that merle coloring can produce health problems.

● *These sturdy dogs have an outgoing nature.*

How much grooming?

Their double coat needs frequent trimming and daily grooming through the overlying long, harsh, straight, and thick outer coat to the soft, thick, short undercoat. The coat knots and tangles easily and sheds constantly, so a stiff pin brush should be used. For showing, the coat needs shaping to look like a ball of fluff with protruding legs.

Do they make good pets?

Pomeranians are typically friendly and loyal to their owners and love their company. They can be equally calm and independent if the owner takes time with training. They are unsuitable for busy families or those with young children, because of the attention and coat care that is required.

What home suits them?

Pomeranians adjust well to city living or country life. Their small size makes them ideal for apartments provided they are taken out regularly or spend time playing with their owner. They make very good companions for elderly people who are housebound.

What type of owner?

Pomeranians develop a strong bond with their owner and can suffer from separation anxiety. They are affectionate, demand plenty of time and attention, and will be jealous and protective of their family. They are not suitable for owners who have no time for grooming, socializing, or training, and may become tyrants if their training is neglected or the owner is overindulgent and spoils them.

How much exercise and stimulation?

Despite their size, their sled-dog background makes them capable of walking some distance, but owners can satisfy them by playing in the yard for exercise and stimulation.

Friendly with other pets?

They are generally friendly and sociable with other pets, but unless trained and socialized as puppies, they can be aggressive or bullying to larger dogs. They enjoy a good chase.

Is puppy training easy?

These are intelligent dogs and

Personality Traits	Poor	Average	Good	Excellent
ttitude toward other dogs				
Quietness				
Behavior at home				
Watchdog ability				
Good with children				
Ease of training				
Obedience to owner				

Time to maturity: 2 years
Male height: 8.5–11 in (22–28 cm)
Female height: 8.5–11 in (22–28 cm)
Weight: 4–5 lb (1.8–2.3 kg)
Average lifespan: 12–15 years

earn quickly, benefiting from egular, patient, and gentle training. Not the most obedient breed, they an be naughty if bored or lonely.

pecial puppy care?

upervise puppies around ther household pets and mall children, as they are ulnerable because of their mall size. Discourage barking when young or this may become a difficult habit o break later. Puppies need o be trained to stand for grooming because the coat needs routine daily care, as it sheds continuously.

ossible health problems?

Patella luxation (dislocating kneecaps), tracheal (windpipe) collapse, black skin disease causing the hair to fall out, entropion (inward-turning eyelashes), Cushing's syndrome, hypothyroidism, and cryptorchidism (undescended testes). Merle colors also suffer from deafness, skeletal, and cardiac problems.

What can we do together?

Poms are excellent watchdogs, companions, and show dogs.

● This 6-week-old ball of fluff will enjoy active play.

Don't forget!

These little dogs have a big personality, and need time devoted to grooming and firm training.

Small dogs

Norfolk Terrier and Norwich Terrier

In 1932, these two working terriers were so closely related that they were regularly interbred and recognized as one breed, the only distinction being their different ear carriage. They were ideal for hunting rabbit and vermin across East Anglia's wide areas of cultivation and woodlands and fields, and were favored as mascots by Cambridge University undergraduates. By 1964, under pressure from breed enthusiasts, the two breeds were separated, distinguished by the Norfolk's drop ears and its slightly softer expression, as opposed to the Norwich's pricked ears. Both have friendly, good-natured characters, and a loveable disposition. Their compact size make them adaptable to most situations, and they suit owners who like a less feisty terrier temperament. Busy, bustling, and with a captivating and outgoing personality, they make ideal family pets for owners who enjoy companionship, and who like caring for dogs with easy grooming and walking requirements.

Color choices?

Shades of red, black and tan, wheaten, or grizzle (red and black hairs mixed). There should be no white markings.

How much grooming?

This harsh, wiry outer coat and soft, warm undercoat benefit from grooming twice a week—especially face and leg hair—using a pin brush, steel comb or hound glove. Hand-stripping will be needed twice a year to remove dead hair and to encourage new growth. Trimming or cutting the hair is not recommended by groomers as it spoils the hair texture.

Do they make good pets?

These are sociable, busy Terriers who enjoy family activities and thrive on company. They will not appreciate being roughly handled by young children, but are tolerant of older children who treat them sensibly. They are exceptionally companionable and make excellent pets for most age groups.

● *Norfolk and Norwich Terriers are distinguished by their different ear carriage.*

What home suits them?

With plenty of exercise, these Terriers settle happily in cities, suburbs, or in the country, provided that their owner never leaves them alone for too long. They prefer country living, because it presents opportunities for hunting and sniffing around hedgerows. A yard with secure fencing is best.

What type of owner?

An owner who appreciates an active, busy life, and allows time for playing and grooming will suit these energetic little dogs. They like their owner to be available most of the time because they do get lonely. Owners must not mind if they indulge in digging in the ground—a true Terrier trait.

How much exercise and stimulation?

Bred for hunting, these Terriers enjoy at least an hour of walking every day. They can be adaptable and cope with shorter walks, but they need stimulating activity at least a few times a week to stop them from putting on weight and to provide valuable mental stimulation.

Friendly with other pets?

Assertive and energetic, but friendly with other household pets, they need early socialization and to learn good manners while puppies to avoid problems later. They may be inclined to hunt small pets or chase the neighbor's cat.

Personality Traits	Poor	Average	Good	Excellent
Attitude toward other dogs				
Quietness				
Behavior at home				
Watchdog ability				
Good with children				
Ease of training				
Obedience to owner				

Time to maturity: 2 years
Male height: 9–10 in (23–25 cm)
Female height: 9–10 in (23–25 cm)
Weight: 11–12 lb (5–5.5 kg)
Average lifespan: 13–14 years

Is puppy training easy?

Like any Terrier they can be willful and disobedient with a mind of their own. Both breeds need to start being trained as soon as possible, and benefit from firm, kind, and reward-based training. Obedience is not their forte, but patient, conscientious owners will achieve a well-behaved dog.

Special puppy care?

Puppies do not appreciate rough play and are inclined to nip small children if they tease. Seeing how puppies can be assertive when very young, this should prompt owners to start training early and to make it consistent and regular.

Possible health problems?

Expect them to be hardy and healthy, but some suffer from eye problems, hip dysplasia (deformity), luxating patellas (dislocating kneecaps), allergies, heart defects, and respiratory problems.

Small dogs

What can we do together?

Both do well in hunting, Earthdog trials, agility, and flyball competitions. They excel as companion pets, too.

Don't forget!

These Terriers can appear hungry, but try not to overfeed them. Buy only from reputable breeders. The ears of the Norfolk need checking weekly to keep them clean.

● *Both of these Terriers enjoy life to the fullest, and have the personality of big dogs in little dogs' bodies. This puppy is 12 weeks old.*

Havanese
Other names: Bichon Habanero, Havanese Silk Dog, Havaneser

This breed is the national dog of Cuba. It is descended from the Bichon and the now extinct Blanquito de la Habana. The Philippines also claim the breed, but it is likely they originated in the western Mediterranean and were taken overseas by Spanish Conquistadors. The most common color, "Havana Brown," inspired their name as they lived mainly in Cuba's capital city. By the 1950s they were almost extinct in Cuba, but a few specimens smuggled into the U created an opportunity for the breed to become popular again. Their greatest popularity in modern times came in the 1990s, when they established a reputation for their lively, affectionate charm and suitability as an excellent children's playmate and family dog. These dogs make ideal companions for apartment living and require very little walking, bu their beautiful coats do need plenty of grooming t keep them looking neat.

Color choices?
Coat colors are white, cream, fawn, orange, red, brown, silver, black, or blue. Color can be solid, or with mixed markings, pied, brindle or parti-colors.

How much grooming?
Some Havanese have dense, curly coats that mat and tangle, needing more grooming; the correct, soft silky coat is less time-consuming. A soft pin brush and wide-toothed comb are best, and coats should not be trimmed or stripped; pets can have shorter coats for convenience. Hair above the eyes can be trimmed, braided, or tied back. Paw-pad hair is trimmed to prevent slipping. Weekly ear cleaning, and eye cleaning is needed to remove tear stains.

Do they make good pets?
These fun-loving pups are happy anywhere. Gentle with children and very much a family member, they are good watchdogs, but never yappy. However, firm handling is important.

What home suits them?
They are robust enough to live and

● *Good temperaments make these delightful pets for the right family.*

exercise in the suburbs and country, but they make happy companions for city-dwelling apartment owners, too. Not demanding, they love human contact and are also happy with other pets.

What type of owner?
Havanese are great companions for owners who lavish affection on them. Havanese can be left for short periods, but prefer attention and company. Owners must be attentive and conscientious about coat care and playtime.

How much exercise and stimulation?
Short walks two or three times a day around town are fine, but

Havanese do enjoy long walks, to Their personality is lively and bright, so play sessions and learni new tricks are good for mental stimulation.

Friendly with other pets?
This is the "love people, love oth pets" dog, although their ideal ma be another Havanese. Some owners may have difficulty with breeding them if they are kept alone, as they prefer to be in breeding "groups" rather than housed individually.

Is puppy training easy?
Always cheerful, Havanese enjoy showing off, and thrive on learnin tricks. Puppies are more likely to retain obedience skills if learned young, and taught with a positive and sensitive approach.

Special puppy care?
Puppies must learn to let their coats be groomed daily and have their ears and eyes cleaned. Lighte coats may need more warmth in winter, so make sure puppies kee

Personality Traits	Poor	Average	Good	Excellent
Attitude toward other dogs				
Quietness				
Behavior at home				
Watchdog ability				
Good with children				
Ease of training				
Obedience to owner				

Time to maturity: 2 years
Male height: 8–12 in (20–30 cm)
Female height: 8–12 in (20–30 cm)
Weight: 7–13 lb (3–6 kg)
Average lifespan: 14–16 years

warm. Teaching obedience early is essential to prevent bad habits that may persist into adulthood.

Possible health problems?

Havanese are particularly hardy with few inherited health problems reported. Most breeders participate in rigorous health testing for potential problems. They can, however, suffer from cataracts, retinal dysplasia, patella luxation (dislocating kneecaps), heart, and liver disease. Tear marks around the eyes can be caused by dietary allergies. Ears must be plucked and cleaned to prevent infections.

What can we do together?

Havanese will participate in flyball, dog agility, freestyle, and obedience trials. They also work as therapy dogs, and assist the hearing impaired.

Small dogs

Don't forget!

The lighter coats are ideal for tropical weather, so some dogs may appreciate more warmth in colder weather.

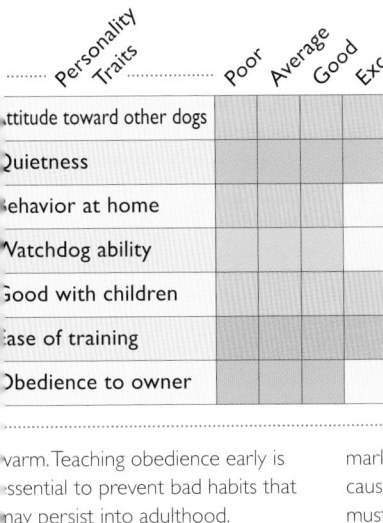

 Start your puppy training early to help this 10-week-old Havanese learn good manners from a young age.

Bichon Frise

Other names: Tenerife Dog, Bichon Tenerife

Bichons originated in the Canary Isles in the 14th century, where they were reputed to descend from Water Spaniels or Barbets. Italian sailors befriended them as sailing companions. Bichons became favorites of Italian, French, and Spanish aristocracy, and were particularly popular at the court of King Francis I, and they were also greatly admired by King Henry III. Bichon-type dogs often appear in paintings of royal families from the past and they resemble the cuddly white ball of fluff with jet black eyes and nose that we see today. The breed later became popular as performing dogs in circuses. In the mid 1900s, they established a place as popular show specimens esteemed for their glamorous looks. Today, this lively and exuberant small dog loves long walks and makes a charming and entertaining family pet. Intelligent, but adaptable and very strong-willed, he does need firm training to be at his best.

Color choices?

Usually white, especially show specimens, but apricot or gray are available. White puppies may have apricot shades or gray in immature coats, but this clears by 18 months.

How much grooming?

One of a group of breeds reputed to have hypoallergenic coats, Bichons need lots of care with a pin brush and wide-toothed comb. Matted coats cause health problems, so daily brushing is essential. Trimming is needed every four to six weeks, with bathing once a month. Continental owners prefer the natural curly look, whereas British and U.S. owners like sculpted, round trims, particularly for showing. Pet owners will find a puppy clip more manageable. The white coat needs attention around the eyes and mouth to prevent stains, and hair on the feet and muzzle must be trimmed neatly.

Do they make good pets?

Bichons love company, and demand attention in abundance. They are good natured, sensitive, affectionate, and

● *Little fluff-ball puppies will grow up to look just like adult Bichons.*

well-mannered if trained properly, but their strong-minded attitude may make them household tyrants. With their high energy levels, they enjoy playing with sensible children and make charming family pets.

What home suits them?

The Bichon size is suitable for most dwellings, provided that he has plenty of exercise, but his preference would be for a yard to play outdoors.

What sort of owner?

Owners must be willing to devote hours of attention, which will be repaid in abundance. Not liking to be left alone, Bichons need an owner who is always around to groom them daily, play with them go on long walks. Owners should not to overindulge, or let bad hab and willfulness take over.

How much exercise and stimulation?

Bichons enjoy long walks, and lots exuberant playing. Their backgrou as circus performers makes them eager for mental stimulation throu learning tricks and obedience task

Friendly with other pets?

Bichons get along well with other household pets, particularly cats and dogs. However, early puppy socialization is important, as this character enjoys being the center of attention and other pets may fi his playful nature too demanding.

Is puppy training easy?

Training should start early for this puppy and owners must be consistent. Bichons are strong-will stubborn, and manipulative, so the can be challenging. Training needs be imaginative—use toys to attrac attention and to maintain interest.

Personality Traits	Poor	Average	Good	Excellent
Attitude toward other dogs				
Quietness				
Behavior at home				
Watchdog ability				
Good with children				
Ease of training				
Obedience to owner				

Time to maturity: 2–3 years
Male height: 9–12 in (23–30 cm)
Female height: 9–12 in (23–30 cm)
Weight: 7–12 lb (3–5.5 kg)
Average lifespan: 12–14 years

Small dogs

Special puppy care?

Puppies who fail to thrive or are underweight should be checked early for liver problems, as later treatment is less effective. Bichon puppies take longer than most dogs to mature, so persistence with training is necessary. Use suitable shampoo according to age and coat type when bathing puppies.

Possible health problems?

Very robust and healthy, they can suffer from dislocating kneecaps, hip dysplasia (deformity), hemophilia, eye, heart, and liver problems.

What can we do together?

Mainly companions, Bichons will enjoy long walks, learning, performing tricks, and showing.

Don't forget!

Firmness really counts with this breed, so early puppy training and socializing is a must. Don't overindulge this puppy because he could become spoiled. It is recommended that all Bichons have an annual eye test.

Five little bundles of week-old cuteness.

Lhasa Apso *Other names: Abso Seng Kyi*

The Lhasa Apso, named after the sacred Tibetan city of Lhasa, is one of the most ancient of dog breeds. Thought to have been domesticated as long ago as 800 B.C., Tibetan nobility and ancient Buddhist monks needed sentinel dogs to guard their homes and monasteries and the Lhasa proved ideal. The Dalai Lama was particularly possessive of Lhasas, presenting them only to the most important visitors, because the Lamas' souls were thought to be preserved in the Lhasa Apso. Consequently, the breed only made its debut in the Western world early in the 1900s. With a beautiful long, flowing coat and a character encapsulated in the Tibetan name that means "bearded lion sentinel dog," Lhasas are reputed to bring good luck. They are lively, independent, courageous, hardy dogs with assertive minds, who can be willful and disobedient if untrained, but they make ideal family pets because of their size and personality.

Color choices?

Golden or lion-like colors are preferred, so sable, honey, dark gray, slate, smoke, black, white, brown, or parti-colors are all acceptable.

How much grooming?

A Lhasa's coat is long and beautiful, and owners need to provide thorough daily brushing with a firm brush and comb through the soft undercoat to the skin. Neglect can cause skin problems, excessive tangles, and painful matting, so owners may prefer to give a puppy clip every six weeks and tie back the hair over the eyes. Lhasas do not enjoy bathing, but coats need regular washing, with particular attention paid to the hair on the face and underbody.

Do they make good pets?

Lhasas make great pets because they are devoted, and they love to please their owners. They can be willful, however, and may snap if treated roughly, and often find it hard if they are not the center of attention. If trained and socialized

● *Always on alert to warn of visitors.*

well, they are versatile, happy, loyal, affectionate, and extremely devoted pets.

What home suits them?

This adaptable dog will live in cities, suburbs, or the country, but his lively spirit needs to be satisfied with a good daily walk or several shorter interesting outings. A yard to play in is ideal, or a large park close by for apartment dwellers.

What type of owner?

With a high-maintenance coat, this dog is suitable only for owners with time to provide the necessary grooming care. Extremely loyal and devoted, these dogs want to please and owners must devote time to training and socializing them.

How much exercise and stimulation?

Lhasas are hardy and lively by nature, so they tolerate plenty of exercise despite their small size. Stimulation is essential for their intelligent minds and they enjoy time spent with their owner.

Friendly with other pets?

Naturally wary and suspicious of strangers, including other dogs, males may be aggressive toward rivals. While they get along well with family pets if socialized early on, cats will be chased and household pets belonging to other families may not be tolerated.

Is puppy training easy?

Lhasas need firm training because they are intelligent, alert, assertive dogs and they may try to be dominant. They love learning; owners who use fun, reward-base training, will achieve the best resul

Personality Traits	Poor	Average	Good	Excellent
Attitude toward other dogs				
Quietness				
Behavior at home				
Watchdog ability				
Good with children				
Ease of training				
Obedience to owner				

Time to maturity: 18 months
Male height: 9–11 in (23–28 cm)
Female height: 8–10 in (20–25 cm)
Weight: 13–15 lb (6–7 kg)
Average lifespan: 13–14 years

● *If you want a pair of Lhasas, don't choose two males or rivalry may develop between them.*

Small dogs

8-week-old puppies enjoy cuddling up together, or sharing a toy.

Special puppy care?

Habituate puppies to grooming and bathing early on. This ensures good coat quality, which will maintain health and prevent skin problems later. Make sure to check kidney function in puppies as they can suffer from kidney problems when quite young. If the puppy seems off-color, consult your veterinarian.

Possible health problems?

They mainly suffer from eye problems, but skin problems occur if they are not groomed regularly, even if the coat is kept short. Some puppies suffer from juvenile kidney disease.

What can we do together?

They are mainly companion dogs, but Lhasas will enjoy long walks with their owner. They make excellent show dogs but have high maintenance needs. Their keen hearing and deep bark make them good watchdogs.

Don't forget!

Regular coat care is essential. Lhasas have big personalities and need early training and socializing to prevent them from becoming spoiled.

Border Terrier

This tough little Terrier derives from a mix of several Terrier breeds, and he hails from the Border country between England and Scotland. The Border was specifically bred to be rugged, courageous, strong to tackle a fox or badger, and have abundant energy to keep up with horses during a day's hunting. Slightly longer legged, Borders are energetic and tireless, and have a reputation for being the most brave and powerful of hunting Terriers. The breed excels in many areas; they are agile, playful, and friendly, and known for not being as aggressive as other Terriers. His daily requirements are relatively low, but attention and stimulation for an energetic mind is essential. Borders hate being left alone at home—when they are, they are likely to be noisy, destructive and mischievous. Generally, they are friendly and loving and make one of the best family pets with a reputation for being good with children.

Color choices?

Red, wheaten, grizzle and tan, or blue and tan are available. There may be white markings on the chest.

How much grooming?

Borders have double coats, a harsh, dense and wiry outer coat that is weather- and dirt-resistant, and a short, soft undercoat. Grooming twice weekly is ideal, using a palm brush to remove dead hairs and combing down to the skin. Hand-strip bi-monthly for showing, or twice yearly for pets. Occasional bathing may be necessary for dogs kept indoors.

Do they make good pets?

Borders' gentler personality makes them less feisty than other Terriers, and their cheerful, friendly nature means that they bond well with sensible children. They enjoy owners who value their company, and in return make loving pets.

What home suits them?

The Border's happy disposition makes it suitable for living in cities,

● *Traditionally these little dogs were tenacious and hostile, but today's Border is an amiable dog. The otter-like head and strong legs are ideal for burrowing in the ground.*

suburbs, or the country, provided that he is well exercised to maintain his health and well-being. They adapt well to all environments, as long as there is plenty of action. A secure yard is important, as they are game for adventure and will seek to escape if life on the other side seems more interesting.

What type of owner?

Borders are great for active families who enjoy being out and about, and who accept their fun-loving, lively personality. Having time to spend playing, exercising, and providing early basic training and socialization should be an important consideration for owners.

How much exercise and stimulation?

These Terriers were bred to hunt all day, so plenty of exercise is needed, particularly for dogs living in smaller premises. Stimulation is essential or they will find mischief. They may become destructive if bored or lonely.

Friendly with other pets?

Generally friendly with low aggression levels, but small household pets (rabbits, guinea pigs, and mice) may be at risk from a Border with hunting instincts. Good socialization and early training helps considerably.

Is puppy training easy?

Borders are not difficult to train, but can be stubborn and strong-willed, so they need firm handling. Puppies need training to respond to commands early, before they develop independent minds and focus on other pursuits. Training should be firm and consistent. Hide-and-seek tasks and agility are ideal training exercises.

Personality Traits	Poor	Average	Good	Excellent
Attitude toward other dogs				
Quietness				
Behavior at home				
Watchdog ability				
Good with children				
Ease of training				
Obedience to owner				

Time to maturity: 3 years
Male height: 10–11 in (25–28 cm)
Female height: 10–11 in (25–28 cm)
Weight: 11.5–15.5 lb (5–7 kg)
Average lifespan: 14 years

task-related activities appeal to their intelligence. They can jump high and run fast, so agility-based activities will be fun. Earthdog trials are a popular way of testing a Border's hunting abilities.

go to ground in pursuit of interesting smells or game, so make sure when you walk there is no danger of them getting stuck in holes.

Small dogs

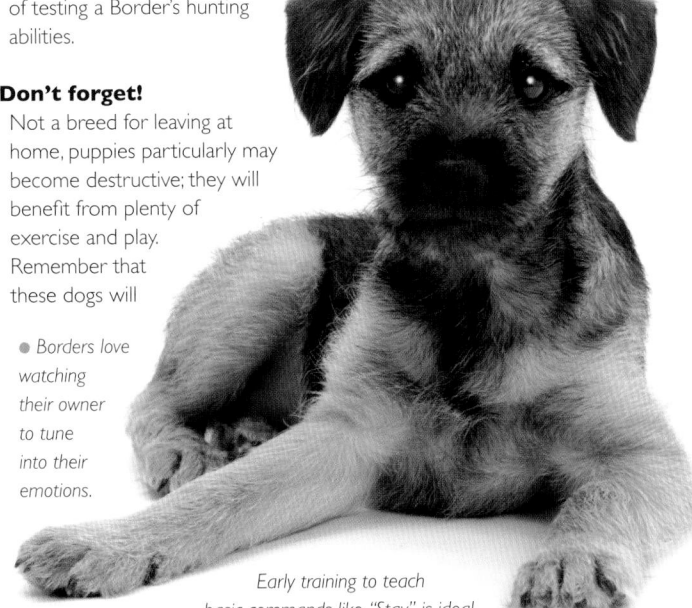

● *Puppies at 5 months are agile and playful.*

Special puppy care?
Puppies won't take kindly to being teased or treated badly, so children need supervising. Be careful with small toys as they may be chewed or eaten—puppies will respond to their natural hunting instinct for small prey.

Possible health problems?
Borders are usually a hardy breed, but they do have some genetic problems that include heart and eye problems, hip dysplasia, Legg-Perthes disease (malformation of the hip joint), and sometimes seizures.

What can we do together?
Learning tricks is not their forte, but

Don't forget!
Not a breed for leaving at home, puppies particularly may become destructive; they will benefit from plenty of exercise and play. Remember that these dogs will

● *Borders love watching their owner to tune into their emotions.*

Early training to teach basic commands like "Stay" is ideal.

Tibetan Spaniel

History tells us that Tibetan Spaniels were used to turn the prayer wheels for the ancient orders of Tibetan monks. Although one of several sacred Tibetan breeds, this one was considered the monks' favorite. Originating in the Himalayas, they served the purpose of sitting guard high up on the monastery walls. Using their excellent vision, they could see intruders approaching and barked well in advance of other watchdogs. Tibetan Spaniels arrived in Brit around 1900, although they did not become popula the United States until the 1960s. Noted for being gentle breed that is good natured and affectionate, they are calm, intelligent, and relatively quiet by comparison to other dogs. With an excellent natura watchfulness, fueled by a mistrust of strangers, they make good watchdogs, but are very unlikely to be aggressive. They need regular coat care, but otherw their needs can be fairly easily met by pet owners.

Color choices?

Several varieties of solid or multi-colors, but the usual colors are black, black and tan, red, gold, fawn, cream or white. Darker colors often have white markings on the paws.

How much grooming?

Tibetans have medium-length, silky, double coats, shorter on the face and legs and with feathering on the ears, toes, and tail. They need brushing daily to maintain health and coat hygiene; grooming with a soft brush and comb is best. Bathing once a month is usually sufficient.

Do they make good pets?

These dogs have great personalities and make excellent pets. They have an outgoing nature and are quite strong physically for a small breed. They enjoy a full life, either running around playing, or sitting quietly indoors with the family. Be cautious especially when they are with young children, as their gentle nature is sensitive to rough play, and their size makes them vulnerable to injury.

● *Coat feathering takes a long time to grow and may not develop for months.*

What home suits them?

Tibetan Spaniels are very adaptable and do well in most household environments. They enjoy homes with a yard where they can run around, but if they are walked daily, they will settle equally well in apartments or suburban locations.

What type of owner?

Tibetans need owners who understand them and appreciate them for what they are: gentle little dogs who have long been closely associated with Buddhism. Owners must also pay attention to regular coat care and walking.

How much exercise and stimulation?

These little dogs enjoy daily exerci and mental stimulation, because they are very positive and outgoin temperamentally. Suitable habitua-tion and socialization helps over-come distrust of strangers, and spending time meeting people should always form part of early puppy activities.

Friendly with other pets?

Kind and gentle, these little dogs ge along well with other household pets, and particularly have no problem with cats, although early socialization with all pets is still needed.

Is puppy training easy?

Training is very easy. It should be gentle and reward-based, as they respond well to kindness. With the delightful temperament, Tibetans are unlikely to take over their household, but generally need guidance in learning what behavior an owner will find preferable and what is not allowed.

Personality Traits	Poor	Average	Good	Excellent
Attitude toward other dogs				
Quietness				
Behavior at home				
Watchdog ability				
Good with children				
Ease of training				
Obedience to owner				

Time to maturity: 18 months
Male height: 10–11 in (25–28 cm)
Female height: 9.5–10.5 in (24–27 cm)
Weight: 9–15.5 lb (4–7 kg)
Average lifespan: 11–12 years

Special puppy care?

Although small dogs, they are full of life and often think they are bigger than they are! Puppies can be vulnerable because of their size. Training must be gentle and sensitive, particularly for puppies in the early stages. A puppy's failure to thrive needs prompt investigation as it could indicate signs of liver problems.

Possible health problems?

Like many breeds, Tibetans have problems with their eyes (progressive retinal atrophy causing blindness), allergies, and liver shunt (a blood supply abnormality that causes problems with filtering out waste in the body and becomes evident in puppies or young dogs).

What can we do together?

Tibetans are great as family pets, or for single owners who want a companionable little dog for taking walks. They make good watchdogs, too.

Don't forget!

Liver shunt is inherited, so remember to ask if tests have been done on relatives and if the puppy's parents are healthy. Their small size and sensitive nature should be respected, particularly if they are handled by small children.

● *This silky coat of this 5-month-old puppy is best groomed by daily brushing using a soft brush. Coat feathering takes a long time to grow.*

Small dogs

Pug

One of the oldest of the short faced (brachycephalic) breeds, the Pug originated in China as a tiny Mastiff dog and was bred as a lapdog during the Shang Dynasty. The name "Pug" is believed to mean "monkey face," although in Latin "pugnus" means fist, which notes the round fist-shape of the head. Traveling west in the 16th century with Dutch East India Company traders, they became favorites among Dutch,

French, and Italian nobility, and from there came to England where they became popular in the 18th century. This is one of the few breeds retaining its original looks with its coil tail, button ears, round black-muzzled head and wizened little face. The vertical wrinkle or "prince mark" on the Pug's head is highly favored. Low maintenance, this breed is neat, obedient, and companionable. The Pug's fortunes have dipped and risen over the years, but appear to be blossoming again.

Color choices?

The smooth, glossy coat is silver, fawn, apricot, or black with well defined markings. The dark mask appears on the muzzle and ears of lighter colors, with a thumb mark or diamond shape on the head, and a black "trace" line down the back from head to tail.

How much grooming?

Grooming is needed several times a week, using a hound glove or chamois cloth to remove shedding hair that may be abundant. Facial wrinkles need gentle cleansing to keep them dry and to prevent infection. Eyes need to be checked, as they are sensitive to dust and injury.

Do they make good pets?

Pugs make excellent family pets, and enjoy playing with children, provided they are gentle. Their good nature and even temper allows them to bond easily and become an essential member of any family.

What home suits them?

Pugs are clean and companionable and suit most homes because they

● *Busy and curious, Pugs have a lot of personality and make very appealing family pets.*

are robust for suburban and country living, but small and neat for apartments. This breed is gregarious, and will want to be around people and not be shut away on their own.

What type of owner?

Pugs sense their owner's mood, and may be quiet and docile or energetic and active. Owners may find this personality demanding, but they are affectionate little dogs and

are happy to follow the owner's lifestyle, providing it does not involve long walks and they do not work away from home.

How much exercise and stimulation?

Pugs need exercise to avoid obesity, so a good walk daily and time to play is usually sufficient. Keeping them active and stimulated maintains their health.

Friendly with other pets?

This is a good breed to mix with other household pets, as they do not have specific natural behaviors likely to cause a problem. Their bulging eyes can be vulnerable to injury by cats. Other pets may find their characteristic snorting and grunting disconcerting.

Is puppy training easy?

Pugs need firm training early on to develop their potential as good-natured adults. They train reasonably easily but are strong-minded, so they may not always be obedient. Persistence is needed.

Personality Traits	Poor	Average	Good	Excellent
Attitude toward other dogs				
Quietness				
Behavior at home				
Watchdog ability				
Good with children				
Ease of training				
Obedience to owner				

Time to maturity: 2 years
Male height: 10–11 in (25–28 cm)
Female height: 10–11 in (25–28 cm)
Weight: 14–18 lb (6.5–8 kg)
Average lifespan: 12–15 years

These pups are about 9 weeks old.

massaging the throat can shorten episodes of breathing problems. Hip dysplasia, Legg Perthes disease (a hip problem), luxating patella (dislocating kneecap), Pug dog encephalitis (affecting puppies from six months to 7 years), hemivertebrae (congenital spinal deformity), obesity, heat sensitivity can occur. The Pug's bulging eyes can be prone to injury.

Small dogs

What can we do together?
Pugs have been known to do obedience, fly ball, agility, and to provide support for disabled owners or the hearing impaired.

With their flat face, bulging eyes and great charm, Pugs will appeal to families who enjoy quieter, less active lifestyles.

Special puppy care?
Encourage your puppy to allow to be cleaned their face wrinkles and eyes when very young, as this needs to be done regularly. Overheating should be avoided. Incorrect feeding can cause flatulence, so the diet needs attention. Pugs can be hard to housetrain, so you'll need patience and understanding.

Possible health problems?
Sniffling, snorting, and breathing difficulty caused by respiratory problems or pharyngeal gag reflex (elongated palate) is common—

Don't forget!
Pugs do not tolerate overheating and must be kept cool on a hot day. Take care of the wrinkles around the face and avoid injury to their protruding eyes.

Scottish Terrier *Other names: Aberdeen Terrier*

These Terriers hail from the Highlands of Scotland, although controversy rages about their exact ancestry and correct name. These Terriers have a long history in the farming communities of the Scottish Highlands, where they were also used as hunting dogs, despite their small size. Today's Scotties are so synonymous with their heritage that they often appear in advertisements for many Scottish products. Reserved and often unfriendly to strangers, as family dogs they make ideal companions and enjoy family life and time spent with close friends. Very territorial by nature, some may be inclined to take over households, but in general they are kind, devoted dogs with a lively, playful, and sensitive temperament. Scotties settle well in any home from an apartment to a country farmhouse, and can adapt well to a variety of lifestyles.

Color choices?

They are nearly always black, but can also be wheaten (pale straw color), or brindle.

How much grooming?

Scotties typically have hard, wiry, waterproof outer coats with soft, thick undercoats, and longer hair on the beard, legs, and under the body. Professional grooming is needed three to four times a year for hand-stripping and clipping, but owners must be conscientious about daily brushing with a hard pin brush, and combing through the longer hair on the face and lower body to keep the coat neat.

Do they make good pets?

Strong-willed, hardy, and courageous, Scotties can be feisty by nature, and have strong hunting instincts. They form strong, loyal bonds with their owners and make good family pets with sensible children, although they avoid young children who may be rough. Scotties seldom bark, but their territorial nature makes them excellent watchdogs.

Small but perfectly formed.

● *A true Highlander, with loads of charm.*

What home suits them?

Scotties suit city, suburban, or country life, but apartment dwellers should provide good daily walks to release their abundant energy. Gardeners beware, this is an enthusiastic digger—they will burrow under fences if the world outside seems more interesting. Secure, high fencing is essential, and in the country, their hunting instinct may become evident.

What type of owner?

Scotties are proud and stubborn—they have strong personalities and occasionally appear quite obstinate. But, owners who handle them firmly and work with this disposition to guide good behavior will be well rewarded. These dogs also like owners who give them plenty of company and provide the necessary regular coat care.

How much exercise and stimulation?

Full of energy, Scotties were bred to hunt, and a lot of exercise and stimulation will be needed. Scotties are intelligent and playful as puppies and time spent bonding through play usually pays dividends in successful training.

Personality Traits	Poor	Average	Good	Excellent
ttitude toward other dogs				
Quietness				
Behavior at home				
Watchdog ability				
Good with children				
ase of training				
Obedience to owner				

Time to maturity: 2.5 years
Male height: 10–11 in (25–28 cm)
Female height: 10–11 in (25–28 cm)
Weight: 19–23 lb (8.5–10.5 kg)
Average lifespan: 13–14 years

iendly with other pets?

cotties expect to rule any ousehold, but with early ocialization they nearly lways get along well with ther family pets, although mall pets may be at risk ecause of their inherent unting instincts.

puppy training easy?

raining is difficult for owners who o not engender respect and bond ensibly with their Scottie puppy. hey are stubborn and may only ooperate on their own terms, so arly socialization is essential. raining must be firm, consistent, nd sensitive, but always kind.

pecial puppy care?

This breed really does need early ocializing. Try o buy from a reputable reeder who starts this process early. Avoid any puppy tress, such as situations when they re lonely or frightened, as this could cause health problems.

Possible health problems?

Scotties have a few health problems ranging from flea allergy, cranio-mandibular osteopathy (a disease of the lower jaw), von Willebrand disease (a blood coagulation abnormality), hypothyroidism (low levels of thyroid hormone), and a higher incidence of cancer than other breeds.

Small dogs

What can we do together?

Scotties enjoy hunting and outdoor pursuits, and have proved successful in the show ring, but otherwise they make excellent companion dogs for the right kind of owner.

Don't forget!

This dog has a strong personality that requires plenty of socializing. Training can be difficult, so owners also need to have strong personalities to handle them.

● *Even at 12 weeks, this Scottie is devoted, playful, and sensitive. Scotties will appeal to families seeking a dog with an honest nature.*

Miniature Pinscher

Miniature Pinschers hailed from Germany several centuries ago. Their exact origins are unknown, but they probably developed from indigenous German Terrier types. Celebrated as the "King of Toys," Pinschers are particularly admired for an elegant high-stepping gait and a clean, dainty body. Often considered the most soundly built of toy breeds, the Pinscher's solid, muscular body can cope with high activity levels when needed. Their fearless nature, coupled with high energy and inquisitiveness, make them enthusiastic watchdogs as well as loving and entertaining companions. Without adequate training, Pinschers become tyra[...] because they are strong-willed and dominant, desp[...] looking small and fragile. They make ideal pets for experienced owners who understand proper socializing and training. The Pinscher's personality lots of "pep," so it is not an ideal choic[...] for novices.

Color choices?
Solid red or stag red, black, chocolate, or blue, or any of these colors with well defined tan markings. Slight white markings on the chest are allowed but not considered desirable.

How much grooming?
Regular brushing once a week will remove dead hair and dander, with a soft cloth polish to finish. This and the occasional bath are all the grooming that is needed.

Do they make good pets?
Pinschers are assertive, outgoing, intelligent, and active. They make ideal pets for experienced owners who know how to deal with an ultra big personality. This is not a particularly good pet for novice owners. Always busy, they are excellent watchdogs, but will be wary of strangers in their home until they get to know them. This breed does not enjoy rough handling by small children and may nip if upset, so it is not the best dog for families with young children.

● *Adult Min Pins (left) could be mistaken for their cousin, the German Pinscher (right), but will obviously not grow as big.*

What home suits them?
The Pinschers' compact size make them ideal for apartment living, but they are equally at home in the suburbs or the country. However, an intelligent and inquisitive mind may cause them to seek diversion in the outside world, so a fenced yard is essential. Warm homes suit them better because their smooth coat is not thick enough to withstand lower temperatures.

What type of owner?
Pinschers are best suited to experienced owners who will appreciate this dog's fearless spiri[...] strong personality, and its "big do[...] attitude. Owners who work away from home for long periods are not ideal for this breed.

How much exercise and stimulation?
Plenty of socializing and training in regular short sessions is needed, along with firmness, gentle handling, and patience, to prevent them from becoming tyrants in their own home. As adults, Pinschers enjoy long walks with their owner.

Friendly with other pets?
In their own household, Pinschers are free from aggression and very friendly if socialized early. Very much a house dog now, they wer[...] originally used for rat hunting, so very small pets may be at some risk.

Is puppy training easy?
Pinschers need firm, consistent training, or they can start behaving badly. Training should be fun, as

Personality Traits	Poor	Average	Good	Excellent
Attitude toward other dogs		■		
Quietness		■		
Behavior at home			■	
Watchdog ability				■
Good with children			■	
Ease of training			■	
Obedience to owner				■

Time to maturity: 18 months
Male height: 10–12 in (25–30 cm)
Female height: 10–11 in (25–28 cm)
Weight: 8–10 lb (3.5–4.5 kg)
Average lifespan: 12–13 years

Small dogs

they quickly become bored and have a short attention span. Generally amenable to discipline, training needs to be consistent and firm. Go with short training sessions and use plenty of rewards to maintain a focus on learning.

Special puppy care?

Pinschers have rather fine, fragile-looking bodies. They are quite sturdy, but be careful when playing with puppies as they are vulnerable to injury. Puppies (particularly) and adults need protection from the cold.

Possible health problems?

Usually a very healthy breed, with patella luxation (dislocating kneecaps) being the main reported problem.

What can we do together?

They have a reputation as good companion dogs, and agility is possible for the owner who can train well and get the best out of their Pinscher. They make an ideal show dog.

Don't forget!

Training is essential for this breed because they can be very animated and have a fearless spirit.

Adolescent puppies at 9 months enjoy playing, but they can also be assertive.

● *Early training, socialization, and patient handling are essential for the first year to support outgoing personalities and to develop good manners. With the right owner, this is a great family dog.*

Shih Tzu

Other names: Shi Xi Quan, Chrysanthemum Dog, Tibetan Lion Dog

The Shih Tzu is associated with the ancient Tibetan religion of Lamaism. With a flowing mane of hair, he is said to have been able to turn into a lion and was depicted in pictures with Manjusri, the Lamaist god of learning. Tibet's spiritual leader, the Dalai Lama, presented them to Manchu emperors living in Imperial China. The last empress in China had Shih Tzu until the early 1900s, although they were not seen elsewhere until 1930. This is a courageous little dog, with a big personality, who is noted for his rather arrogant posture. An excellent watchdog, he has a gentle, affectionate, and intelligent temperament making him a good family dog. The rich abundant head coat has led to the name of "Chrysanthemum dog," and he needs plenty of grooming to keep looking good. The American and European standards show distinct variations in type.

Color choices?

Various shades of solid colors in gold, white, brown, and liver are available, or combinations of black, gray, silver, white, and brindle. Parti-color dogs can be gold with a black mask, black and white, liver and white, brindle and white, or gray and white. Parti-colors with a white flare on the forehead and white markings on the tail are particularly popular.

● *Shih Tzu have beautiful coats, but this often proves impractical because of the grooming required.*

How much grooming?

Grooming is a big commitment, and needs daily attention. A good brushing right down to the skin is essential with regular bathing once every two weeks. Many pet owners prefer the coat trimmed to a "puppy clip" every six weeks even when adult, but they still need daily grooming.

Do they make good pets?

Shih Tzu are lively, active, and independent, needing plenty of love and attention. They have a willful charm and personality, which makes them a favorite family pet, but the grooming may be too much for some families. They make a great companion and affectionate playmate, and will want to be involved in all family activities.

What home suits them?

This breed adapts to city, suburban, or country living. Apartment living necessitates a short walk several times a day. They are usually happiest with a house and yard, and participating in regular family outings.

What type of owner?

Playful and companionable, they need someone willing to spend time enjoying their company and who will groom them daily to keep them in optimal health and condition. They can become tyrants if allowed, so they need an owner who is firm with training and makes time for socialization.

How much exercise and stimulation?

Shih Tzu enjoy long walks and playing in the yard, but are equally happy with several short daily walks. This breed needs entertaining to keep them stimulated or they will find their own ways of making mischief.

Friendly with other pets?

They are generally friendly with other pets, but they do need time and good handling to become well socialized.

Is puppy training easy?

This is a strong-minded breed, and quite outgoing, so puppies need firm, but kind handling in training. Not the most obedient of breeds, so a more playful approach in training would suit them better.

Personality Traits	Poor	Average	Good	Excellent
Attitude toward other dogs			✓	
Quietness		✓		
Behavior at home			✓	
Watchdog ability				✓
Good with children			✓	
Ease of training		✓		
Obedience to owner		✓		

Time to maturity: 2 years
Male height: 10 in (25 cm)
Female height: 10 in (25 cm)
Weight: 10–17 lb (4.5–8 kg)
Average lifespan: 11–16 years

The 3-month-old puppy will soon begin to be groomed and trimmed in the lighter style seen on his adult companion.

Special puppy care?

This breed does not tolerate heat well, so be careful not to overheat them. Regular baths and eye checks are needed, and the hair needs to be kept out of the eyes. Puppies can be difficult to housetrain, so patience is needed.

Possible health problems?

Shih Tzu can suffer from liver problems, hypothyroidism (a reduced level of thyroid hormone), and intervertebral disc disease. Breathing problems due to the shape of the head may need surgery later.

Small dogs

What can we do together?

These dogs are very good as children's playmates, or a companion dog for adults, and they make excellent watchdogs.

Don't forget!

The Shih Tzu coat needs plenty of grooming, maybe as much as 30 minutes daily, and frequent baths. Pet owners may want to trim the coat every six weeks, so consider the cost implied by this.

Pembroke and Cardigan Welsh Corgis

Popular folklore tells of woodland fairies giving Corgis to Welsh farmers. Fairy warriors were reputed to have ridden them around on the hills, leaving the saddle marking that is visible on their backs. Considered the oldest breed in Britain, hill farmers interbred them over many years until they separated into two breeds in 1934. Pembroke Corgis are the most common, possibly because they became popular in the 20th century with the British Royal Family. The Cardigan is believed to have moved into the Welsh hills with the Celts, while Pembroke Corgis originated among Flemish weavers. Differences are subtle: the Pembroke is slightly smaller and longer bodied, with a naturally shorter tail. Whatever their background they have striking similarities, both performing the same task of herding cattle, ponies, sheep, pigs, and even geese and hunting rabbits or vermin. More recently they have been used as search and rescue dogs.

Color choices?

White is limited and never predominates on either breed, only marking the chest, head, and foreface as a blaze—and white feet. Most colors are acceptable for Cardigans, but Pembrokes should be red, sable, fawn, or tri-color (black, tan, and white).

How much grooming?

Both breeds have easy care double coats, and need grooming regularly each week into the undercoat, or daily when undergoing their twice-yearly molt. The slightly thicker, harsher coat of adult Cardigans does better with a stiffer brush.

Do they make good pets?

Welsh Corgis make excellent pets when raised with children—they are fun-loving, confident, and even-tempered. Puppies are excitable, so they need supervision with young children, but they have an excellent reputation for being good family pets. Wary of strangers, they make excellent watchdogs.

● In the foreground, a Pembroke Corgi and her pup, while behind sits a Cardigan Corgi. The Cardigan's head has more of a foxy look than the Pembroke's.

What home suits them?

Better suited to country homes because of their farming background, Corgis need plenty of walking or somewhere to run loose. They can fit into city or suburban life if owners walk them regularly in a park, allowing them a good run to burn off energy.

What type of owner?

Corgis are loyal, affectionate, and friendly, but need sensible owners; Pembrokes are particularly inclined to heel-nip to round up the family. These are active, strong-minded breeds, so owners must be prepared to spend time walking and playing from the start, while maintaining a firm early training regime.

How much exercise and stimulation?

Gradually building up to longer walks with some running and active play is appreciated. Their active minds need variety to stimulate them, as they can quickly become bored.

Friendly with other pets?

Early socialization within households prevents dominance from developing among males. Their background as vermin hunters may place other small pets at risk. Otherwise, early socialization and suitable introductions creates the right environment in which they are generally friendly with other pets.

Personality Traits	Poor	Average	Good	Excellent
Attitude toward other dogs				
Quietness				
Behavior at home				
Watchdog ability				
Good with children				
Ease of training				
Obedience to owner				

Time to maturity: 2 years
M/F height: Cardigans c.12 in (30 cm)
Pembrokes 10–12 in (25–30 cm)
Weight: 30 lb (14 kg) and 28 lb (13 kg)
Average lifespan: 12–14 years

s puppy training easy?

Approached with intelligence and firmness, Corgi puppies are easy to train. They do not enjoy repetitive training, but usually comply with plenty of reward-based training techniques. More complex activities are suggested as training progresses, and later they enjoy activities in which owners can participate.

pecial puppy care?

Training puppies not to nip should start early to prevent bad habits from forming. Young dogs need reward-based training to motivate them. They can have a tendency to be obese if overfed, which often causes back problems later in life.

ossible health problems?

Corgis, particularly Cardigans, are a healthy breed with few inherited problems, but long backs and short legs may make them prone to back problems such as canine degenerative myelopathy or intervertebral disc problems. Some suffer from hip malformation (dysplasia), von Willebrand's disease (a blood-clotting disorder), and inherited eye problems (progressive retinal atrophy). Pembrokes may also suffer from epilepsy.

What can we do together?

Corgis are intelligent, and with the benefit of their herding background they can take part in agility, herding trials, tracking events, obedience competitions, flyball, and showing.

Small dogs

● *Two Pembroke Corgi puppies at just 9 weeks of age. This breed has a working ancestry as a hunting and farm dog, and so it relishes having tasks to do.*

Don't forget!

These breeds need training early on to prevent them from developing bad habits like nipping. Be careful not to give too many treats to puppies because of the risk of obesity.

West Highland White Terrier

Poltalloch Terrier, Roseneath Terrier

Commonly known as the "Westie," the origins of this Terrier are not clear. Some stories suggest it descends from Spanish dogs that arrived when a Spanish Armada ship was wrecked on the Scottish coast in 1588. Others credit the 16th Laird of Poltalloch, who, around 1900, wanted to produce a strain of white hunting dogs to prevent them from being mistaken for foxes and shot in error.

He developed the Poltalloch Terrier, which was renamed the West Highland White in 1908. The breed quickly found recognition in Britain and the United States. Westies are a family's dream of a four-legged playmate with a great sense of fun that endears them to any family. Reasonably good as watchdogs, Westies are lively and happy, and have great personalities, but can turn on the dignity in the blink of an eye. They are also rustic, courageous, independent, and sometimes stubborn, but all in all an affectionate dog who is good with children.

Color choices?

Only pure white is available, although some puppies appear more cream-colored than white.

How much grooming?

Westies have weatherproof, straight topcoats over short, thick, undercoats, which shed continuously and need grooming with a pin brush and combing to remove tangles and dead hair. Professional grooming is needed every three or four months for bathing and hand-stripping, when coats may be sculpted for showing or left shaggy. Hair on the face and ears needs trimming, and ears and eyes should be cleaned regularly.

Do they make good pets?

Charming, fun-loving, playful, family dogs, Westies are happy to join in anything. They don't like being handled roughly, but they make great companions for sensible children. Tremendous house dogs, they are alert and protective of their family.

● *Not quite ready to leave home, at 7 weeks, puppies are still dependent on their mother for love and protection.*

What home suits them?

Intelligent and inquisitive, Westies particularly enjoy country living and long family walks, but they are equally happy in cities or suburbs if they get a good daily walk with time to explore the local area.

What type of owner?

Frequently a one-person dog and often a good choice for single or active older people, they are tremendous family dogs, despite their sometimes bossy Terrier nature. Westies make great companions for sensible owners who allow them the leeway for self-expression and accept their playful, affectionate personality, but are also firm with training and consistent about providing regular grooming.

How much exercise and stimulation?

Westies' hunting background makes them active and energetic and they really do enjoy long walks, but are equally happy playing in their yard. City-dwelling Westies will need two or three decent walks every day, and preferably somewhere to explore off-leash in safety.

Friendly with other pets?

Westie puppies need early socializing with other pets, as their strong hunting instinct may put small pets at risk. Generally, expect reasonable relationships after early introductions, but supervise the behavior of puppies carefully.

Personality Traits	Poor	Average	Good	Excellent
Attitude toward other dogs				
Quietness				
Behavior at home				
Watchdog ability				
Good with children				
Ease of training				
Obedience to owner				

Time to maturity: 2 years
Male height: 10–12 in (25–30 cm)
Female height: 9–11 in (23–28 cm)
Weight: 13–22 lb (6–10 kg)
Average lifespan: 10–18 years

puppy training easy?

Westies can be willful and stubborn, and training should start early to establish who is in charge. Short reward-based sessions, involving fun activities and new challenges to sustain interest, are best. They are unlikely obedience champions, but they do make well-behaved family pets if treated with a firm, kind approach. Some may be possessive of food and toys, so train carefully to prevent this from becoming an issue.

This litter of 7-week-old puppies looks cute, but they also can be mischievous!

Special puppy care?

Training must start early or you can expect a puppy's bossy nature to assert itself and take control. Coat care is needed early on, as this helps to promote bonding and establishes who is in charge. Check and clean ears regularly.

Possible health problems?

Generally robust and healthy, Westies can suffer from inherited skin disorders (hyperplastic dermatosis), white dog shaker syndrome, and globoid cell leukodystrophy—both inherited

Learning to submit is part of growing up.

neurological disorders that puppies may suffer up to 30 weeks—Legg-Perthes disease (hip problems), and Westie jaw (a bone overgrowth).

What can we do together?

These dogs make excellent companion dogs, as well as great family pets who will get along well with children in the household.

Don't forget!

Buy only from reputable breeders, never from puppy mills, to avoid risks of health problems or the consequences of poor early care. Training, socializing, and grooming should start early!

Cavalier King Charles Spaniel
Other names: English Toy Spaniel

In the reign of King Charles II the English toy spaniel was brought to the U.K. from France, where it was used for sporting purposes. The king became so devoted to them as his soulmates and companions, that he called them King Charles Spaniels. Today's Cavalier originated as a separate breed from those dogs; it is a little larger, with a slightly different head shape, although very similar. Although

Cavaliers were only recognized in 1945, they are one of the most popular toy breeds, and are loved all over the world. Considered a lapdog, Cavaliers make ideal family dogs because of their size, gentle nature, good manners, ease of handling, relatively low maintenance, and loving and affectionate nature. Cavaliers are sociable, and enjoy family life and playing with children; they hate being left out. Their sporting background lends them to long walks while their size makes them good companions for older people.

Color choices?
There are four color choices: black and tan, ruby (solid red—there should be no white markings) chestnut markings on white (known as Blenheim), and tri-color (white with black and tan markings).

How much grooming?
Coats are long and silky with only a slight wave, and require brushing every few days with a slicker brush and comb, with special attention to combing ear, feet, leg, and tail feathering. Ears need checking and cleaning regularly.

Do they make good pets?
They are exceptionally good pets, as they are sweet-natured, easy to handle, mix well with all ages, and are patient, eager to please, kind and affectionate. They are not good watchdogs because they enjoy company and are rarely shy.

What home suits them?
Cavaliers are very versatile and will live in city, suburbs, or the

● *This dam will use play opportunities to teach her puppies some manners and social skills before they leave home.*

country, as long as they have some form of daily exercise that includes a vigorous walk. Puppy walking should be carefully graded to prevent damage to young bones. Off-leash they may be distracted by scent trailing.

What type of owner?
Owners must include their Cavalier in family social activities, as they are fun-loving and gregarious. These dogs adapt well and fit into family life or life with single or elderly owners, and do not enjoy being left alone. They will adore owners who dote on them, enjoying time spent

either in active pursuits or just cuddling together.

How much exercise and stimulation?
The breed's sporting ancestry encourages Cavaliers to enjoy walking off their almost boundless energy. They are active and enthusiastic about walking and following a scent, but a good walk and play session in the local park should suffice. Long walks are always enjoyed, but be careful not to over-walk an enthusiastic pupp

Friendly with other pets?
Very friendly with household pets, this breed enjoys living with his own kind and other smaller or larger animals. Small pets may be seen as game for chasing or playing, but early puppy socialization will encourage respect and tolerant friendship.

Is puppy training easy?
Cavaliers are always eager to please, so training is welcomed. However, start early. They are not

Personality Traits	Poor	Average	Good	Excellent
Attitude toward other dogs				
Quietness				
Behavior at home				
Watchdog ability				
Good with children				
Ease of training				
Obedience to owner				

Time to maturity: 2 years
Male height: 13–18 in (33–46 cm)
Female height: 10–12.5 in (25–32 cm)
Weight: 12–18 lb (5.5–8 kg)
Average lifespan: 9–14 years

overly intelligent, so patience and time are needed for success. It is unlikely that they will star in agility competition or obedience.

Special puppy care?

Keep an eye on puppies for symptoms of early onset heart disease, and also "air scratching" (the dog scratches with his hind leg in mid-air) or spinal scoliosis (curvature of the spine), as these could be indicators of syringomyelia (see below). Puppies are very playful, so make sure that they are not treated roughly.

Possible health problems?

This breed has potential for visual (cataracts, retinal dysplasia) and hearing problems, patella luxation (dislocating kneecaps), mitral valve problems, and some inherit a serious neurological condition called

syringomyelia in which fluid-filled cavities develop within the spinal cord. Check that your breeder tests for syringomyelia.

What can we do together?

Not being the brightest pups on the block, walking, good companionship, and cuddling are the things they excel at most.

● 6 weeks old and nearly ready for a new home.

Don't forget!

Breeding protocols recommend that Cavaliers should be medically checked for heart problems before being bred, so make sure to buy from a reputable breeder who has tested their breeding stock.

Small dogs

Cairn Terrier

One of the oldest of the Scottish Terriers, this breed originated in the Isle of Skye and Western Highlands early in the 15th century. A small and compact working Terrier, Cairns hunted in rocky crags and fells where rabbits and foxes lived. It is from this skill of hunting in "cairns" (outcrops of rock and stone) that the breed gained its name. The Cairn temperament is excellent for a family dog and they do not usually display aggressive tendencies, although they do make good watchdogs. This breed adapts well to wherever his owner lives, but they are most at home in the country rather than the city, because they enjoy an active life and will happily walk for miles. Cairns are happy, lively pets and good family companions, particularly for children. Cairns respond well to firm training and usually do well for owners who want a companion, a dog to show, or both.

Color choices?
Red, sandy, gray, brindled, or nearly black to blend with the color of heather or bracken in the native Highlands are the usual colors.

How much grooming?
The Cairn's double, weather-resistant coat requires less grooming than other Terriers, and brushing two or three times a week is sufficient. Bathing is needed every six to eight weeks. Professional help to hand-strip the coat may be needed, but owners can easily learn this technique if they want to. Early training to accept brushing and hand-stripping is sensible.

Do they make good pets?
Cairns are good watchdogs and also good pets for families, although some may prefer bonding with just one person. This breed loves children, but puppies do not appreciate rough treatment.

What home suits them?
This puppy adapts to wherever his owner lives, although he prefers

● With patience and fun training, some Cairns can learn tricks that will delight and amuse their owner.

the suburbs and country to the city because adult Cairns like plenty of walking.

What type of owner?
Cairns love owners who spend time on outings or long walks. Owners need to be firm with their puppy, making sure they are in charge and not the Cairn! This lively and intelligent breed is one to test his owner's limits because of his natural instincts for hunting.

How much exercise and stimulation?
Cairns will take as much exercise as they are given, although puppy walking should be gradually built up to avoid straining growing bones and tendons. Games, play, and training will stimulate his mind.

Friendly with other pets?
Cairns get along well with other pets, although careful supervision needed around smaller ones—rabbits and guinea pigs—because of the Cairn's natural hunting instinct. Some may take exception to cats if not socialized well as puppies.

Is puppy training easy?
Training should be fun and reward based to encourage learning. Owners must keep sessions short and interesting to maintain their focus. Not the ideal dog for obedience, although firmness and consistency bring rewards for patient owners. Training Cairns not to

● These 6-week-old puppies have a lot of growth and change ahead of them.

Personality Traits	Poor	Average	Good	Excellent
Attitude toward other dogs				
Quietness				
Behavior at home				
Watchdog ability				
Good with children				
Ease of training				
Obedience to owner				

Time to maturity: 18 months
Male height: 11–12 in (28–30.5 cm)
Female height: 11–12 in (28–30.5 cm)
Weight: 13–14 lb (6–6.4 kg)
Average lifespan: 12–14 years

chase squirrels, cats, and rabbits is essential as the instinct to hunt will take over at any opportunity.

Special puppy care?

Cairns enjoy long walks, but they should not be introduced too early or health problems may occur later. Some puppies have a tendency to bark, but early remedial work should reduce any such problems. Training must start early because puppies can be willful and stubborn if not firmly handled. Supervise puppies during play because they may be vulnerable to injury.

Possible health problems?

Generally a healthy breed, there are some health problems such as eye problems, Krabbe disease (a disorder of the nervous system), Legg-Perthes disease (malformation of the hip joint), and von Willebrand disease (affecting the blood). Some also suffer from hip dysplasia and patella luxation (dislocating kneecaps).

What can we do together?

Cairns make useful hunting dogs and good family companions.

Don't forget!

Cairns need careful training and handling while they are puppies to ensure that they grow into great little family dogs.

Chinese Crested

Other names: Crested Chinese Hairless, Powder Puff

Archaeologists have found 10,000-year-old remains of the Crested, and believe they originated in Africa. Early examples were unknown outside China until 1880, when they appeared in the United States and the U.K. Cresteds were not seen in Europe until the 1970s, so they are relative newcomers on the continent. Although seemingly two different breeds, the Crested can either come in hairless or coated "powder puff" form and both can appear in one litter. Hairless looks as you would expect, but they have a "crest" of hair on the head and ears, "socks" on the feet and a "plume" tail. The hairless body is soft, humanlike, and warm, without a "doggy" smell. Powder puffs have long, soft, silky, double "veil" coats, with very little molt; both are ideal for allergy sufferers. Although pretty, they are famous for winning ugly dog competitions. Cresteds make delightful pets because of their gentle, affectionate nature and adaptability for apartment living.

Color choices?

Any combination of colors are available, the skin often being spotted or dappled; base skin colors are blue, lilac, gold, or pink. Spotted puppies are born pink and develop spots in the early weeks of life—the colors showing a seasonal darkening in summer and lightening in winter.

● It takes a lot of time to prepare an adult powder puff for showing, but their beauty makes it worthwhile.

How much grooming?

Hairless puppies need their skin cleansed and creamed daily and after bathing. The use of oil-free moisturising cream to prevent dryness, and sunscreen in summer is recommended. If neglected, their skin is susceptible to acne and blackheads; hair on other parts needs regular brushing to remove tangles. Powder puffs' long hair needs daily grooming with a soft bristle brush to remove shedding coat that does not molt.

Do they make good pets?

Cresteds make lively, alert, energetic pets, but this graceful, dainty dog may find boisterous, noisy families too much. They love playing with sensible children and being cuddled, but they need the family to respect their sweet, honest nature. Sociable and affectionate, they expect these qualities in abundance from their owner.

What home suits them?

Cresteds must spend a lot of time indoors because they are sensitive to cold and heat. Adaptable to most types of home—apartments, suburban, or country homes—their kind, loving nature yearns for constant family company.

What type of owner?

Owners must appreciate that they need to spend time playing with their Crested every day. Daily skin care and grooming are also essential. These dogs want to spend time with an affectionate and sociable owner and do not like being left alone.

How much exercise and stimulation?

While this breed enjoys long walks, they are happy to fit in with owners who enjoy only short walks or outings, but they still need plenty of stimulation with suitable play activity.

Friendly with other pets?

Chinese Cresteds are very friendly with other family pets if introduced and socialized properly while young. They are gentle companions, lacking any hunting instinct, so other family pets are not likely to be at risk.

Is puppy training easy?

Crested puppies need firm, gentle, and consistent training. They do have a mind of their own, and can be stubborn, but early training will pay dividends. As a breed they have the potential to be tyrants, but this is avoided if they are trained early.

Personality Traits	Poor	Average	Good	Excellent
Attitude toward other dogs				
Quietness				
Behavior at home				
Watchdog ability				
Good with children				
Ease of training				
Obedience to owner				

Time to maturity: 2 years
Male height: 11–13 in (28–33 cm)
Female height: 9–12 in (23–30 cm)
Weight: 10–12 lb (4.5–5.5 kg)
Average lifespan: 13–15 years

Special puppy care?

Never overwalk this puppy because they can suffer dislocation of the kneecaps early on. The hairless types are susceptible to temperature extremes, so puppies need to be protected from heat and cold.

Possible health problems?

Cresteds are a very healthy breed, but a few have developed a progressive movement disorder (canine multiple system degeneration) and may succumb by six months. Some also suffer patella luxation (dislocating kneecaps)

quite early. Other conditions include eye problems or skin allergies. Some are allergic to the use of lanolin in daily creaming regimes.

What can we do together?

These affectionate little dogs, if trained well, make great companions and playmates.

Don't forget!

Check out the breeder's heath check regime, and make sure that young puppies are not overwhelmed by a busy family.

Small dogs

● This 6-week-old litter includes three hairless puppies and one powder puff.

French Bulldog

This breed developed in France from the unwanted by-products of the English bull baiting sport that was outlawed in 1835. These smaller Bulldog versions were bred as companion dogs. Suitable for city life, these diminutive, short-coated, sweet tempered, comical, bat-eared little dogs became popular with French aristocracy and fashionable Parisiennes. Crossing the Atlantic, they were soon sought after in the United States by influential families where their popularity grew and grew. Frenchies make excellent family pets, taking an active part in family life. The breed is often likened to a sweet-natured clown who loves to entertain his owner. Ideal for apartments, he is a handy compact size, lively without being too boisterous, low maintenance, and quiet (he does not bark), but still a good watchdog. Not built for active life, he loves company and being part of all that is going on.

Color choices?

Narrow choice in color of mainly brindle or fawn with only a small amount of white on the head, or pied—white with brindle markings—or entirely white.

How much grooming?

This is a low-shed coat, but it will molt at certain times of the year, so a regular weekly brush will suffice, with a daily brush when molting is occurring. The eyes and head folds of the skin need to be wiped daily. Bathing needs to be done about once a month.

Do they make good pets?

Frenchies make very good pets, being good-natured and fun-loving. Families should make sure not to allow him to overheat or be too active with him.

What home suits them?

Ideal for city homes, the Frenchie settles especially well in apartments. Their compact size suits smaller homes. Low-maintenance care and limited walking requirements often appeal to city dwellers.

● *Very devoted to their owners, Frenchies soon find their niche in family life.*

What type of owner?

These dogs appreciate the type of owner who will want to take their Frenchie to work with them. Someone who will appreciate their affectionate and gentle nature and enjoy their company is ideal, valuing and being entertained by their sociable nature. They will appreciate an owner who will give them plenty of love and attention.

How much exercise and stimulation?

Due to their short foreheads and associated breathing difficulties, they do not need active walking for more than a short distance; a short walk once or twice a day should suffice. They do, however, need plenty of socializing to stimulate their active and intelligent minds. Overheating when exercising is a danger because of their breathing problems. Play is essential for their well-being but it should not be too strenuous.

Friendly with other pets?

It is important to socialize this breed well, as they can be very possessive and territorial around the home. They do get along well with other pets if introduced and socialized properly from early puppyhood.

Is puppy training easy?

Their training sessions should be treated as fun times to enjoy together—they will learn obedience more quickly this way. They are fun-loving so need to be treated appropriately; generally they tend to be fairly easy to train.

Personality Traits	Poor	Average	Good	Excellent
Attitude toward other dogs				
Quietness				
Behavior at home				
Watchdog ability				
Good with children				
Ease of training				
Obedience to owner				

Time to maturity: 2 years
Male height: 11–13 in (28–33 cm)
Female height: 11–13 in (28–33 cm)
Weight: 24–28 lb (11–12.5 kg)
Average lifespan: 9–12 years

Special puppy care?

Keep the eyes and head folds clean and try to accustom puppies to this regularly.

Possible health problems?

Frenchies can suffer compromised airways causing respiratory collapse. Chondro-dysplasia (spinal disc disease), eye problems including cherry eye, juvenile cataracts, corneal ulcers, retinal fold dysplasia, thyroid problems.

What can we do together?

Frenchies make great companions and some have done well in obedience trials.

● *The ears of 8-week-old puppies look too large, but they soon grow into them and achieve the correct proportions.*

Don't forget!

This breed does not appreciate extremes of temperature due to their restricted airways. Some airlines will not accept Frenchies as passengers because of fatalities from breathing problems while they were airborne.

Small dogs

Italian Grayhound

This delightful "miniature grayhound" is thought to be one of the oldest breeds in history. Well known during the Roman Empire and the Middle Ages, they later found favor among nobility in the Italian Renaissance and appeared in many famous paintings of that time. The Italian Grayhound came to England around the 17th century as a companion to royalty, and remained popular in royal circles well into Victorian times. His debut in the United States, however, did not occur until the 19th century. His popularity declined during the Second World War. He has changed little since his origins as the smallest of the sighthounds, although modern breeding has produced a much sturdier dog, capable of being more than just a companion animal. As puppies, their dainty physique requires more care while they mature than other breeds, and they need plenty of gentle training or may lack confidence. They make delightful family pets in the right home.

Color choices?

Recognized colors are shades of fawn, white, cream, blue, black, and fawn/white pied.

How much grooming?

Italian Grayhounds have very easy coat care: the short, fine, sleek-as-satin coat needs gentle brushing to remove the small amount of hair shed. An occasional bath or wipe down will usually suffice, as these dogs are virtually odorless. Dental cleaning is essential, as they can suffer periodontal disease, but daily brushing will prevent teeth problems.

Do they make good pets?

They make delightful pets. They are intelligent, loving, happy, and very playful. Preferring a quieter life, Italian Grayhounds may suit older or childless couples, but they can also make super pets for families with considerate children.

What home suits them?

This dog likes space to be active and lively, and his slim, compact build suits apartment or city living,

This breed has a long and distinguished history.

● *Delicate to look at, but bold and speedy, this dog needs plenty of exercise to use up his surplus energy.*

provided that he has ample opportunity for exercise and play. Owners in apartments should guard against the risk of the dog jumping over the balcony railing inadvertently.

What type of owner?

Italian Grayhounds need quiet, considerate owners who will be happy to indulge their need for warmth, comfort, affection, and plenty of company.

How much exercise and stimulation?

Despite his fragile appearance, Italian Grayhounds are capable of speeds up to 25 mph (40 kph), so they need space to burn off this energy, but without the risk of injury. Generally quiet and reserved, firm but gentle handling is needed because of their timid nature. They need socializing and stimulation to prevent any lack of confidence. Early training and stimulation, with plenty of variety, is essential because of their short attention span.

Friendly with other pets?

Always prepared to be friendly with other pets, some care is needed as his sighthound origins might encourage him to chase cats and small animals. For this reason, this breed needs to be kept on a leash in open areas where he might otherwise be tempted to give chase.

Is puppy training easy?

Italian Grayhounds need short, sharp, regular training sessions with plenty of encouraging praise to

Personality Traits	Poor	Average	Good	Excellent
Attitude toward other dogs				
Quietness				
Behavior at home				
Watchdog ability				
Good with children				
Ease of training				
Obedience to owner				

Time to maturity: 2 years
Male height: 12.5–15 in (32–38 cm)
Female height: 12.5–15 in (32–38 cm)
Weight: 7–14 lb (3–6 kg)
Average lifespan: 13–14 years

maintain their concentration. Patience is essential as they are not inclined toward obedience.

Special puppy care?

Puppies tend to be lively and athletic, and their high level of activity may cause the risk of broken bones, so puppies should not overexert themselves. Try to get into the habit of cleaning their teeth daily from an early age to help prevent the onset of tooth decay and gum problems.

Possible health problems?

As with many breeds, these little dogs can develop eye, orthopedic, liver, and thyroid problems. Also Legg-Perthes disease (malformation of the hip joint), epilepsy, auto-immune hemolytic anemia, and hair loss can occur in some color types.

A loving companion, even from this early age.

What can we do together?

Lure coursing, agility, and great companionship are the usual reasons why people love having these dogs around.

Small dogs

Don't forget!

Fragile bones can easily be broken in active puppies, and they need a coat to keep them warm in cold weather. As the long, thin head is the same width as his neck, a "martingale style" harness is best to prevent strangling or slipping out of the leash.

● *Caring owners who indulge this 6-week-old puppy's need for extra warmth, and provide plenty of play, exercise, and training, will suit him well.*

Miniature Schnauzer

Miniature Schnauzers are smaller versions of Standard Schnauzers that were bred 500 years ago in the German provinces of Württemburg and Bavaria. The Miniature has proved more popular in the U.S. and Europe, perhaps because its smaller size suits apartment living. It also has a less powerful and dominant nature compared to the larger types. Miniatures conform to the same basic breed standard as the bigger sizes, and were also used as vermin hunters and guards for farms, factories, or homes. Created in the 19th century, Miniature Schnauzers have been popular with American families only since around 1920, a even later in Britain—the 1960s. Robust, active, and intelligent, Miniature Schnauzers are sometim described as "a terrier without the attitude," and they make an ideal family pet who enjoys compar and is content to be a loyal and affectionate companion. These Schnauzers are particularly qui to learn and are ideal for obedience trials or agili

Color choices?

Black, salt and pepper, black and silver, with dark masks and no white markings. White and parti-color Schnauzers have been bred, but they are only accepted in Europe, not in the United States and Great Britain.

How much grooming?

These pups have high-maintenance coats, and need hand-stripping preferably about every eight weeks, which retains the wiry top coat and protects the soft, warm undercoat. Puppy owners may prefer trimming for convenience. Starting daily as puppies, a stiff brush through the coat is needed, and the whiskers and legs should be combed. The beard needs washing after meals. Bathing will be needed every four to six weeks.

Do they make good pets?

This breed can be energetic and bossy, but is not usually aggressive. This is a versatile dog that matches perfectly with single and inexperienced owners, or families

● *Always on the lookout for mischief.*

with young children. Miniature Schnauzers are obedient and devoted to their owners, and their size often suits modern living better than larger breeds.

What home suits them?

This Schnauzer, unlike the larger versions, will adapt to life in apartments or small homes with yards, provided that there are good places for walking.

What type of owner?

Miniature Schnauzers have a lively, live-to-please personalit. Owners must be responsive to their lovi nature, but also be firm and kind, and not allow the to become bossy. They should nev be left at home by working owne as they easily become bored and lonely and could be destructive.

How much exercise and stimulation?

Puppies need gently increasing exercise levels, with short activity sessions and play times until they mature, when they will need arour an hour's walk daily. Like most dog Schnauzers do not like being confined indoors alone, and need be stimulated to prevent boredom Either take them with you on fami outings or make sure they are not left alone for too long. They can be task-oriented, so teaching them to fetch the newspaper or your slippe is something they will readily learn

Friendly with other pets?

Usually good natured, they need to be introduced to other family pets

Personality Traits	Poor	Average	Good	Excellent
Attitude toward other dogs				
Quietness				
Behavior at home				
Watchdog ability				
Good with children				
Ease of training				
Obedience to owner				

Time to maturity: 2.5 years
Male height: 13–14 in (33–36 cm)
Female height: 12–13 in (30–33 cm)
Weight: 13–15 lb (6–7 kg)
Average lifespan: 13–14 years

...s puppies, and supervised while learning how to behave. Male dogs may try to be dominant with other dogs, but early socialization will help.

puppy training easy?

These dogs are fun to train, and plenty of rewards encourages quick learning. Owners should use a firm, calm, and confident approach.

pecial puppy care?

Puppies need less walking initially, gradually building up more time. Try to incorporate play into training, as it makes obedience more fun. Schnauzers are good watchdogs, but can bark a lot, so dealing with this issue early may prevent problems later.

Possible health problems?

Schnauzers may suffer from hypothyroidism (lack of thyroid hormone), hemophilia, and von Willebrand's disease (both

At 12 weeks, these puppies are old enough to learn how to behave for grooming. The coat will need hand-stripping later on.

blood disorders), Legg-Perthes disease (degeneration of the hip joint), epilepsy, eye problems (cataracts, progressive retinal atrophy), skin disorders, digestive disorders, and liver shunt.

Small dogs

What can we do together?

Devoted, loyal companions, their love of learning often makes them successful in obedience competitions and agility trials.

Don't forget!

Buy only from reputable breeders who do health checks on their stock, particularly eye testing.

Parson Russell Terrier

Other names: Jack Russell, Russell Terriers

The original Terrier was developed by Parson Jack Russell of Devon in the 1800s for hunting, and had to be sturdy enough to keep up with horses over some distance. Once the prey went to ground, this lively and rustic little fellow's job was to dig underground, courageously face up to the quarry, and flush it out for the hunters. Parson Russell Terriers are recognized in most parts of the world, but there are other Terriers bred from the same source. Recognition 1990 of the longer-legged version, now named the Parson Russell Terrier, standardized the breed into a dog more closely resembling the original type. The non-registered versions, known as Jack Russell Terriers, are not officially recognised, and have slightly different physical proportions with shorter legs. However, their similar characteristics and uses as working Terriers make them equally suitable as companion pets.

● *Somewhat longer legged than the Jack, this adult Parson more closely resembles the original type.*

Color choices?

Usually white with black and/or tan patches, or solid white, sometimes with dark ticking.

How much grooming?

These Terriers have harsh, dense double coats in three different combinations: rough, smooth and broken coated (rough and smooth combined), which can occur in the same litter. Rough coats need hand-stripping, but puppy owners may prefer to trim as puppies may not stand still for stripping. Rough and broken coats benefit from weekly "raking" with a rubber curry comb. Although clean by habit, regular brushing is preferable to bathing. Check ears and between paws for grass seeds that may have worked their way into the coat after walking through long grass.

Do they make good pets?

Friendly and outgoing, Parsons make affectionate pets. Rough handling is not appreciated, but they are kind and attentive if treated well, and also good with children.

What home suits them?

Mainly suburban and country lovers, these dogs will also fit into apartment life, but need daily outings to stimulate their active minds. Homes with a large yard for play and activity are ideal.

What type of owner?

An owner who provides regular exercise and plenty of attention is essential. Puppies left alone for too long are likely to want to escape in search of adventure and mischief. Parson Russell Terriers are best suited to active owners who enjoy walking and who are happy to involve their dog in family activities.

How much exercise and stimulation?

By nature they appreciate working the field all day, using their abundant energy and tenacious skills, so plenty of exercise and stimulation is needed, although this should be carefully graded for puppies. Boredom will encourage them to find their own way of exercising their energy and intelligent minds.

Friendly with other pets?

These Terriers have a natural instinct for hunting or chasing, and can be aggressive or predatory with other pets unless well socialized early on. Other smaller household pets may be at risk, as Parsons are by nature hunters of small animals.

Is puppy training easy?

The natural spirit of these Terriers make them either easy or difficult to train as puppies, depending on the owner. Training needs to be firm, patient, consistent, and respecting of their independent spirit. Some are harder to train than others, but patient owners will be rewarded.

Personality Traits	Poor	Average	Good	Excellent
Attitude toward other dogs				
Quietness				
Behavior at home				
Watchdog ability				
Good with children				
Ease of training				
Obedience to owner				

Time to maturity: 18 months–2 years
Male height: ideal 14 in (36 cm)
Female height: ideal 13 in (33 cm)
Weight: 12–14 lb (5.5–6.35 kg)
Average lifespan: 13–16 years

Special puppy care?

A puppy with a rough coat is better trimmed rather than hand-stripped. Otherwise they are easy to care for, requiring few baths, some grooming, and sensible nutrition.

With high energy levels it may be tempting to overwalk puppies, but short walks and active play sessions are better, gradually extending to longer walks.

Possible health problems?

Generally a healthy and hardy breed, but they may suffer from eye problems such as cataracts, primary lens luxation (the lens slips out of position), also deafness, patella luxation (dislocating kneecaps), Legg Perthes disease (degeneration of the head of the femur), and von Willebrand disease (a blood-clotting disorder).

Small dogs

What can we do together?

These Terriers do well at agility, Earthdog trials, obedience, and hunting.

Don't forget!

Puppies need firm handling to prevent their independent spirit from taking over family life and ruling the roost. This breed's extroverted personality is its most important feature, but it needs training to become the ideal pet. Only Parson Russell Terriers can be officially registered with the AKC.

● These 6-week-old Jack Russell puppies will make super pets with the same disposition as their cousin, the Parson Russell Terrier.

Beagle

A happy little dog popular in America since 1840, this is an old English breed that is one of the smallest of the hounds. These dogs are excellent scent hounds and they were bred by the Elizabethans for hunting. Called "singing hounds," the yeomen of the time walked on foot behind small packs hunting hares and rabbits. In the 1860s they became popular for "beagling," and later found a place in Field Trials. They have a strong hunting instinct and will go scent tracking, often disregarding the owner's call to return. Many are used for working purposes, their ability to scent being utilized for drug and bomb detection. Beagles make great additions to most families, being good companions and adaptable to most lifestyles and activities, as well as smart show dogs. His tail-wagging and ear-flapping enthusiasm for life make him a popular choice.

Color choices?
Usually black, tan, and white (tricolor) is the most common, but also lemon and white, red/tan and white, or occasionally mottled. The short, slightly curved tail (the stern) is white-tipped. The position of color markings is relevant when choosing a puppy for showing.

How much grooming?
This short, dense, and weatherproof coat sometimes produces a pungent "doggy" smell. Easy to care for, it needs regular brushing to keep clean and neat. Grooming with a hound glove or stiff brush removes dead hair, which sheds profusely. Regular attention is needed to keep the large, floppy ears clean and infection-free.

Do they make good pets?
This versatile, energetic hound is happy, brave, and intelligent. His affectionate, good-natured manner and gentle disposition make him a great family pet. Sometimes too bouncy and mouthy for small children, he is quite mischievous as a puppy, but well-trained mature Beagles adore children.

● Beagles easily put on weight, so keep an eye on rations.

What home suits them?
Beagles generally prefer the country, but they are happy in the suburbs with a securely fenced yard. Regular daily walks to let off steam discourage escape artists from finding their own amusement. This is not a suitable breed for apartments for this reason.

What type of owner?
Beagles love people and fit in well with most age groups. They love playing rough, and are usually good natured and affectionate with everyone. Owners may need to be more easy-going and tolerant of their mischievous ways, as strict training is not appreciated. They are not suitable for working owners because they enjoy company so much.

How much exercise and stimulation?
Beagles are intelligent and energetic dogs, so exercise and stimulation with plenty of play sessions is essential. They enjoy a good, long walk with plenty of activity to satisfy their natural instincts. Some make their own exercise regime if bored, and may run for miles in pursuit of an interesting scent.

Friendly with other pets?
Beagles generally get along well with most other household pets, but enjoy a chase if encouraged.

Is puppy training easy?
Intelligent and single-minded, this breed needs moderate firmness in training. Mostly obedient, but they are easily distracted by scent so a good recall is essential. Training should start early, using reward-based techniques, but trai

Personality Traits	Poor	Average	Good	Excellent
Attitude toward other dogs				
Quietness				
Behavior at home				
Watchdog ability				
Good with children				
Ease of training				
Obedience to owner				

Time to maturity: 2 to 4 years
Male height: 13–16 in (33–40 cm)
Female height: Marginally smaller
Weight: 18–35 lb (8.2–16 kg)
Average lifespan: 12–15 years

sparingly and with plenty of patience because they can be stubborn.

Special puppy care?

Don't overdo rewards in training as they can be greedy—even puppies! The large, floppy ears need careful cleaning to keep them dry and infection-free. Start ear care early—it will train them to accept such care later.

Possible health problems?

Physically they are a healthy breed, although they can suffer obesity. They are usually free of most health defects, although epilepsy, ear infections, eye problems, and "Beagle pain syndrome" (usually in puppies) can sometimes occur.

What can we do together?

Beagles are great walking companions, good show dogs, and are also suitable for Field Trials.

Don't forget!

This dog is bred for hunting and following scent; he will be tempted to go off alone, particularly if he gets bored and finds a way out of the yard.

Small dogs

● *Just 4 weeks old, these Beagle puppies will rapidly grow into sturdy and compact hounds.*

Cocker Spaniel *Other names: American Cocker Spaniel*

English Cocker Spaniels arrived in the U.S. on the *Mayflower* in 1620, but it was not until later in the 1880s when they were introduced as gun dogs that the American Cocker developed. Quick to nurture their natural ability for hunting, American sportsmen trained them to flush out and retrieve woodcock. The Cockers' boldness and willingness to please charmed owners and won them a proud hunting heritage. The modern conformation Cockers is more compact than the English Cocker, slightly heavier with a squarer, more domed head, a shorter back and legs. His distinguished looks and thick, silky coat have repeatedly won the breed popularity as a proficient and smart show dog. This a most beautiful dog, but the consequence of fame is the high-maintenance required to keep him looki the part. This little dog's glamorous appearance is unsuitable for working, so life for him tends to be a a companion and show dog.

● *A fine specimen of an adult, this dog aims to impress in the show ring.*

Color choices?

A variety of colors are available in three main groups: black, black and tan, solid colors other than black—brown, liver, red, golden, sable, cream, silver; and parti-colors that are white with distinct patches of solid colors, including roan. Some merle colors are produced, but these are not recognized.

How much grooming?

This breed will keep owners busy with coat care every day. They need dedicated care for coat maintenance, which will be time-consuming and costly because professional assistance is required, even for short coats. Daily brushing and combing through the luxuriant coat with special attention to feathering on ears, legs, and underside is a must. Bathing is needed, if not twice a month, then at least once.

Do they make good pets?

This easy-going, good-natured, happy little dog is an eye-catching charmer who loves his family and wants to be a part of all activities. They make gentle playmates for children who make sure not to be rough.

What home suits them?

This is an active breed, so suburban or country locations are appreci-ated. However, town houses with yards and walking space are fine, too. Apartment living with access to parks or walking trails may be acceptable with the right owner.

What type of owner?

Not recommended for owners who work long hours, these dogs enjoy family company, or an older person who gives the time necessary for long walks, training, and essential grooming. They are very responsive to an affectionate owner, but need firm handling.

How much exercise and stimulation?

Plenty of walking will suit ther fine, together with play and stimulation as they are an active intelligent breed.

Friendly with other pets?

Always friendly with other dogs a cats, they do have a hunting instinc so socialization from an early age necessary.

Is puppy training easy?

Essentially bred from a working or hunting line, Cockers are extreme bright, quick to learn, and eager to please, but they can be stubborn. Firm, gentle handling is ideal with suitable rewards and no harsh

Personality Traits	Poor	Average	Good	Excellent
Attitude toward other dogs				
Quietness				
Behavior at home				
Watchdog ability				
Good with children				
Ease of training				
Obedience to owner				

Time to maturity: 4 years
Male height: 13.5–15.5 in (34–39 cm)
Female height: 13.5–14.5 in (34–37 cm)
Weight: 24–30 lb (11–14 kg)
Average lifespan: 12–15 years

0 weeks
d and
cute.

tones. Games that test their intelligence and draw on their background as retrievers are ideal to include in puppy training sessions.

● He will be eager to please.

Special puppy care?

Start brushing and combing as soon as possible, as puppies need to learn patience to stand still long enough for grooming. Training should not be harsh, but fun and playful, exercising the dog's bright and happy nature to develop a good foundation of learning.

Possible health problems?

Cockers can suffer from many different conditions: cancer, liver disease, heart problems, glucose deficiency problems, epilepsy, eye problems (progressive retinal atrophy, glaucoma, and cataracts), hemolytic anemia, patella luxation (dislocating kneecaps), hip malformation (dysplasia), ear infections, and skin allergies.

What can we do together?

Ideal as a companion dog, they also make excellent show specimens for owners who have plenty of time to spend on the coat.

Don't forget!

This breed is not for the faint-hearted when it comes to coat care. Attention to grooming is a must, and if professional attention is sought, it is likely to be costly if required on a regular basis.

Tibetan Terrier

Other names: Chrysanthemum Dog, Phassa Terrier, Dhokhi Apso

As the name suggests, this breed comes from the high Tibetan mountains where they were much more than just temple dogs, but also used for farming work as well. Tibetans are hardy dogs and were frequently used to herd livestock and accompany caravans from place to place. Their long, thick, water-resistant coats proved ideal for coping with harsh weather conditions. Bred in the West from two dogs given as a gift to a British doctor by a Tibetan princess in 192... they are now a popular breed around the world. Tibetan Terriers are classic shaggy dogs, solid and robust, with a happy temperament. Medium-sized, with glamorous coats, they are not true Terriers, although they do have the same energy, intelligence spirit, and stubborn streak. They can be distrustful strangers, which makes them good watchdogs, but they are very appealing as family dogs because they are gentle with children and extremely devoted to all members of the family.

Color choices?

There are many including black, gray, gold, cream, white, parti-colors, and tri-colors. Chocolate and liver are not acceptable in the show ring.

How much grooming?

Tibetans have soft, warm, thick undercoats with a topcoat similar to human hair. The coat needs daily attention to remove tangles and dead hair, using a good pin brush and a comb. Take particular care around nine months when the puppy coat sheds and the adult coat grows. Face hair needs wiping after meals. Some owners opt for short puppy clips, although daily brushing will still be needed, and bathing is needed once a month.

Do they make good pets?

Tibetans are delightful, compact family pets with an outgoing nature. Rarely nervous, they fit easily into most homes and family life. They demand attention, and if treated well, happily go with the flow. They are good tempered without vices, and have a reputation for

● *This terrier is a distinctly shaggy dog and the coat needs regular grooming.*

being amenable and affectionate companions.

What home suits them?

Home is where the heart is, and with family for company, they are always happy, adapting well to city, suburban, or country homes.

What type of owner?

Owners must be equally loving and need to spend time returning affection; they cannot expect sole devotion, however, because Tibeta... love all members of their family. Owners should be willing to inclu... their Tibetan in all family activities.

How much exercise and stimulation?

Tibetans have plenty of energy an... enjoy as much exercise and stimulation as their owner has tim... for. They will, however, accept shorter or longer walks according... the circumstances, and are an idea... size for sensible children to take o...

Friendly with other pets?

Other household pets may not appreciate this puppy's exuberant friendly nature, so early socializatio... is important for teaching good behavior. They must learn manner... and how to treat other animals w... respect. Some can be jealous, whic... may be hard for other pets.

Is puppy training easy?

Perhaps not the best "first" dog fo... novice families—some are strong-willed, but they usually want to

Personality Traits	Poor	Average	Good	Excellent
Attitude toward other dogs				
Quietness				
Behavior at home				
Watchdog ability				
Good with children				
Ease of training				
Obedience to owner				

Time to maturity: 2 years
Male height: less than 17 in (43 cm)
Female height: Slightly smaller
Weight: 18–30 lb (8–13.5 kg)
Average lifespan: 13–14 years

● It takes time for coats to grow long, but experience with grooming is essential for a puppy.

● This 3-month-old puppy should prove to be a quick learner.

Small dogs

Possible health problems?

Tibetans are fairly robust, but they still have health problems such as hip dysplasia (malformation of the hip sockets), patella luxation (dislocating kneecaps), eye problems, hernias, heart murmurs, and an inherited condition called canine neuronal ceroid lipofuscinosis that affects the nervous system. Some are allergic to dairy products and certain grain foods.

What can we do together?

This breed enjoys a lot of activities, such as obedience, flyball, showing, tracking, and even participating in non-competitive herding trials.

Don't forget!

Being firm but kind will pay with this puppy. Make sure that breeders have done health checks on all their stock before buying.

please. Intelligent and quick to learn, puppies need early training that adopts a sensible and consistent approach to curb their bouncy nature. Advanced training often brings out the best in them.

Special puppy care?

If left alone, these exuberant puppies can be hyperactive and noisy, so time spent on early training and socialization is advised. Puppies must not over-exercise, and the length of walks should be built up slowly to allow bones and joints to mature properly.

Fox Terrier (Smooth and Wire)

Fox Terriers are classic British dogs and are one of the most ancient breeds in the British Isles. Originally developed for fox hunting, these Terriers would unhesitatingly go to earth to drag foxes out for the hunt. The breed arrived in America around 1875, and at intervals both coat types have swapped the lead in the popularity stakes. Fox Terriers became famous in the music industry—the HMV (His Master's Voice) record logo features one, and some won enviable army service commendations, but now the are most often associated with Snowy, the cartoon companion of Tintin. These dogs are inquisitive and mischievous, shouldering their way into the limelight. With their jaunty disposition, Fox Terriers are entertaining characters: cheerful, happy, and sociable family dogs for either city or country families, and also vigilant watchdogs. They still have a strong hunting instinct, so other pets may not far well when sharing a home with them.

Color choices?

Solid white, or predominantly white with tan, black, or black and tan markings; other colors are not permitted.

Fox Terriers are noted for their colored "saddle" on the back.

How much grooming?

The smooth coat needs brushing twice a week to remove dead hair and dander. Wire coats, which feel like coconut matting, require daily attention, using a stiff brush and wide-toothed comb. Wire coats also need hand-stripping; pet owners may prefer trimming but this can change the texture of the coat. Both coats benefit from occasional bathing.

Do they make good pets?

Fox Terriers are fast, active, and energetic, with a true Terrier personality and temperament, being courageous, bold, and always game for a scrap. They are considered one of the most affectionate Terriers, and are prized for being family-oriented and gentle with children. In the right home they make excellent pets.

Adult wires need daily grooming.

Smooth coats need less maintenance.

What home suits them?

Fox Terriers were bred to hunt and run, and while they adapt to city life, with energy levels this high they will need long daily walks. Ideally, the better option is a suburban or country life with long, active walks and a yard to explore.

What type of owner?

Their fast, active, strong personalities need firm, strong-minded owners, who enjoy plenty of walk to keep them under control and t avoid clashes of personality with others. Owners will become devoted to this great, fun-lovin pup, but he will deman constant attention.

How much exercise and stimulation?

Fox Terriers love plenty of exercise and have loads of energy. They nee stimulation for their intelligent, acti minds, with task-oriented activities to maintain interest. Playing in the yard is not enough, as they can become nervous or aggressive without exercise and stimulation.

Friendly with other pets?

Early puppy socialization is essentia although they may still be unfriend to other pets or dogs. Fox Terriers have strong hunting instincts so sm household pets are at some risk, a cats may be chased.

Is puppy training easy?

With good handling this dog does well, but owners must be firm and

Personality Traits	Poor	Average	Good	Excellent
Attitude toward other dogs				
Quietness				
Behavior at home				
Watchdog ability				
Good with children				
Ease of training				
Obedience to owner				

Time to maturity: 2 years
Male height: 14–16 in (36–41 cm)
Female height: Slightly less
Weight: 15–21 lb (7–9.5 kg)
Average lifespan: 10–14 years

Tiny puppies need weaning before they can leave their mother.

consistent. Training should be task-oriented and fun, and consist of short sessions because they have low boredom thresholds. Positive, reward-based training to maintain interest helps. Training a good recall is essential as they are independent thinkers and will happily head off on their own missions!

Special puppy care?
Puppies are likely to be energetic, so exercise with care and establish boundaries for playtimes to prevent damage to growing bones. Terriers have an instinct for digging, so it helps to train puppies not to do so.

Possible health problems?
Usually a healthy breed and frequently long-lived, Fox Terriers can get Legg-Perthes disease of the hip joint and von Willebrand's disease (a blood-clotting disorder). Skin allergies also affect some, but diet can improve or prevent this.

What can we do together?
These companionable dogs are great pets and good watchdogs.

Don't forget!
Given the opportunity, Fox Terriers are great car and bicycle chasers. Sensible diet helps to prevent skin problems. Socialization is essential to prevent aggression toward other dogs, and other unwanted behaviors.

Small dogs

● *Socialization will be essential for this puppy at 6 months old.*

Shetland Sheepdog
Other names: Sheltie, Miniature Collie, Shetland Collie

Charming, quick-witted, nimble little dogs, they hail from the Shetland Isles off the north coast of Scotland. The stern, rugged, and weather-beaten environment produced a working breed with a dense coat and a Lilliputian size; perfect for herding in rocky, storm-swept pastures or guarding crofters' cottages and flocks for well over a century. Today's breed is thought to have developed from crossing the original Shetland Collie with Greenland's whale fishermen "Yakki" dogs, together with Scandinavian fisherme spitz dogs. The breed went relatively unnoticed ur the early 1900s when English and U.S. dog fancier took an interest. From its origins as a general farm dog and sheep herder, this loyal and affectionate breed shows similarities with the Rough Collie in terms of his elegance and popularity as an obedie and loyal family member. This is an active dog, affectionate, devoted to his owner, and a wonderf companion to live with.

Color choices?
The most common colors are shades of sable—mahogany sable, shaded sable, and sable merle, also tri-colored (black, gold, and white), blue merle, and sometimes black and white, or black with tan. All colors have white markings on the collar and chest, legs, tail tip, and a forehead blaze.

How much grooming?
Shelties have a double coat with long, rough, water-repellent hairs lying over a soft thick undercoat, which retains coolness in summer and warmth in winter. Molting in spring and autumn, the hair is gently teased out in clumps and combed. Daily use of a stiff brush and comb to penetrate through both coats to remove dead hair and tangles is necessary. The soft hair around the hind legs (the skirt), and inside the thighs and armpits is particularly susceptible to tangles. Bathing more than once a month is not recommended.

Do they make good pets?
Shelties make wonderful pets, but

● *Adult Shelties have profuse double coats. Prospective owners must be prepared for a lot of grooming.*

they dislike noisy households or boisterous children, so they may react badly and nip in response to chaotic or busy homes. They are affectionate and gentle and easy for family members to train, but can be vocal, which may not suit all families.

What home suits them?
Suburban or city life suits them equally, provided that their need for exercise and freedom in open spaces is met. Country life is preferable because they love open space. Expect Shelties to be reserved, but not fearful, with strangers.

What type of owner?
Shelties are unsuitable for workir owners, as they are affectionate, sensitive dogs who will miss their owners if they are away from home every day. Owners shou be prepared to spend time on grooming and exercise, and be gentle and sensitive with training.

How much exercise and stimulation?
Shelties are active, intelligent little dogs who enjoy long walks and playing in the yard. They can be noise-sensitive, so walk venues should be chosen with this in mind, as they may bolt if startled. Early socialization to prevent nervousness and high levels of stimulation are important.

Friendly with other pets?
Most Shelties get along well with other pets; however, they enjoy a chase if encouraged.

Personality Traits	Poor	Average	Good	Excellent
Attitude toward other dogs				
Quietness				
Behavior at home				
Watchdog ability				
Good with children				
Ease of training				
Obedience to owner				

Time to maturity: 2 years
Male height: 14–16 in (36–41 cm)
Female height: 14–16 in (36–41 cm)
Weight: 11–31 lb (5–14 kg)
Average lifespan: 12–13 years

Is puppy training easy?

Highly intelligent and retaining lots of original characteristics, Shelties can be vocal and excitable, but they like to please and work hard for sensitive owners. Responding well to encouragement and reward-based training, they dislike harshness or scolding, which makes them sensitive.

Special puppy care?

It is important that this breed is socialized early because their natural shyness could develop into nervousness. Puppies should learn to accept handling as their thick coats need grooming daily.

Possible health problems?

Deafness in puppies from merle parentage can occur. Progressive retinal atrophy (PRA), Collie eye anomaly (CEA), von Willebrand's disease of the blood, heart problems, hypothyroidism, epilepsy, hip dysplasia, patella luxation (dislocation), and skin allergies can also occur. Many of these can be checked with parental blood tests.

What can we do together?

Shelties make excellent companions and train well for obedience, agility, flyball, showing, tracking, and herding.

Small dogs

Don't forget!

They are sensitive and dislike loud noises or busy households with boisterous children. Regular coat care is a necessity.

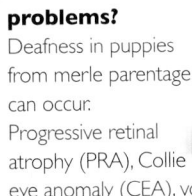

● *Just a few weeks old and absolutely irresistible.*

Boston Terrier

Other names: Boston Bull, Boston Bull Terrier, Boxwood American Gentleman

The Boston Terrier is the result of all-American breeding, and the first non-sporting dog produced exclusively in the U.S. in the 1870s. Originating from bull and Terrier specimens crossed with French Bulldogs, the modern breed does not reflect either the rat-catching tenacity or fighting-dog tendencies of the Bully breeds or the querulous Terrier nature that his name suggests. The Boston Terrier has captivated people's hearts, and his early fighting background has been replaced with courtesy and irresistible charm. His gentle, happy-go-lucky disposition and his good nature have earned him the title of the "American gentleman." A compact little dog, he fits well into city life in an apartment, and makes a delightful companion for most age groups. His ease of training, low-maintenance care, and lack of demand for regular walking makes him a favorite for modern lifestyles.

Color choices?

Color is important and markings should be even and specifically placed on show puppies. Usually brindle or black over the body, every dog carries a "shirt" with a handsome white blaze on the face, collar, breast, forelegs, and the hind legs below the hocks.

How much grooming?

The coat is short, smooth, and lustrous with the advantage of minimal shedding; brushing once a week should suffice. The face and eyes need to be wiped and cleaned more regularly.

Do they make good pets?

An intelligent and affectionate little dog, his good nature and low maintenance makes him an excellent companion dog for a modern lifestyle. Bostons make good friends and playmates for children in a family, but will equally enjoy life in a more sedentary situation. He demands company and attention and will be unhappy if left alone too long.

The Boston is a very good-natured companion.

● *Like other short-faced breeds, Bostons can suffer from breathing problems.*

What home suits them?

The Boston Terrier, as the name suggests, is a city dog, and fits well into apartments or houses with small yard situations. He does not require much walking, so he fits into a modern city lifestyle very readily. He prefers homes where there is someone around for company most of the time.

What type of owner?

This breed is happiest with an owner who is prepared to give plenty of love and attention. He makes an ideal companion for older people who appreciate his gentle, courteous disposition, but can also be lively and sociable within younger, more active families.

How much exercise and stimulation?

Bostons do not enjoy excessive walking and would rather be carried, but will want to go everywhere with their owners. They should walk at least a short distance daily to maintain good health and to stimulate and socialize them outside their home. Regular playtime in the yard or home will exercise their intelligent and active minds.

Friendly with other pets?

Early socialization is always necessary, but they are friendly and fit in well with most other household pets. Some males may show aggression toward other males.

Personality Traits	Poor	Average	Good	Excellent
ttitude toward other dogs				
Quietness				
ehavior at home				
Watchdog ability				
Good with children				
ase of training				
Obedience to owner				

Time to maturity: 2 years
Male height: 15–17 in (38–43 cm)
Female height: 15–17 in (38–43 cm)
Weight: 10–25 lb (4.5–11.5 kg)
Average lifespan: 11–13 years

puppy training easy?

Training can be easy if the owner appeals to this highly intelligent mind, making training more like fun than serious work. Bostons are stubborn, so a firm and consistent approach is needed to bring out the best in them. Tricks and obedience tasks will be well received if owners show patience and consistency in their training.

pecial puppy care?

Most puppies are delivered by caesarean section because of the head's shape and size, so smaller puppies may need continued nurturing. Avoid extremes of heat or cold, and make sure to provide correct nutrition from early on, as Bostons can suffer from flatulence.

ossible health problems?

Breathing problems associated with the short face are common. Cataracts (affecting puppies or adults) and other eye problems can occur. Also, they can suffer from luxating patellas (dislocating kneecaps), deafness, heart murmurs, allergies heat intolerance, and intolerance to anesthetics.

What can we do together?

Great companion dogs, some do really well in obedience, or for showing.

Don't forget!

Feed puppies correctly from the start, or they will produce a lot of wind! This breed does not enjoy very hot or very cold weather.

Make sure that eyes do not get injured during boisterous play.

● At 6 weeks old, play gives this puppy the confidence to enjoy life.

English Cocker Spaniel *Other names: Cocker Spaniel (U.K.)*

An old English breed, this Spaniel's ancestors have been used for hunting wildfowl since the 14th century. The U.K. officially recognized the breed in 1892, at which time some were exported to France and the United States, where their skills for "cocking" (hunting woodcock) were developed. Cockers are the most well known of Spaniels and are popular throughout the world. As sporting dogs, working strains are smaller and stocky, and not bred to the same standard, but are recognized for their working abilit[y] they are trained to flush, drive, and retrieve the gam[e] As family pets, the happy little English Cocker with h[is] non-stop wagging tail is full of life, exuberant, good-natured, affectionate, and gentle. Devoted to his fam[ily] he is a faithful companion, but strong-willed and independent. With their outgoing personality and working ability, they can be trained as hearing dogs, [to] provide support for the hearing impair[ed] and also as police search dogs.

Color choices?

There are a wide variety of colors to choose from: black, liver, red, golden, sable, silver, black and tan, black and white, liver and white, tri-colors (black, tan, and white) and roan (solid color patches and white with ticked areas) colors—blue, liver, orange, and lemon, but never all white. White on solid colors is not allowed except as a small patch on the chest. Working Cockers can come in any color, there is no restriction.

● *Maturity is reached by two years as these handsome dogs show; feathering on their bodies is already grown.*

How much grooming?

The thick silky coat needs grooming with a brush and comb daily, with particular attention paid to the feathering around the ears, legs, chest, and underside. He should be bathed about once a month. The long ears should be checked regularly, as they can become dirty.

Do they make good pets?

The English Cocker is a most charm-ing pet; with his constantly wagging tail he really is a "happy Cocker." Exuberant, active, playful, affection-ate, and gentle, he appeals to all age groups. They are particularly family-oriented, but do not like rough treatment from children.

What home suits them?

Apartment living is possible but it may be a little too small; generally they suit a home with yard space for playing and long walks.

What type of owner?

Any sensible and responsible owner will suit this breed; someone who includes their dog in family activities and takes care of his physical needs. He is best suited to an owner who spends time training and enjoys his learning development from puppy to adul[t]

How much exercise and stimulation?

Cockers can become frustrated and obese without adequate amounts of exercise, so plenty of walks are needed. It is best to star[t] puppies on short walks initially an[d] build up to long walks with play sessions. Highly intelligent, this breed needs mental stimulation from training.

Friendly with other pets?

Good with other animals, althoug[h] their hunting instincts may surface if a chase is available.

Is puppy training easy?

This breed's intelligence makes training a pleasure, but it must start early before bad habits form. Cockers can be strong-willed and independent, but harnessing this trait through firm but gentle

Personality Traits	Poor	Average	Good	Excellent
Attitude toward other dogs			■	
Quietness		■		
Behavior at home			■	
Watchdog ability		■		
Good with children				■
Ease of training			■	
Obedience to owner			■	

Time to maturity: 2 years
Male height: 15.5–16 in (39–41 cm)
Female height: 15–15.5 in (38–39 cm)
Weight: 29–32 lb (13–14.5 kg)
Average lifespan: 12–14 years

training as a puppy molds them into excellent family companions.

Special puppy care?

Training needs to start early or an owner's commands may be disregarded in favor of their own activities. Frustration can cause destructive behavior so make sure a puppy cannot be injured if he chews. Check ears regularly to avoid dirt build-up.

Possible health problems?

Usually quite healthy, but they do have their share of eye problems (progressive retinal atrophy), deafness, kidney disease, heart problems, and dislocating kneecaps. At one time, solid colors (mainly reds), had a problem with rage syndrome, but this has largely disappeared.

What can we do together?

Cockers (and owners!) will enjoy agility, flyball, obedience competitions, walking, and games that involve retrieving.

Small dogs

Don't forget!

Make sure ears are checked and cleaned regularly as they can become smelly and painful. Firm but gentle training will prevent this puppy from getting the upper hand.

● *Affectionate and gentle at 8 weeks old, this puppy is ready for a loving family.*

Bedlington Terrier

Other names: Rothbury Terrier, Rodbery Terrier, Gypsy Dog

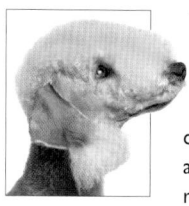

This lamb-like dog has a lion's heart, and was originally bred by miners in the 13th century in Northumberland, England to clear rats out of coal mines. In addition to a reputation for ratting, the Bedlington, named after the village where it originated, was famed for his speed and became known as the "miner's racehorse" in field racing. His speed, agility, and hunting skills also made him an attractive dog for poachers. The breed was not recognized in England until the early 1870s and was unknown in the United States until the 20th century, but it quickly became popular as a show dog and loyal family companion. Docile and devoted to their owner, Bedlingtons make loving pets. The roached back and soft, linty wool coat with ear fringes and topknot is distinctive because of its shade of blue. This delicate-looking dog is nevertheless a game Terrier, not inclined to fight but quite capable of looking after himself.

Color choices?

Mainly blue, but also liver or fawn (sandy) with or without tan markings. Topknots in adult dogs should be lighter colored than the shade of the main coat.

How much grooming?

Expert groomers need to do the first coat clipping. Subsequently, pet owners should brush this low-shedding coat with a wide-toothed comb and slicker brush regularly to remove dead hair. The coat may need to be professionally clipped two or three times a year into a "pet clip" suitable for easy maintenance; for show puppies, the coat is sculpted into a specific style, which can be rather difficult for novices to maintain.

Do they make good pets?

Charming and loyal pets, Bedlingtons are very friendly but also make good watchdogs; they tend to attach themselves to a family or one member of a family. Calmer and less boisterous than other Terriers, they are affection-

● *Adult Bedlingtons usually get along well when kept in pairs. They may look delicate, but they are feisty Terriers.*

ate, good-natured pets with mild manners, and normally play gently with children.

What home suits them?

Owners prepared to give them an outlet for their high energy levels will find them suitable for apartment living, but homes with space and access to good walks are best. Bedlingtons should not be left home alone, as they can be destructive when bored and will find their own entertainment.

What type of owner?

This breed needs owners who return affection and loyalty, and devote time to releasing high energy levels through exercise. A conscientious owner prepared to allocate regular time for grooming and training is necessary.

How much exercise and stimulation?

Bedlingtons need a daily walk, grading the distance and timing for puppies and progressing to longer walks as they mature. A bored Bedlington could be destructive and aggressive so mental stimulation is essential, as they have active, intelligent minds.

Friendly with other pets?

Bedlingtons need to be well socialized as puppies to get along with other household pets, and there may be gender issues between males. Households with small pets should be cautious because of their natural instinct to hunt rats and small vermin.

Personality Traits	Poor	Average	Good	Excellent
...ttitude toward other dogs				
...uietness				
...ehavior at home				
...atchdog ability				
...ood with children				
...ase of training				
...bedience to owner				

Time to maturity: 2 years
Male height: 16.5 in (42 cm)
Female height: 15.5 in (39 cm)
Weight: 17–23 lb (8–10.5 kg)
Average lifespan: 13–14 years

...puppy training easy?

...lways eager to please, this breed ...oes really well with firm but ...entle training, and can be trained ...or a wide variety of activities that ...wners may enjoy.

...ecial puppy care?

...uppy coats must be clipped close ...o the skin by a professional for ...asy care. Plenty of early socializing ...s essential to ensure puppies fit ...nto a home with other pets.

...ossible health problems?

...hey can suffer from heart murmur, ...ye problems, and copper toxicosis ...the inability of the body to elimi-...nate copper—this disease has ...almost been eradicated in the U.S.); ...or breeders, reproductive prob-...ems have caused concern, too.

...hat can we do together?

...Owners can participate in several ...activities, such as agility, Earthdog ...rials, obedience, showing, and ...other performing tasks. Working ...Bedlingtons need to express their ...natural ability for hunting.

Don't forget!

Only buy from reputable breeders who provide evidence of DNA testing or liver biopsy results proving that the puppy's parents are unaffected by copper toxicosis. This is not an easy breed for novice groomers who want to show.

Small dogs

● *Puppies can appear scruffy by 16 weeks old, and need trimming to bring out their good looks.*

Medium dogs

Medium-sized breeds offer the best of both worlds and are often very popular as family companions. They are an ideal size for handling, and not too big for the average home. There are a number of possible choices: from the low-maintenance coats of Bulldogs and Dalmatians to fluffy Chows and Soft-coated Wheaten Terriers, and plenty of coat types in between!

Bulldog

Other names: English Bulldog

The first references to the Bulldog in literature come from around the 1500s, when their use for bull baiting is described. Characterized as a "compressed Hercules," the Bulldog's longer-legged and more agile 19th-century gladiator ancestors were also used for fighting. The more modern version of this very British dog has been bred to have a very sturdy body, massive chest, loose wrinkled skin, and pendulous flews. Distinctive features are the Bulldog's short, broad face with lower jaw jutting and a foreshortened upper jaw, bowed legs, and a naturally short tail. Sadly, breed exaggerations have caused significant health problems as well as difficulties with whelping caused by the size of the head. Carefully bred, Bulldogs are happy, strong-minded dogs but also affectionate and humorous. Not ideal for novice owners, but experienced owners will find a soulmate in the calm, quiet nature of this excellent breed.

Color choices?

Most colors are available, although they are usually solid red, fawn, white, brindle (often waves or color stripes), with/without black masks and muzzles, or piebald (white with another color).

How much grooming?

Coats are short, flat, and sleek and need minimal care. Weekly brushing with a hound glove and bristle brush removes dead hair. Facial wrinkles, particularly the "rope" wrinkle over the nose, need cleaning daily with a dry cloth to remove dampness and to prevent sores or eczema from developing.

Do they make good pets?

Despite their fierce looks, Bulldogs make excellent companions, with no vicious or aggressive tendencies. They have affectionate demeanors and a calm, dignified presence. Particularly noted for their kind temperament and patient nature, they get along well with children, other dogs and pets, but they are boisterous and mischievous puppies.

● *This 3-week-old puppy still has a lot to learn from his mother.*

What home suits them?

A Bulldog's home is where his heart is—with his owner. Adaptable to cities, the suburbs, or the country, they do need space for a daily walk. Shady yards are best because Bulldogs are sensitive to heat.

What type of owner?

These puppies are devoted to their owner, and are affectionate with their family. Ideal for owners who want to walk for some exercise, but not too far, this dog is an individual and needs to spend time in his owner's company. Firm handling is best, as Bulldogs are physically strong, stubborn, and are unlikely to be obedience stars.

How much exercise and stimulation?

Bulldogs are content as couch potatoes, but they need two half-hour daily walks to keep fit. Their short legs, heavy bodies, and breathing problems do not make long walks a favorite pastime. Bulldogs need to move at a steady pace on all walks and should avoid hot or humid weather. Stimulating a Bulldog's mind in active and interesting ways is a good idea, too.

Friendly with other pets?

Bulldogs are very good natured and get along well with other family pets, although there may be dominance issues between males.

Is puppy training easy?

Strong-minded, obstinate, and with no interest in obedience, this can be a difficult dog to train. They are sensible, though, and reward-based

Personality Traits	Poor	Average	Good	Excellent
Attitude toward other dogs				
Quietness				
Behavior at home				
Watchdog ability				
Good with children				
Ease of training				
Obedience to owner				

Time to maturity: 2.5–3 years
Male height: 12–14 in (30–36 cm)
Female height: 12–14 in (30–36 cm)
Weight: 49–55 lb (22–25 kg)
Average lifespan: 8–12 years

...training is a big motivator for good behavior. Firm, patient handling is best; harsh training gets nowhere. Owners must be patient, positive, and confident in demeanor.

Special puppy care?

Socialization and regular walking should start early so that puppies don't get used to a couch-potato life. Teeth cleaning and daily wiping of facial folds will accustom puppies to these necessary procedures.

Possible health problems?

Not the most robust breed because of overexaggeration of features through their breeding, Bulldogs can suffer from cardiac defects; cancer; hip dysplasia (malformation); elbow and patella dislocations; vertebral deformities; interdigital cysts; and dental, skin and eye problems. Their short "screw" tail can be malformed causing bowel problems, and they suffer badly from overheating.

What can we do together?

Good companions and watchdogs. Some have attempted obedience and agility, although not many!

Don't forget!

It is important to buy from reputable breeders only.

Medium dogs

● 8 weeks old
and ready
for play.

Basset Hound

Bassets are an ancient French breed originating from 16th-century St. Hubert hounds. Used as pack hounds for hunting because of their excellent scenting ability, noblemen followed them on foot. Short-legged and low-slung for use in heavy cover ("basset" means "rather low" in French), their endurance, courage, and ability to trail and flush out game such as roe deer, wolf, fox, and bear was remarkable.

Introduced into Britain and the United States in the late 19th century, modern breeding has not been always to their advantage, with some exaggerated features developing. They are, however, delightful family dogs with peaceful, mild dispositions and good natures. Despite short legs, they love an active life; exercise is necessary, as is training, as they are stubborn to recall if they find a good scent. Bassets deserve their rise in popularity and their placid, affectionate, and gentle nature makes them prized as family companion dogs.

Color choices?

Usually black, tan and white tricolor, or tan and white bicolor. White tips to tails and a white face blaze.

● Adult Bassets' long ears need care to prevent injury or infection.

How much grooming?

A Basset's long, smooth, short coat is easy maintenance, but sheds constantly so needs brushing twice weekly with a stiff brush and hound glove. Their long pendent ears, designed to sweep up scent, need checking and cleaning frequently. The folds of supple, elastic, hanging skin should be dried to prevent sores from developing.

Do they make good pets?

These gentle, friendly, non-aggressive dogs make excellent pets. Great companions, Bassets love people and are gentle with children and other pets. Powerful and stubborn dogs, they are unsuitable for leash walking by children or elderly people who may not be strong enough. Bassets use affectionate, murmuring whines to gain attention and "talk" to their owners.

What home suits them?

Although short-legged, Bassets are big dogs and benefit from larger homes with yards. Long daily walks are preferred, but they adapt to apartment life provided that they have company. Solitude is not appreciated, and Bassets will tell the world about this by using a deep, melodious bark, which may upset neighbors.

What type of owner?

Suitable for tolerant owners only, Bassets drool, shed hair, may smell strongly, and, because they are low-slung, bring a lot of dirt into the home. Owners should be patient and appreciate their placid nature, independent personality, and occasional stubbornness.

How much exercise and stimulation?

Plenty of exercise is needed for adult Bassets, but be careful with puppies, as too much exercise can cause back problems. Puppies should have gradually increasing exercise time from six months old, preferably provided in shorter walks several times a day, with time for off-leash running and plenty of active play.

Friendly with other pets?

Bassets are non-aggressive dogs and are well disposed to other household pets. They are hunting dogs and have a hunting instinct, however, so early socialization and introductions to smaller house-hold pets will be advantageous.

Is puppy training easy?

Bassets' strong will and stubbornness is legendary, and firm training is a must. Teaching a good recall is the most important objective, but this breed is not good at obedience, so anything else learned is a bonus.

Personality Traits	Poor	Average	Good	Excellent
Attitude toward other dogs				
Quietness				
Behavior at home				
Watchdog ability				
Good with children				
Ease of training				
Obedience to owner				

Time to maturity: 2 years
Male height: 13–15 in (33–38 cm)
Female height: 11–14 in (28–36 cm)
Weight: 40–66 lb (18–30 kg)
Average lifespan: 10–12 years

Special puppy care?

Never overexercise a puppy, and introduce recall training early to avoid problems later. Avoid overfeeding—obesity can cause back problems. Walking too soon after meals can cause gastric problems—wait at least an hour before you go for a walk.

Possible health problems?

Physical exaggerations in breeding have caused eye problems, hip and elbow dysplasia (malformation), dermatitis in skin wrinkles, and ear infections. Bassets also suffer from gastric torsion (bloat), weight problems, arthritis, cancer, cardiac problems, von Willebrand's disease (blood coagulation abnormality),

● *9 weeks, and already sporting long ears and the soulful looks of a friendly, confident puppy.*

Medium dogs

hypothyroidism (insufficient levels of thyroid hormone), and foreleg lameness.

What can we do together?

Bassets are companion dogs mainly, but small game hunting is available in organized clubs.

Don't forget!

Only buy from reputable breeders because of the health issues in this breed. Highly sociable, Bassets enjoy company, and should not be left alone.

● *At 8 weeks old, this Basset puppy is ready for a world of new experiences.*

Staffordshire Bull Terrier

This dog's ancestors came from 19th-century Staffordshire, and were bred by crossing Old English Bulldogs and various Terriers to produce a dog with strength, tenacity, quick-wittedness, and agility. The Staffie's wide body, sturdy physique, and calculated aggression made them ideal candidates for bull baiting, and later for the sport of rat killing. When bull baiting was banned, the fiercest of them, being highly prized for level headedness and courage, were used for dog fighting until that too was banned. Their other attributes so began to be prized—friendly, docile, and ideal companions for owners, they quickly found a place people's hearts. Formal breed recognition in Britain came in 1935, and in the U.S. in 1974. Although the still hold an inherent grudge against other dogs, the are obedient, good-natured, and well-respected fam dogs. They are often called the "nanny" dog because the trust placed in them to look a young children.

Color choices?
Colors can be solid red, fawn, black, blue, and brindle, or any of these with white.

How much grooming?
This dog's smooth, short coat is low maintenance, and it shines beautifully if brushed with a pin brush or hound glove for a few minutes daily. Occasional bathing is sufficient.

Do they make good pets?
Staffies are faithful, gentle, and affectionate, and wholly devoted to their owners. These are brilliant family dogs, trustworthy, and fond of children, with a great sense of fun. Puppies love playing games that involve chasing and fetching.

What home suits them?
Although Staffies are muscular, powerful, and athletic, they can adapt to most homes provided that they get plenty of exercise. A yard or open space nearby that can accommodate off-leash play and long walks is desirable.

● *Well-trained adults make great pets.*

What type of owner?
These dogs are unsuitable for the housebound or elderly, but ideal for owners who live alone and want close companionship, or for families with children. They are devoted, loyal dogs and deserve the right owner who will appreciate their unswerving loyalty. Owners must commit to regular exercise, constant companionship, and entertainment. Staffies may have gotten into the wrong hands and developed a bad reputation, but with the right owner they thoroughly deserve to be regarded as excellent family dogs.

How much exercise and stimulation?
Staffies are athletic and powerful, and need plenty of exercise and space for uninhibited play to keep them in good condition as they mature. Highly intelligent, they also need mental stimulation, but some of this will come from playing.

Friendly with other pets?
All puppies need socializing and careful introductions to other household pets, and Staffies are no averse to conflict, so there may be confrontations with other dogs. Owners may need to walk them in quieter places or keep them on the leash. Proper socializing within the first weeks of arrival should settle puppies into family life, but they still need careful supervision until they know their place.

● *Hold youngsters l this 4-week-old pup cupped safely in both hands.*

Personality Traits	Poor	Average	Good	Excellent
Attitude toward other dogs				
Quietness				
Behavior at home				
Watchdog ability				
Good with children				
Ease of training				
Obedience to owner				

Time to maturity: 2 years
Male height: 18–19 in (46–48 cm)
Female height: 17–18 in (43–46 cm)
Weight: 24–38 lb (11–17 kg)
Average lifespan: 12–14 years

The best of friends at 6 weeks, but early socialization will be needed to prevent dominance issues between these two puppies later on.

thrives on plenty of energetic exercise, this should not be introduced too early to allow young bones and joints to mature.

Possible health problems?

Staffies can suffer from eye problems (cataracts, distichiasis, ocular lens problem), kidney stones, and metabolic disorders (causing behavioral changes and dementia symptoms), as well as being at higher risk for tumors (mastocytoma).

Medium dogs

What can we do together?

Staffies are primarily good watchdogs, affectionate pets, and wonderful playmates or walking companions.

Is puppy training easy?

Staffies are very intelligent, but can be stubborn if they are trained harshly. Firmness and consistency with praise, rewards, and encouragement will work best; responding with anger and reprimands will not achieve the desired goal of good behavior.

Special puppy care?

Puppies need socializing from the start to prevent problems with other pets. Although this breed

Don't forget!

This is a breed that happily takes on bigger dogs. Make sure to always keep them on leash. They need an attentive owner to maintain them as an even-tempered, reliable companion.

Shiba Inu
Other names: Shiba Ken, Little Brushwood Dog

This ancient Japanese breed came from Honshu Island, and in 1937 it was honored as a "Natural Monument" of Japan. Shiba Inu literally means "small dog," and their size and agile movement was ideal for hunting and flushing out small game in mountainous terrain and wild shrub land. Some speculate that "Shiba" means "brushwood" in recognition of their red color, which is similar to that of the wild shrubs. Frequently crossed with other breeds, today's Shiba is one of the most popular breeds in Japan. Shibas are fastidiously clean grooming their coats by licking like a cat, and particularly easy to housetrain. If they are upset, startled, or excited, they respond with high-pitched screaming rather than barking. They do not tolerate other dogs well, and are better suited in homes without children. This good-natured dog with its "spirited boldness" can be reserved toward stranger but the Shiba is a loving and affectionate pet for owners who earn their respect.

Color choices?
Colors are usually light red, sesame (red with black tips to hair), red sesame, black sesame, black and tan, brindle, or light gray. White is not considered acceptable. Cream, buff, or gray hair should be on the sides of the muzzle, cheeks, under the jaw, chest, under the body, under the tail, and on insides of the legs.

How much grooming?
A Shiba's naturally waterproof, double coat consists of stiff, straight hair with a soft, thick undercoat, with some parts, like the tail, thicker. Although Shibas tend to be clean dogs, daily brushing is needed, particularly when the coat is shedding. They also need occasional bathing to keep them clean.

Do they make good pets?
A Shiba's normal behavior is lively, alert, and independent; they make good pets with the right owner because they are good-natured and dignified with a natural beauty. Expect them to be reserved with strangers, but loyal and affectionate to owners.

● *Bold even at 8 weeks, puppies must learn manners before leaving home.*

What home suits them?
Shibas adapt well to life as house dogs, but because they have so much energy for long walks or playtime, they do better in homes with a yard where they can run.

What type of owner?
Shiba owners will need to earn this breed's respect and be ready to take frequent, long, daily walks to enjoy this companionable dog. They should be firm and attentive to the Shiba's need for training, exercise, grooming, and family companionship.

How much exercise and stimulation?
A Shiba's robust and naturally independent disposition, as well as its ancestry as a hunting dog, means that exercise is essential. They are also intelligent, so stimulation should be provided either by long walks or play. Daily exercise helps to maintain good health.

Friendly with other pets?
Shibas have a strong prey drive and can be aggressive toward other dogs, although this usually occurs between females. Although Shibas tend to do better in homes without other household pets, they often get along well with cats if raised together from youngsters and well socialized.

Is puppy training easy?
Training needs to be with firm, but gentle handling. If other household pets are kept, training a Shiba to accept them must begin early.

Personality Traits	Poor	Average	Good	Excellent
Attitude toward other dogs				
Quietness				
Behavior at home				
Watchdog ability				
Good with children				
Ease of training				
Obedience to owner				

Time to maturity: 2 years
Male height: 14–16.5 in (36–43 cm)
Female height: 13.5–16 in (34–41 cm)
Weight: 15.5–24 lb (7–11 kg)
Average lifespan: 12–15 years

Special puppy care?

Shibas should not be walked too far or too long when they are puppies, to allow time for joint and bone growth. Regular health checks should be made when they are puppies to watch for joint and bone problems as they mature. Start grooming early to establish a regular brushing routine.

Possible health problems?

This breed does not suffer from many inherited problems; however, they can be affected by allergies, eye problems, hip dysplasia (malformation of the hip sockets), and luxating patellas (dislocating kneecaps). Joint problems are likely to occur in puppies and young dogs, which should be checked regularly.

What can we do together?

Shibas make good watchdogs, but owners may also enjoy hunting for birds and small game with them. Otherwise, they make very companionable pets.

Don't forget!

This dog is unsuitable for novice owners and not likely to fit into a household with other pets or children very easily.

● Shiba puppies (even from 8 weeks) are easy to housetrain if put outside at regular intervals.

Medium dogs

Nova Scotia Duck Tolling Retriever

Tollers are the smallest of the retrievers. The breed became the provincial dog of Nova Scotia in 1955, where it first developed early in the 19th century. The Canadian Kennel Club registered them starting in 1945. The name Toller relates to the dog's ability for "tolling," which is to trick and lure geese and ducks to approach them at the water's edge. The curious birds come over to investigate the disturbance on the shore, and put themselves within gunshot range. The Toller then retrieves the bird and returns to his owner. They have an appealing fox-like appearance and outgoing personality, but can be destructive when bored, or if left alone too long. They benefit from plenty of exercise to keep them stimulated. Tollers are intelligent, high-energy dogs, and although very affectionate as family pets and patient with children, they have a strong retrieving drive and are happiest when they work.

Color choices?

Any shade of red from red-gold to copper with lighter colored feathering on the underside, the backs of the legs, and under the tail. White markings are acceptable only on the chest, feet, tip of the tail and a face blaze.

How much grooming?

Regular grooming with a comb and firm pin brush removes seasonal shedding, mud, and undergrowth debris from the longer hair on the body, and feathering on the tail and backs of legs. Tollers love swimming and have double coats with natural oils that make the coat water repellent. Only bath them very occasionally or you risk washing out these oils. Check between toes as their webbed feet may pick up debris and cause infection.

Do they make good pets?

Tollers are natural Retrievers and love to play games. They are excellent family pets and get along with everyone, as well as other household pets. They are patient

● Adults normally get along well together.

and friendly with children, but may not be suitable as watchdogs, as they only give a warning bark.

What home suits them?

Tollers are a high-energy breed and confining them to apartments or small yards without adequate activity or amusement can cause them to turn destructive. Ideally, a reasonable amount of space and company is needed.

What type of owner?

Strong-willed and sometimes difficult to train, Tollers need owners who demonstrate good leadership and encourage them to behave well. Owners will need to enjoy retrieving games and generally take part in activities that appeal to their natural behaviors.

How much exercise and stimulation?

Tollers have plenty of energy and great endurance. They need long, brisk, daily walks with extra physical activities, such as running after a ball, and swimming, to provide them with sufficient exercise and mental stimulation.

Friendly with other pets?

Small pets may be at risk of being "retrieved" but Tollers are generally friendly with other household pets.

Is puppy training easy?

If Tollers learn as puppies that their owner is in charge, they are likely to be quite easy to train. They can be strong-willed, and need firm, but kind, training to establish obedience and good habits. Training that draws on their natural behaviors is best: for example, recalls can best be taught by using their natural ability to retrieve.

Personality Traits	Poor	Average	Good	Excellent
Attitude toward other dogs				
Quietness				
Behavior at home				
Watchdog ability				
Good with children				
Ease of training				
Obedience to owner				

Time to maturity: 2 years
Male height: 17–21.5 in (43–55 cm)
Female height: 17–21.5 in (43–55 cm)
Weight: 37–55 lb (17–25 kg)
Average lifespan: 10–13 years

● *Submission in play is typical of a puppy with a low dominance trait, and is an ideal sign in young puppies being chosen for a family.*

Medium dogs

Special puppy care?

Teach puppies basic skills in obedience, as this will be a major benefit in controlling this strong-minded breed. Tollers are very active, and owners should make sure that they do not overexercise them to avoid injuries.

Possible health problems?

With increasing popularity and a limited gene pool, Tollers are starting to develop health issues. These include Addison's disease (a hormonal disorder), hip dysplasia (malformation), progressive retinal atrophy, thyroid, and autoimmune problems. Cancer is presently the highest cause of death in this breed.

What can we do together?

Tollers are excellent at canine activities such as agility, obedience, and hunting.

Don't forget!

Tollers are dogs with natural behaviors developed for hunting and retrieving. With only a limited gene pool to draw upon, owners should make sure they buy only from experienced and reputable breeders.

● *This puppy is the ideal age (16 weeks) for learning who is the boss in his life, and for training to control his strong-willed nature. Starting with a "Sit" and using treats for rewards should work well, or try clicker training.*

Welsh Springer Spaniel

Other names: Welsh Springer, Welsh Starter

In the early 18th century, Welsh Springers were bred in the Welsh valleys for their ability to follow scent to "spring" rabbits, birds, and game—especially woodcock—from undergrowth and then flush them out for hunters with falcons (and later guns). The breed was first recognized in Britain in 1902 and in the U.S. in 1906, although it then declined and was reintroduced to America in

1923. A Welsh Springer's attractive red and white coat distinguishes it from black and white English Springers. Unlike other working sporting dogs, size is no different between working and pet strains. Welsh Springers will readily involve themselves in their owner's life and activities. They have a kind disposition, show no aggression or nervousness, and suit family life well because they thrive on human companionship. They are high spirited, affectionate, intelligent, and perceptive, but they can be a challenge to train.

Color choices?

The Welsh Springer Spaniel's most distinguishing feature is its coat—rich red markings on a white background, and any pattern is acceptable. White areas may be flecked with red ticking.

How much grooming?

This thick, straight, silky coat will need regular grooming to remove tangles and debris from the undergrowth. Special attention is needed when brushing through the thicker feathered parts of the body: the backs of legs, chest, underbody, ears, and tail. Ears need to be checked and cleaned regularly.

Do they make good pets?

Welsh Springers are conveniently sized, have companionable personalities, and make sensible pets. They are active, loyal, affectionate, bold, friendly, and make excellent housedogs. Although very good natured, they are independent, strong-willed, and sometimes stubborn, so they need firm handling to keep them compliant.

● *An adult and two half-grown puppies. These attractive dogs have a lot of energy.*

What home suits them?

Not suited to apartment living, this breed suits suburban or country life best, with a yard and a lot of places to exercise. This is a breed that owners will enjoy taking out on long walks when adult, so you need space available close by.

What type of owner?

Welsh Springers have a reputation for being friendly, happy, and demonstrative with all family members. They get along well with children, are kind, gentle and never aggressive. They need owners who handle them kindly but firmly,

because they are strong-willed. Owners should be active and provide plenty of walking, and activities that appeal to their high-energy activity levels.

How much exercise and stimulation?

These are active, hard-working dogs built for endurance. High spirited with boundless energy, they need plenty of exercise. They are well suited to running in mountainous terrain, and they particularly like water. They were bred for an active outside life and lot of stimulation will help their mental well-being.

Friendly with other pets?

A Welsh Springer's kind disposition is accepting of other household pets, and they generally react to them with a friendly, playful attitude.

Is puppy training easy?

This breed can be challenging to train, and is easily bored. Training is

Personality Traits	Poor	Average	Good	Excellent
Attitude toward other dogs				
Quietness				
Behavior at home				
Watchdog ability				
Good with children				
Ease of training				
Obedience to owner				

Time to maturity: 2 years
Male height: 18–19 in (46–48 cm)
Female height: 17–18 in (43–46 cm)
Weight: 35–45 lb (16–20 kg)
Average lifespan: 12–15 years

essential to mold them into sociable dogs, and it should be firm, gentle, and patient to achieve the best results. Puppies can be headstrong, but with good training they will be extremely obedient.

Special puppy care?
Welsh Springers can have a tendency for overexercising as puppies, so exercise should be graded to allow for bone and joint growth to prevent injuries. Puppies and adults can suffer from separation anxiety; training should start early to prevent this problem from developing later in life.

Possible health problems?
Small numbers of Welsh Springers suffer from seizures, hip dysplasia (malformation of the hip sockets), eye problems (entropion and glaucoma), and they are prone to ear infections. Breeders and owners are encouraged to check for these problems.

What can we do together?
These are very versatile dogs and are often involved with showing, agility, obedience, and freestyle. They are also trained as therapy and hearing dogs.

Don't forget!
Without sufficient exercise Welsh Springers will become hyperactive, so exercise and stimulation are essential for this energetic breed.

● At 1 year old, this puppy is finding his feet. He will respond to firm but patient handling to achieve the best results in training.

Happy to oblige with a Sit!

Medium dogs

Welsh Springers are ideal working dogs and also make great family pets.

Soft Coated Wheaten Terrier

This happy, lively breed originated as Irish crofters' dogs used for guarding, herding livestock, and hunting vermin. Breed recognition in Ireland came in 1937, in Britain in 1943, and in the U.S. in 1973. They have energetic, intelligent, cheerful personalities and gregarious natures, and relate well to people, especially children. Their exuberant, sometimes stubborn, and occasionally dominant nature makes training essential. Puppies look quite different from their parents, without their distinctive, soft, flowing coat, until maturity at around two. The softly waved, silky hair, reflecting the color of ripening wheat, needs regular attention to maintain non-shedding properties without matting. Wheatens are less feisty than most Terriers, devoted to their owners. They have loads of personality, and are always willing to join in family events, because they enjoy being the center of attention. Carefully trained, they make exceptional family pets.

Color choices?

Puppies are black or dark brown when born, shading white by 18 months, before darkening to honey colors with black muzzle, ears, and other points or clear wheaten—like ripening wheat.

How much grooming?

The loosely waved, but never curly, coat needs daily grooming with a pin brush and wide-tooth comb to prevent the non-shedding coat from tangling. Sometimes trimmed short, especially around the eyes to help vision, Wheatens are never stripped, as hair regrowth will be orange-colored. Grooming daily between 12 and 24 months is essential as adult coats grow. Ears need regular checking and cleaning.

Do they make good pets?

Wheatens are not for quieter families. They have "big" personalities, but are easy to live with when trained well. Wheatens are mischievous and may learn bad habits, though they are rarely aggressive. They are delightful companions and often

● *This adult Wheaten's coat is trimmed, not stripped, to present a neat outline.*

jump up for kissing and affection. Their loyal, playful nature and happy exuberance delight young and old, and they make excellent pets.

What home suits them?

Wheatens appreciate suburban or country living with good walks nearby. They love travel and adjust to changes well. Adaptable to most homes, though owners should have a yard where they can play and explore. Secure fencing is needed, as they may escape if bored.

What type of owner?

Wheaten owners should be gentle, firm, and consistent with discipline, but equally appreciate a exuberant and extroverted nature. Owners need to adopt positive and sensitive approaches to training, must take regular walks, and provide suitable toys to prevent boredom. Wheatens enjoy digging, so they are not ideal choices for gardening enthusiasts.

How much exercise and stimulation?

Puppies will need around a 15-minute walk twice daily, gradually building up time and distance; hour-long walks are needed for adults. A consistent, firm approach taken early on is best, because they are highly intelligent, quick to problem-solve, and may take advantage. Mental stimulation using canine toys or activities is ideal.

Friendly with other pets?

Early introductions are essential for good relations with other family pets, as their lively, inquisitive, and

Personality Traits	Poor	Average	Good	Excellent
Attitude toward other dogs		■		
Quietness		■		
Behavior at home			■	
Watchdog ability			■	
Good with children			■	
Ease of training			■	
Obedience to owner		■		

Time to maturity: 2.5 years
Male height: 18–19.5 in (46–49.5 cm)
Female height: Slightly less
Weight: 35–45 lb (16–21.5 kg)
Average lifespan: 12–14 years

...bouncy nature may not be appreciated. Small animals may be at risk because of their typical Terrier prey drive. Wheatens are often kept in pairs, although very occasionally this can lead to rivalry and jealousy.

Is puppy training easy?

Firm, patient, reward-based, fun training is best; harsh training methods are ineffective. Ideally play-learning suits Wheatens rather than formal training, because life is for fun, not obedience!

Special puppy care?

Digestive problems caused by feeding puppies incorrect diets can occur. Puppies need early gentle persuasion, so they do not dictate their owner's life.

Possible health problems?

Wheatens are generally healthy dogs, but can suffer from protein wasting disease; eye, liver, and kidney problems; and hip dysplasia (malformation of the hip sockets). Dietary and allergy problems occur if

● Irish-bred puppies have less coat than shaggier English-bred Wheatens.

At 5 months, this puppy is already growing a longer coat.

Medium dogs

diets are wrong. Some are intolerant of anesthetics.

What can we do together?

Wheatens are good watchdogs, enjoy long walks, agility or obedience, and working as therapy dogs. They are amusing companion dogs.

Don't forget!

Wheatens are a handful unless properly trained and supervised. Coat care and checking ears are essential.

Chinese Shar-Pei
Other names: Chinese Fighting Dog

Known for their distinctive face, body wrinkles, and a blue-black tongue, this ancient Chinese breed originated 2000 years ago during the Han Dynasty. The breed was mainly used for temple or herd guarding, fighting, and hunting boar. The Shar Pei's bristly "horse coat" is a distinctive feature and the name literally translates as "sand skin." Its favor declined with Chinese peasant farmers when China increased its dog tax, but it w saved from near extinction by breeders in Hong Kong and the U.S. in the 1970s. Numbers increase and interest soon developed in Europe. Its hippo-li head, bristly fur, and heavily wrinkled skin give it ar eccentric appearance. The Shar Pei's calm persona however, means it is sought after by dog fanciers a families alike, its reputation as a fighting dog long gone. Despite the scowling expression, these are intelligent, affectionate, and playful dogs who make great companions and family members.

Color choices?
Black, chocolate, isabella (light fawn), blue, red, sable, red-fawn, apricot, and cream in solid colors are acceptable, while spotted ("flowered coats") or black and tan are not. Some have darker shading on the back and the ears, with a lighter shaded underbody.

● *A Shar-Pei puppy at 7 weeks starting to develop the wrinkles so distinctive of his parent (left).*

How much grooming?
There are three different coat types: horse, brush, and bear coats, although bear coats are only found in China. Horse coat is prickly, rough, and stands off the skin. Brush coats are smoother and longer. Both coats are low maintenance, but need brushing with a hound glove or stiff pin brush, separating folds and penetrating to the skin, once weekly. Molting occurs twice yearly, and brushing should increase to remove the shed. Ears need cleaning regularly using cotton swabs.

Do they make good pets?
Shar-Peis are reserved and aloof with strangers, but are especially good with children and are happiest living with families. They rarely bark, but when they do, it is with good reason. Overall, they are devoted, loyal, affectionate, and capable of calm companionship. They make excellent pets if well trained and socialized early.

What home suits them?
These puppies appreciate homes with yards for playing and running, but either suburban or country living suits them provided that there are good walks and family company.

What type of owner?
Shar-Peis need owners with firm and sensitive leadership, with time for training, exercise, and mental stimulation. These dogs are not ideal for novice owners because they are strong-minded.

How much exercise and stimulation?
Shar-Peis are adaptable and enjoy long or short walks, although any exercise in hot weather should be avoided. Shar-Peis are highly intelligent and enjoy the stimulation of two daily walks. Active play each day also provides exercise and benefits their health.

Friendly with other pets?
Early socialization is important, as puppies develop their natural guarding senses; usually they are good with other dogs, although aggression may occur between males. Shar-Peis are fine with famil cats, but have strong chase instincts so beware of neighbors' cats and farm livestock.

Is puppy training easy?
Strong-minded and independent dogs, they are amenable and intelligent for training to high

Personality Traits	Poor	Average	Good	Excellent
Attitude toward other dogs				
Quietness				
Behavior at home				
Watchdog ability				
Good with children				
Ease of training				
Obedience to owner				

Time to maturity: 2–3 years
Male height: 18–20 in (46–51 cm)
Female height: 18–20 in (46–51 cm)
Weight: 40–60 lb (18–27 kg)
Average lifespan: 8–10 years

standards of obedience. Firm, gentle training and early socialization will prevent aggressive traits or other behaviors. Repetition causes boredom and Shar-Peis learn best with varied training sessions to maintain interest, and owners who foster mutual respect.

Special puppy care?

Shar-Peis' suspicion of strangers needs addressing when young to prevent this from causing territorial and protective behavior. Puppies may need special attention to their diets.

Possible health problems?

Their popularity has caused problems with breeders exaggerating excessive wrinkles and skin folds. They also suffer from allergy-induced skin infections, recurring familial Shar-Pei fever (swollen hock syndrome), amyloidosis (kidney problems), hip dysplasia, eye problems (entropion, ectropion, blocked tear ducts), low levels of thyroid hormone, Vitamin B12 deficiency, gastric torsion, and chronic ear problems.

Medium dogs

What can we do together?

Obedience, agility, herding, and tracking events.

Don't forget!

Make sure to only buy from reputable breeders who address potential health issues.

● *Puppies at 8 weeks look cute, cuddly, and playful, but they are old enough to go out into the big wide world to start learning good manners.*

Australian Cattle Dog

Other names: Blue or Red Heeler, Queensland Heeler

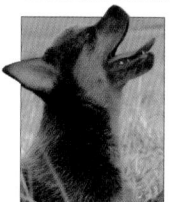

This breed embodies a cocktail of qualities derived from other dogs combined to make one species. Its historical antecedents include the Smithfield (now extinct), the Dingo, Collie, Kelpie, and Bull Terrier. Australian Cattle Dogs were bred to drive cattle over long distances in the harsh terrain of the outback. They are also called Heelers because their method of driving cattle is to nip at their heels, without causing injury. Courageous, intelligent, dynamic, always alert, and extremely hard-working, this is an active dog that will need plenty of exercise. They rarely bark and when they do it sounds like owls hooting. This breed is not meant for the city, but will prosper in the country, particularly when doing what it does best— herding livestock. Very loyal and protective of their owners, they are devoted to their families, but will always need an active working life to be happy.

Color choices?

Born white, puppies color up as they mature. Adult coloring is brown (red) or black (blue) hairs evenly distributed in white hair. Blue coloring is blue; blue mottled; or speckled, with or without black, tan, and white markings. Red coloring is speckled with solid red markings. Symmetrical markings of solid colors are preferred in dogs that are bred for showing. Chocolate and cream colors occur occasionally.

How much grooming?

Easy to groom and to keep clean, ACDs have little doggy odor. Coats molt once yearly, but daily brushing and occasional bathing, particularly when shedding, works well. Attention to nails, ears, and teeth keeps this puppy healthy.

Do they make good pets?

ACDs are very devoted to their owners, and love being part of the family. Highly protective, loyal, and wary of strangers, they are quick to respond to their owner's emotions. They are happy, playful, and affectionate dogs, but they can

● A strong muscular breed which benefits from plenty of working activity, but also enjoys canine sports with his owner.

develop undesirable habits, such as chewing, nipping, barking, digging and chasing. Training should be used to prevent these behaviors.

What home suits them?

Country and suburban homes or farms are best, with plenty of space to run and expend their large amounts of energy. A securely fenced yard is necessary because they like to wander.

What type of owner?

They are very protective and never far from their owner's side. Owners should train their dog not to be possessive to prevent problems. Training is essential with children around, as play and active movements may encourage nipping and herding behavior.

How much exercise and stimulation?

This breed has high energy levels, sharp intelligence, and an independent spirit. Plenty of exercise is needed and preferably a "job" or herding activity that engages their mind and body. Lack of space or activity encourages mischief and bad behavior.

Friendly with other pets?

ACDs introduced as puppies respond well to other family dogs or those that they come to know. However, this breed does not enjoy living as a pack and natural aggression among them is a strong possibility while a pecking order is established.

Is puppy training easy?

Well-structured training with rewards, challenging activities to

Personality Traits	Poor	Average	Good	Excellent
Attitude toward other dogs				
Quietness				
Behavior at home				
Watchdog ability				
Good with children				
Ease of training				
Obedience to owner				

Time to maturity: 2 years
Male height: 18–20 in (46–51 cm)
Female height: 17–19 in (43–48 cm)
Weight: 44–62 lb (20–28 kg)
Average lifespan: 11–14 years

create interest, and purposeful tasks are best. Training must be consistent, and never repetitive or boring; it is a good idea to use games and a lot of encouragement to assist training.

Special puppy care?

Puppies will need careful training to prevent them from developing bad habits. Close supervision and mental stimulation will also be needed from the start, as boredom may cause puppies to be mischievous and badly behaved.

Possible health problems?

This robust, hardy breed may suffer from deafness, eye problems (blindness), hip dysplasia, PRA (progressive retinal atrophy), OCD (osteochondritis dissecans) and accidental injury brought about by its highly energetic and active lifestyle.

What can we do together?

Owners will enjoy their ACD if they enjoy active sporting events. Structured activities such as non-

competitive herding tests, agility, and rally obedience, or any other athletic or endurance competitions, are popular. These dogs are also used as assistance dogs and in the armed services.

Don't forget!

Training to avoid the puppy from developing its natural habit of herding and nipping will be needed from the start. These puppies need plenty of activity from early on, but don't let them over-exert and damage young bones and joints.

Medium dogs

● Puppies like this at 11 weeks need to grow into their pricked ears!

● Symmetrical markings are preferred for show specimens, but any color or marking is suitable for pets.

Border Collie

Borders have been the shepherd's working partner for centuries, arriving in the British Isles with the Vikings. Used for herding sheep in the border regions between England, Scotland, and Wales, Borders are incredibly intelligent and very trainable. Guided to obey their owner's whistles, they group, separate, and herd sheep over hillside terrains and can take the initiative to bring flocks safely home. Borders

work patiently with extreme focus. This breed real is the canine Einstein, excelling at many activities including search and rescue and police work. Borders need early socialization, intense training, and sensitive handling to reach their true potential Committed owners who work their minds will find them to be exemplary dogs, very intelligent and highly responsive, but they must be prepared to commit time and attention to them. This is not a dog for a novice owner.

Color choices?

Usually Borders are bicolor—white with either brown, black, or red (the most common); or tricolors—black, brown/tan, and white. They can also be red or blue merle (marbled color on white), sable, brindle, and some are solid black or brown.

How much grooming?

Borders either have thick, double, long coats that are soft, silky, and shed; or smooth coats that need less attention. Keeping thicker coats in good condition needs more regular grooming with attention to feathering on the legs, the tail and around the head. Check ears once a week to keep them clean. Bathing may be needed occasionally, although regular grooming should suffice.

Do they make good pets?

These dogs need to be on the go, working and herding or undertaking meaningful activities, which is what they are happiest doing. They are devoted and affectionate pets, but perhaps not for busy families.

● *A lovely group of mother, father (right), and their 6-week-old puppies.*

What home suits them?

This is an active, energetic dog and country or suburban homes with plenty of space and an enclosed yard with secure fencing are best. These are not ideal city dogs, and definitely not suited to homes that cannot offer them enough exercise or activity.

What type of owner?

These dogs were used to spending long working days with only their owner for company. Owners will need to be active, keen on long walks and intensive training, or happy to be involved in energetic

activities that interest their Borde Definitely not a dog for novice owners, nor is a Border suitable fc owners who don't appreciate the pleasures of exercise.

How much exercise and stimulation?

Borders need plenty of exercise a mental stimulation to keep them happy. Daily activity with play, train-ing, and supervised exercise and company are best. If these are not provided for them, they can becom neurotic, aggressive, and territorial.

Friendly with other pets?

Early socialization is recommende so that they get along well with other pets, but their instinct to her may be a problem for smaller pets Training and socialization around livestock for farm dogs is also recommended.

Is puppy training easy?

Borders are very trainable, but the need to be trained in the right wa by an owner who keeps one step ahead of their response to differer

Personality Traits	Poor	Average	Good	Excellent
Attitude toward other dogs		●		
Quietness		●		
Behavior at home			●	
Watchdog ability			●	
Good with children			●	
Ease of training				●
Obedience to owner				●

Time to maturity: 2 years
Male height: 18–21 in (46–53 cm)
Female height: Slightly less
Weight: 30–49 lb (14–22 kg)
Average lifespan: 12–14 years

...ituations. Highly intelligent and very quick to learn, they can be sensitive and need sensitive, responsive training to do well.

Special puppy care?

Good socialization is essential for this puppy may become neurotic. Some may find their own entertainment, and because they are motion-sensitive may develop a habit of chasing moving vehicles, which should be curbed.

Lovely puppies, but not the best choice for inexperienced owners.

Possible health problems?

Generally very hardy, Borders can suffer from hip and elbow malformation, eye problems (collie eye anomaly), epilepsy, deafness, and hypothyroidism (lack of thyroid hormone). Some merle-coated dogs may have eye or hearing problems.

What can we do together?

Energetic owners will enjoy a variety of activities with their Border such as flyball, competitive obedience, agility, and sheepdog trialling/herding.

Don't forget!

This is a breed only for owners willing to lead an active life, and not for novices.

Medium dogs

● With unlimited energy, training must start soon for these 8-week-old puppies.

Whippet

This graceful, slender little sighthound was "the poor man's racehorse," bred by miners in northern England a little over a century ago. Trained to run like a "scared spirit," Whippets can achieve speeds of 35 mph (56 kph), and love the sprint to a finish line. They entertained their owners by competing in coursing, racing, and hunting hare for the pot. Recognition of the breed came in Britain in 1888 and in the U.S. in 1890. Whippets are ideal companion pets because they are quiet, very home loving, affectionate couch potatoes, and appreciative of their creature comforts—warmth and a good bed. Their medium size makes them ideal for most types of homes, and their undemanding, sweet natures and easy-care coat makes them an excellent choice for most families. Whippets' exercise requirements are very reasonable and they develop an excellent rapport with children and adults.

Color choices?

Whippets are available in several colors from solid black to solid white, or red, fawn, cream, brindle or blue, with spots, blazes, and particolors.

How much grooming?

A Whippet's short, smooth coat is excellent for families who do not want to commit to regular daily grooming. Occasional use of a rubber hound glove, finishing with a silk cloth or chamois leather, will keep coats looking good. Whippet coats are quite thin and not weatherproof, so make sure to keep them warm in cold weather.

● *These graceful and elegant dogs are well respected for their speed. This young adult still retains his inborn hunting instinct and may follow an interesting scent when out walking.*

Do they make good pets?

These are quiet, affectionate, gentle dogs who love children and make excellent family pets. Puppies are mischievous at first and demand lots of attention, but eventually they mature and grow into sensible dogs. They are quite adaptable to varying amounts of exercise.

What home suits them?

Whippets enjoy active country lives but can live quite happily in a suburban or city environment. If well exercised, they will adapt to living in apartments, but homes with yards or space to run off-leash are best.

What type of owner?

A Whippet's calm, loyal, and friendly temperament may suit active older people, although families with children for playmates are ideal. Owners who enjoy active lifestyles will enjoy a Whippet's sweet and good-natured companionship.

How much exercise and stimulation?

Whippets are often content to spend the day quietly at home, but they still need at least an hour's walk, plus about 20 minutes of free running and play as well. Ideally they should be on leash at certain times, when near livestock, for instance, and definitely near traffic as they have no road sense. Stimulation through off-leash sessions and play is recommended.

Friendly with other pets?

These are gentle, friendly puppies, who get along well with other household pets. However, they are bred for chasing rabbits, so smaller pets or neighbors' cats may be at risk.

Is puppy training easy?

Whippets are easy puppies to train for patient and conscientious owners. They are intelligent, alert, and willing to please if training is presented positively with plenty of rewards and encouragement. Harsh training will not be effective.

Personality Traits	Poor	Average	Good	Excellent
Attitude toward other dogs				
Quietness				
Behavior at home				
Watchdog ability				
Good with children				
Ease of training				
Obedience to owner				

Time to maturity: Up to 4 years
Male height: 19–22 in (48–56 cm)
Female height: 18–21 in (46–53 cm)
Weight: 20–40 lb (9–18 kg)
Average lifespan: 12–15 years

because of the sensitive nature of his puppy. Whippets have a strong instinct to chase, so a good recall will be an essential part of early training.

Special puppy care?
Puppies can be naughty, often behaving like small whirlwinds, so patience and attention is needed early to train them to have good habits. Whippets suffer quite badly from the cold, so owners need to provide them with warm coats in cold weather.

Possible health problems?
Whippets are healthy and long-lived, but can suffer from heart problems, undescended testicles, and often have difficulty with anesthetics. Their thin skin is prone to cold and damage by thorny undergrowth when out exercising.

What can we do together?
Whippets are ideal for activities to do together, and enjoy showing, lure coursing, racing, obedience, agility, and flyball.

Don't forget!
Whippets have no road sense so they must be on leash near traffic. Their thin skin means that they are sensitive to the cold in winter.

Medium dogs

● At 9 weeks this puppy (left) looks similar to his 6-month-old friend (right), but has lots of growth and development to catch up on.

Bull Terrier
Other names: English Bull Terrier

This "gladiator" of the dog world was bred from Terriers and Bulldogs for bull and bear baiting and fighting in the 19th century. Endowed with great courage and stamina, they were totally fearless with a driving determination to match their muscular, solid, powerful bodies. Later breeding produced the modern, more elegant show strain, with distinctive triangular eyes and egg-shaped heads, but with the same characteristics of physical power and strong will. Bullies are loveable clowns, fun-loving, and people-oriented. They enjoy playing the fool, but are boisterous and may become destructive when bore Experienced owners will enjoy their robust, eager-t please, stable temperament, but they are hard to liv with if not properly trained. Their strong personalit make them unsuitable for novices, and owners should consider public opinion concerning Bully breeds and current bree specific legislation about owning one.

Color choices?

Bull terriers are available in all white, or white with colored patches on the head, also black, brindle, red, or tricolor. In colored dogs, the color must predominate over white, which can take the form of markings on the chest, under-body, tail tip, socks, and face blaze.

How much grooming?

Weekly brushing with a hound glove or a pin brush to remove dead hair should suffice.

Do they make good pets?

Bullies make excellent pets in the right hands, and are very people-oriented. They can be boisterous, exuberant, independent, stubborn and willful, and so are not suitable for inexperienced or older owners. Bullies are playful and affectionate and make outstanding pets if properly trained, but are unsuitable for families with young children who may tease them.

What home suits them?

Adaptable to either suburban or country living, sturdy fencing around the yard is essential. Access to space for walking is important, as Bullies need time to run off-leash to burn off their excess energy.

What type of owner?

These puppies need an owner with an assertive demeanor, who will be firm in training and not stand for any nonsense. Owners will appreciate their comical, mischievous ways, but need to be experienced to handle their intelligence and stubborn streak.

How much exercise and stimulation?

Bullies are active and need plenty of exercise. They may, however, enjoy lazing around their home, and often need encouraging to go for a walk or they may suffer from obesity. Their intelligent minds nee plenty of exercising, too.

Friendly with other pets?

This breed needs to be very well socialized as puppies to mix with other family pets. Some may be per fectly happy in their company, othe may need to be kept alone. Bullies have strong prey drive, and may be unsafe around cats. Male and femal Bullies usually live together quite happily, but be cautious when introducing second dogs at a later date; dogs of the same gender may caus disruption to family dynamics.

Is puppy training easy?

Strict, firm, but gentle handling is needed, as they can be difficult to train. Reward-based training with a lot of positive reinforcement using food and toys is best. Bullies are not likely to be outstandingly obedient, but with patience they can achieve satisfactory levels of obedience.

● The powerful physique of adult Bullies means they need to be supervised around other dogs.

Personality Traits	Poor	Average	Good	Excellent
Attitude toward other dogs	■			
Quietness		■		
Behavior at home			■	
Watchdog ability				■
Good with children			■	
Ease of training	■			
Obedience to owner	■			

Time to maturity: 3 years
Male height: 18–24 in (46–61 cm)
Female height: 18–24 in (46–61 cm)
Weight: 52–62 lb (24–28 kg)
Average lifespan: 11–13 years

Special puppy care?

These puppies have powerful jaws and will happily chew literally anything, so strong toys need to be carefully selected to keep their interest away from valuable belongings. Pure white puppies may suffer from deafness; it is not immediately apparent when very young, so this needs to be checked before buying.

Possible health problems?

Bull Terriers can suffer from kidney and heart problems, patella luxation (dislocating kneecaps), skin problems (allergies to certain foods, fleas, and mites), and deafness can occur in white dogs.

What can we do together?

Great watchdogs, Bullies will also enjoy time spent walking with their owner or just being loyal companions.

Don't forget!

These dogs can exhibit behavioral problems if training is inadequate. As a powerful breed, Bull Terriers can arouse negative public opinion when taken out, so owners have a responsibility to be conscientious with training.

● *Until these 6-week-old puppies are older, their true nature and temperament may be difficult to determine.*

Brittany *Other names: Brittany Spaniel*

Descending from the historic Chien d'Oysel from northern France, Brittanys were depicted in hunting scenes in many tapestries of the 17th century. Later versions of these Breton farm dogs, sometimes known as Fougeres meaning "high spirited" and possibly bred with English Setters, were valued for their unique qualities of hunting, pointing, and retrieving game. Their excellent ability for scenting and tracking, along with their medium size, made them popular in the U.S. in the 1930s for hunting woodcock. Hard-working, tireless, and willing to work most terrains Brittanys are versatile dogs. Brittanys did not reac Britain until the 1970s, but they are now prized there as good-natured companions. Their energeti enthusiasm for life demands a suitable outlet for their high energy, but with an intelligent, even temper they make gentle and affectionate companions as family pets.

Color choices?
Usual colors (with spots, ticking, or flecks) are orange and white, liver and white, black and white, tricolor (black, tan and white, or liver, white and orange). Black is considered a fault in the U.S.

How much grooming?
The medium-length, single, flowing coat sheds very little, and is usually low maintenance. Ten minutes of brushing and combing twice weekly and regular attention to cleaning and checking ears is fine. Feathering on the ears and legs needs attention, particularly after working in under-growth, as debris will need to be removed. Bath only when needed.

Do they make good pets?
Brittanys make excellent pets if they have plenty of exercise, appropriate activity, and a "job in life," otherwise they can be hyperactive and too energetic to live with. Puppies can be too exuberant and boisterous for small children, although they respond well to older children who can maintain better control.

● With good training and socialization, Brittanys will become well-adjusted adults.

What home suits them?
They suit suburban life best because they need space for off-leash running, long walks, and organized activity. A reasonably sized, well-fenced yard is the ideal solution. Although suitable in terms of size, Brittanys are too active for apartment living and are not indoor dogs.

What type of owner?
Ideal for active owners, this puppy needs a lot of energy-busting walking in all weather, together with training and stimulating activity to appeal to their intelligent minds.

Only owners prepared to accept the commitment of a high-energy dog should consider this breed.

How much exercise and stimulation?
Plenty of exercise is needed on a daily basis. Long walks of one to two hours' duration including free running is ideal, as well as activitie designed to stimulate the mind an use up their boundless energy.

Friendly with other pets?
Friendly with other dogs if well socialized as puppies, Brittanys are also good with cats. However, sma pets such as rabbits and guinea pigs may be at risk because of the hunting background.

Is puppy training easy?
Brittanys are gentle-natured, sensitive puppies and respond we to calm, consistent, reward-based learning. Eager to please, quick to learn and highly trainable, they should not be handled roughly, and they will respond best if given plenty of encouragement.

Personality Traits	Poor	Average	Good	Excellent
Attitude toward other dogs				
Quietness				
Behavior at home				
Watchdog ability				
Good with children				
Ease of training				
Obedience to owner				

Time to maturity: 2 years
Male height: 19–20 in (48–51 cm)
Female height: 18–19 in (46–48 cm)
Weight: 30–40 lb (13.5–18 kg)
Average lifespan: 12–13 years

Special puppy care?

Puppies need plenty of socializing with gradually increasing levels of activity to prevent them from becoming hyperactive. Insensitive training can be detrimental to their well-being, so be gentle and kind while using plenty of encouragement and rewards to achieve success.

Possible health problems?

Generally healthy and hardy as a breed, Brittanys can be susceptible to epilepsy, eye problems, hip dysplasia (malformation), hemophilia, and some skin disorders.

What can we do together?

Brittanys' bright, intelligent minds will respond to owners who encourage them in activities such as flyball, obedience, fieldwork, and agility.

Don't forget!

Plenty of exercise for adults and sensitive training are essential. Brittanys sometimes have a

 *Cute as can be at only
6 weeks of age.*

reputation for being unmanageable, but this is usually the result of lack of exercising and poor training.

English Spring Spaniel

A larger Spaniel used for hunting, the Springer was developed for scenting and retrieving game, or flushing out birds to trained falcons that brought them to the hunter. Springers are good all-around bird dogs, their slightly webbed toes making them powerful swimmers for retrieving water birds. Officially recognized in Britain in 1902, they became the most popular hunting dog.

Springers are available in two strains: working dogs which have a strong working drive, and are sturdier smaller, and less suitable as family pets; and show strains, more suited to family life. Active, energetic dogs with vitality and stamina that love to work an play, Springers are excitable, strong-willed, and boisterous, so they need firm training. Excellent companion and family dogs, they must have plenty physical exercise or "jobs" to do. They are exceller police dogs used for detecting anything from drugs to illegal immigrants.

Color choices?

Coat choices are black or liver (dark brown) with white markings, white with black or liver markings, or tricolor with additional tan markings. White areas can be flecked or ticked.

How much grooming?

Working-strain Springers have shorter, coarse coats that shed in autumn; show-bred dogs have softer, silkier coats that shed twice yearly. Daily brushing with a pin brush and comb removes mud and debris picked up on walks. Ears need checking daily and cleaning weekly, with hair carefully trimmed under their pendulous ears allowing air circulation.

Do they make good pets?

Temperamentally, Springers are easy-going family dogs; they love children and are patient, tolerant, and always willing to play. Not ideal for busy families, puppies are energetic whirlwinds needing a lot of time and attention for training and care.

● *Adult Springers are happiest when given a job or activity to do.*

What home suits them?

Best with a house and secure yard to play in, and owners who are tolerant of their passion for digging. Apartment life would be impossible for this energetic and active dog.

What type of owner?

Ideal companions for people who enjoy long walks, jogging, or biking, Springers are unsuitable for older, less active types. Owners must be firm, patient, and gentle with this emotionally sensitive dog. Above all, they must have a sense of humor to cope with a Springer's rambunctious behavior.

How much exercise and stimulation?

Springers are tough, hardy, vigorous, active, and swift, and need moderate amounts of exercise daily, come rain or shine.

Friendly with other pets?

This sociable breed with its gentle expression and wagging tail is excellent with other dogs and most household pets if well socialized early. He may not pass up the opportunity to chase the cat, though.

Is puppy training easy?

Springers are delightful to train because they are intelligent, quick to learn, and eager to please. They are sensitive, so training must be firm, gentle, encouraging, and with plenty of praise to maintain motivation and interest. Training must start early to harness their exuberant energy, but must never be harsh. Generally, Springers are willing, non-aggressive dogs that are biddable and devoted to owners when suitably trained.

Personality Traits	Poor	Average	Good	Excellent
Attitude toward other dogs				
Quietness				
Behavior at home				
Watchdog ability				
Good with children				
Ease of training				
Obedience to owner				

Time to maturity: 2.5 years
Male height: 19–20 in (48–51 cm)
Female height: 19–20 in (48–51 cm)
Weight: 49–53 lb (22–24 kg)
Average lifespan: 13–15 years

Special puppy care?

Early training is essential to prevent problems with overexuberance, which can make puppies a nuisance. Be careful not to overwalk puppies to try to tire them out, as young bones and joints can suffer. Springers' inclination to flush game may encourage puppies to ramble in thickets, which can cause injury.

Possible health problems?

Springers are quite a healthy breed but may suffer eye problems, fucosidosis (a metabolic disorder), phosphofructokinase deficiency (causing muscle cramps), and hip and elbow malformation. All these illnesses tend to be rare, and can be tested for prior to purchase.

Medium dogs

What can we do together?

Springers are great companion pets for long walks or jogging and biking. Hunting trials for working specimens, obedience, therapy, and service training are also ideal activities for this energetic breed.

Don't forget!

Start training puppies early to prevent behavioral problems

● *These two pups don't look like potential canine whirlwinds at 8 weeks, but they may become that if not trained properly!*

Norwegian Elkhound
Other names: Norwegian Moose Dog

The Elkhound is one of several ancient Spitz breeds, but this one is acknowledged as Norway's national dog. It dates back to the time of early Scandinavian hunters who kept Spitz-type dogs with thick coats to withstand subzero temperatures for hunting large game in snow-bound forests and rugged mountains. Even earlier, remains suggest that Elkhounds were Viking farm dogs, although they now have a more modern conformation in breeding. A sporting breed, they are courageous, hardy, energetic, friendl and loving to their owner, with a reputation for bei child-friendly. They are excellent watchdogs who kn when to take action, but are also independent and strong-willed, so they need firm handling in training Elkhounds are particularly people-oriented dogs, ve protective of small children, and great playmates for families. Their friendly disposition, unswerving loyal and affection for their owner make them ideal family pets.

Color choices?
They are available in silver or gray, with black tips on longer hair, and lighter gray on the chest; or brilliant black with lighter markings on the chest, front legs, and feet. Both colors have areas of darker marking between the shoulder and elbow.

How much grooming?
This harsh, thick, abundant coat is virtually indestructible and without smell, but it sheds continuously, and molts copiously twice yearly. Grooming daily with sturdy brushes and combing is necessary. Twice weekly suffices otherwise. Pay particular attention to thicker hair on the neck and underbody to prevent matting and dirt build-up. Elkhounds will tolerate "vacuum cleaning" to remove loose hair.

Do they make good pets?
Compact and powerfully built, Elkhounds are friendly and intelligent, and their medium size is ideal for families. They make good pets because they are good-natured, very people-oriented,

● *The Norwegian Elkhound needs firm handling to manage its independent nature.*

patient, tolerant, and protective toward children.

What home suits them?
Elkhounds need homes in the country or suburbs, with well-fenced, large yards. These active, powerful dogs need space for exercising or they are likely to become bored, destructive, and noisy. Their sharp, loud bark may upset close neighbors.

What type of owner?
Elkhounds form inseparable bonds with their owners, who should not leave them at home alone. The best owners are outdoor types who love walking and who understanc this breed's exercise requirement Owners should be prepared to groom regularly while being toler of the Elkhound's copious molting

How much exercise and stimulation?
This breed needs lots of exercise (or two hours daily), which should include off-leash running and activ play. Be careful if they pick up inte esting scents as they will go off hu ing. Elkhounds can be trained to r beside a bicycle for exercise, but no puppies. To avoid risk of bone and jo problems, wait until the Elkhound has matured to train for this activ

Friendly with other pets?
Most Elkhounds are good with other pets, provided that introdu tions and socializing are done ear Rabbits, guinea pigs and other sm domestic pets may be at risk.

Is puppy training easy?
Their independent streak and high intelligence could be challenging fo novices. Respect must be earned a

Personality Traits	Poor	Average	Good	Excellent
Attitude toward other dogs				
Quietness				
Behavior at home				
Watchdog ability				
Good with children				
Ease of training				
Obedience to owner				

Time to maturity: 3 years
Male height: 19–21 in (48–53 cm)
Female height: 19–21 in (48–53 cm)
Weight: 43–50 lb (19.5–23 kg)
Average lifespan: 10–12 years

...aining with a firm but kind approach best, as they are sensitive if treated ...arshly, although they do need to ...nderstand their family rank position. ...essions should be short to avoid ...oredom, and should include plenty ...f rewards to maintain interest and ...nthusiasm. If trained appropriately, ...lkhounds do learn obedience, but ...rying to make them "Come" when ...hey catch a scent may be difficult.

...ecial puppy care?

...uppies need training not to pull on ...he leash before they grow into ...owerful adults. Start grooming early ...o encourage bonding and to ...repare for dealing with molting.

...ssible health problems?

...enerally a healthy breed, Elkhounds ...uffer from hip dysplasia, kidney ...isease, eye problems, and some ...ave problems with sebaceous cysts ...blocked pores or hair follicles).

...hat can we do together?

...hese good-natured companion dogs ...re excellent trackers, and could ...e trained for agility; however ...bedience trials are not their forte!

● *Already powerful at 7 months, this puppy needs to be carefully trained and encouraged in obedience.*

Don't forget!

Essential early training encourages suitable levels of obedience. Grooming daily during the molt will reduce hair shed at home.

Medium dogs

Chow Chow

Popular in its native land of China, the Chow has been around for over 2000 years and is thought to be the oldest breed originating from gray wolves. Chows were used for war, hunting, guarding, and as draft dogs by the Huns, Mongols, and Tartars. Its first introduction to England in 1760 was as a zoo animal, although later Queen Victoria's gift of a specimen Chow assured them of popularity as household pets. In the U.S., Chows became popular with the rich and famous during the "Roaring Twenties," to the extent that modern breeding practices have unfortunately led to several health problems. This aristocratic teddy bear of a dog is highly civilized, aloof, strong-willed, stubborn, dominant, and very reserved. They are, however, absolutely devoted to their family, very protective, well mannered at home, and a loyal companion.

Color choices?

Chows are black, blue, cinnamon (light tan to brown), red (light gold to deep red-brown), cream, or white, with lighter coloring on the underside of rumps and tails. Sometimes nuanced, never spotted or particolored. A Chow's most distinctive feature is its blue-black or purple tongue and gums.

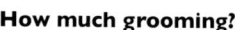

● *Fully grown, Chows resemble dignified teddy bears.*

How much grooming?

A Chow's dense, double coat can be smooth or rough, needing daily grooming to keep it clean. Brushing and combing is best for denser coats, reaching into the fur down to the skin, with more attention paid to thicker areas. A curry comb is easiest during the twice-yearly molt. Extra care is needed with puppy coats during shedding. Grooming smooth coats, which are upstanding plush hair, takes less time.

Do they make good pets?

Some Chows make great family dogs, others not; a lot depends on the puppy, and the methods of early training and socializing. Chows are one-person dogs, and are not particularly affectionate or demonstrative. They need owners who really understand them, and are not a good choice for novices.

What home suits them?

Quiet, orderly homes with an established routine are best. Chows enjoy suburban and country life, but can adapt to cities or apartments if given long, daily walks to burn off energy.

What type of owner?

Owners must appreciate a Chow's individuality—this is an independent breed. Time spent on grooming, training, and socialization teaches puppies to reach their true potential as loyal companions. Owners must earn their Chow's respect and be experienced, assertive, and confident enough to demand it. Strong bonds can be formed, but even so, Chows are distant and not naturally demonstrative.

How much exercise and stimulation?

Chows do not enjoy being active, and exercise needs are moderate, but they do enjoy daily walks, maybe half an hour twice daily. Care in hot weather is necessary, as Chows have a tendency to overheat under their heavy coats.

Friendly with other pets?

Chows are not ideal for forming friendships with smaller household pets, as they have a strong prey drive; early socialization as puppies should allow tolerant relationships to develop satisfactorily between other household dogs. They occasionally show aggression to dogs of the same gender.

Personality Traits	Poor	Average	Good	Excellent
Attitude toward other dogs				
Quietness				
Behavior at home				
Watchdog ability				
Good with children				
Ease of training				
Obedience to owner				

Time to maturity: 2.5 years
Male height: 19–22 in (48–56 cm)
Female height: 18–20 in (46–51 cm)
Weight: 45–70 lb (20–32 kg)
Average lifespan: 14–15 years

puppy training easy?

Chows need firm, patient, consistent, and gentle training from a young age. As puppies, they appear well behaved, and inexperienced owners may assume that this is the norm, but neglecting early training causes problems later. Adults can be independent, obstinate, and dominant, only cooperating when it suits them. It may be difficult for inexperienced owners to change bad habits.

Special puppy care?

Early training must not be neglected, and early socialization helps to overcome their extreme suspicion of strangers.

Possible health problems?

Poor breeding practice in some lines has caused eye problems, lymphoma (malignant tumor), hip dysplasia (malformation), diabetes, cancer, autoimmune disease, and skin melanoma. The thick coat can lead to flea problems.

Medium dogs

What can we do together?

Hunting and being a loyal companion are the Chow's forte. They are also good watchdogs.

Don't forget!

Home insurance in the U.S. has increased for Chow owners, due to badly trained, aggressive Chows. Generally, public perception is poor and Chows are included in breed-specific dog control legislation.

● *Less than 3 months old, but the thick, plush coat already needs regular grooming.*

Portuguese Water Dog
Other names: Portuguese Fishing Dog

True water dogs, they originally came from the Algarve in Portugal, where they worked with fishermen by herding fish into their nets and retrieving tackle. Early stories from 1297 describe a Portuguese Water Dog saving a drowning sailor. They accompanied the fishing fleet to colder waters around Iceland, where their long coats were ideal for the extremes of temperature that they endured. Excellent swimmers and divers, they can be used for hunting water game. By 1930 the bree was on the decline, but it has become popular agai recently and one was chosen as President Obama's family dog. This breed is energetic, impetuous, and tough, needing lots of exercise, but they make grea pets because they are loving, intelligent, and easily trained with firm handling. They enjoy their owner companionship both indoors and out, and make good watchdogs, although they are friendly towa strangers.

Color choices?
They are available in solid white, black or brown, or black or brown with white markings. Particolored Portuguese Water Dogs are rare, but they are found in the United States. In Portugal, white markings rarely cover more than 30 percent of the body.

How much grooming?
These dogs are high maintenance. They have single, hypoallergenic coats, either wavy or curly, and some have both types on different parts of their body. They never shed, and the coat grows indefinitely if not trimmed, which sometimes causes problems around the eyes. Daily grooming is needed, with complete trimming bi-monthly to prevent tangles or skin allergies. Usually a "lion" cut is favored with the hindquarters, muzzle, and base of the tail shaved; or a "retriever" cut, which is trimmed short all over.

Do they make good pets?
These are biddable dogs and quiet in the home, and make excellent

● Energetic, impetuous, and tough, adults will need plenty of walking and exercise to satisfy their need for activity.

family pets. They have a loud, distinctive bark, and invite play and interaction with their owner with an appealing "expressive panting" sound like "ha-ha-ha." Very intelligent, they make ideal companions, and are sometimes used as assistance dogs for the hearing impaired.

What home suits them?
Ideal for suburban and country living, Portuguese Water Dogs enjoy yards for activity and play, with long walks close by. They are excellent jumpers, making high fencing

necessary, and intelligent—if they cannot go over fences, they go under them! True to their name, they are excellent water dogs, so expect lakes, rivers, and oceans to be viewed as potential swimming pools. Owners may need suitable outdoor drying space.

What type of owner?
People who want their dog constantly at their side, and who appreciate an intelligent, independent dog who needs an intense, loing bond would be best. Owners should be prepared to commit to a lot of coat care, and enjoy engaing in plenty of activity. Owners must also appreciate that PWDs enjoy "counter surfing" if food is around! Puppies are bouncy and active, so they are unsuitable for older or less active owners.

How much exercise and stimulation?
Plenty of exercise through walking playing, or swimming is needed, and their high intelligence require adequate mental stimulation.

Personality Traits	Poor	Average	Good	Excellent
ttitude toward other dogs				
Quietness				
ehavior at home				
Watchdog ability				
Good with children				
ase of training				
Obedience to owner				

Time to maturity: 2 years
Male height: 19.5–22.5 in (50–57 cm)
Female height: 17–20.5 in (43–52 cm)
Weight: 35–55 lb (16–25 kg)
Average lifespan: 10–14 years

iendly with other pets?

These dogs are always friendly with other family pets if introduced properly, but do remember their hunting origins. Portuguese Water Dogs are gregarious, so loneliness can cause boredom and destructive behavior.

puppy training easy?

Training skills are quickly learned, and they can master numerous tasks including supporting the hearing impaired and those with epilepsy. However, firm handling is essential because they are willful.

pecial puppy care?

Be careful with toys, as puppies are destructive; rawhide toys are often safer for playing. Puppies failing to thrive should be checked for genetic conditions that may affect them when young.

ossible health problems?

Generally healthy, but they can suffer from juvenile dilated cardiomyopathy (puppies aged from two weeks to seven months) which causes heart failure, and hip and eye problems. Also, hip dysplasia and PRA (progressive retinal atrophy) can occur.

What can we do together?

Obedience taught early is best, but they also do well in agility and hunting.

Don't forget!

Remember to make sure puppies know who is boss, and only buy from a reputable breeder.

● At 8 weeks old, this beautifully marked puppy will make a lovely specimen for showing.

Samoyed
Other names: Nordic Sled Dog, Bjelkier

Samoyeds are a working breed that originated among Samoyedic people of Siberia who were nomadic reindeer herders. They used them for sledding, herding, guarding, and keeping their owners warm. Samoyeds date from at least 3000 years ago, and are one of the most ancient dog breeds, although they were unknown in the West until 1889. They are energetic, active dogs and enjoy taking part in a wide variety of activities, such as sledding, mushing, agility, and tracking. If denied suitable activity, they may become bored and destructive. Samoyeds have hypoallergenic coats, and when groomed, the Angora-like hair can be used for fly-fishing lures or for knitting warm sweaters. However, this coat does require lots of grooming, which may not be ideal for busy families. They are versatile and adaptable, and their sparkling white coat, charming characteristic "smile," and friendly temperament contributes to a happy, sweet natured, and perfect companion dog.

Color choices?

Typically white, but cream or biscuit-shaded are acceptable. A range of other colors (black, brown, and spotted) were once included, but white predominates.

How much grooming?

Samoyeds have double-layer coats that molt copiously twice yearly. They need daily brushing and combing through to the soft warm under-coat and skin to keep them clean and free from mats and tangles. Curry combs are best when the coat is shedding. Neglected coats may get into such a state that they need professional help to rectify. Owners need to tolerate molting because hair sheds everywhere.

Do they make good pets?

These are friendly, gentle, sensitive, and affectionate dogs, that make excellent pets for the right owner. Good with children, they love family life and enjoy being the center of attention. They have sensitive, fun-filled, gregarious temperaments, and do not like being ignored or left alone.

● *If kept well groomed, these beautiful dogs grow into ideal show companions.*

What home suits them?

Samoyeds need sufficient space in a country or suburban home with a yard. A well-fenced yard is ideal, as their energetic working life reflects the need to run around in open space, and they are inclined to escape from the yard if bored.

What type of owner?

This dog needs an owner who is prepared to accept daily coat maintenance and still have hair to clear away during molt seasons. They thrive on affectionate humans who keep up with their energy levels. A demanding breed, they are unsuitable for those leading sedentary lives who just seek canine companionship.

How much exercise and stimulation?

Samoyeds are not satisfied unless they get plenty of exercise and appropriate mental stimulation. They are intelligent dogs and benefit from being involved in energetic and stimulating activity with their owner.

Friendly with other pets?

Samoyeds usually get along well with other household pets, but any introductions should be made while puppies are still young. Some males can be a little dominant, and some are inclined to chase rabbits or neighborhood cats.

Is puppy training easy?

Not always easy to train, Samoyed can be willful, but if training starts early and owners find an activity that suits them both, all will be well. They have no natural inclination to obedience and need firm,

Personality Traits	Poor	Average	Good	Excellent
Attitude toward other dogs				
Quietness				
Behavior at home				
Watchdog ability				
Good with children				
Ease of training				
Obedience to owner				

Time to maturity: 2 years
Male height: 20–22 in (51–56 cm)
Female height: 18–20 in (46–51 cm)
Weight: 50–66 lb (23–30 kg)
Average lifespan: 10–12 years

consistent handling with lots of patience and attention.

‍pecial puppy care?

Puppies will need grooming and training from the start if their owner is to accustom them to continuous coat maintenance and good behavior. Be careful not to overexercise puppies, as it could harm their growing bones.

‍ossible health problems?

Samoyeds do have some health issues such as kidney problems (Samoyed hereditary glomerulo-pathy); hip dysplasia (malformation of the hip sockets); diabetes; and eye, heart, and skin problems. Generally, however, they are healthy and robust.

What can we do together?

There are lots of activities that energetic owners will enjoy, such as sledding, agility, carting, obedience, showing, flyball, tracking, and mushing. Also, non-competitive herding tests and herding trial competitions.

So easy to love at 7 weeks old!

Don't forget!

Samoyeds have heavy shedding coats and require a lot of daily grooming. Always buy from reputable breeders who health-check their stock.

Medium dogs

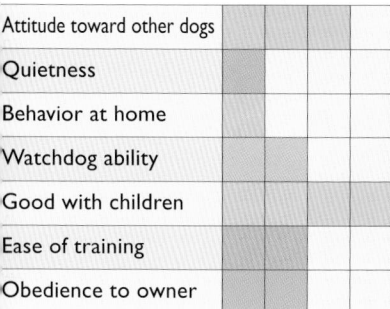

‍ Sporting
‍haracteristic "Sammy"
‍miles, these puppies love
‍eing the center of attention.

Australian Shepherd

Surprisingly, Aussies are an American breed, not Australian as their name suggests. After the Californian gold rush caused mass migration, several arrived on the west coast of the United States, together with the herds of Australian sheep that they worked. These "little blue dogs" earned themselves a reputation for being active, hardy, and fast. They were exceptional working dogs. Closely resembling a Border Collie, they are bred in very attractive colors of marbled (merle) and pastel shades. An intelligent, tenacious breed with strong herding and guarding instincts, they enjoy open spaces, have unlimited energy, and are capable of covering up to 40 miles (60 km) a day. They need plenty of exercise to satisfy their needs. Although friendly, loyal, and affectionate, they can be strong-willed and need proper socializing and firm training. They make ideal family dogs if properly trained, but this is not a good choice for novice owners.

Color choices?

A large variety of colors are available: blue merle (marbled gray and black), red merle (marbled cream and liver red) either solid, or sometimes with tan points, and/or white markings on the face, collar, legs, chest and under-body; red or red bicolor with white; black or black and tan; or tricolor (black, tan, and white). Eye colors offer varieties of brown, blue, or different colors (one blue, one brown).

● *Between 8 weeks (right) and maturity, there is a lot of growing to be done.*

How much grooming?

Aussies have medium-length coats, straight or wavy hair with manes, leg, and tail feathering. Use a stiff brush and groom several times a week to remove any dead hair.

Do they make good pets?

Aussies make excellent pets because they are affectionate, gentle, good-tempered, and very loyal, but they need plenty of exercise to maintain this good nature. Unsuitable for busy families, small children may not cope with Aussies' rough play. They expect to spend most of their time with their owner.

What home suits them?

Not made for an indoor life, apartments and city dwellings are unsuitable for Aussies. Open spaces and suburban or country living are best with somewhere to run off-leash and where long walks are available.

What type of owner?

This breed needs experienced owners, who are prepared to walk long distances or jog several miles daily. Ideally, an owner who is happy to do agility, who has sheep to herd, and who is not out at work all day, would be best. Nicknamed "velcro" dogs, Aussies need company.

How much exercise and stimulation?

Typically high energy, an Aussie wants a lot of exercise. Two to three hour walks a day may be needed, and other activities should be included to stimulate their minds. They enjoy working and learning, and are ideal for owners who jog daily, but remember to also include obedience and tricks, which is great for mental stimulation.

Friendly with other pets?

Early socializing is best to introduce puppies to other pets successfully, usually they get along well. Some are dominant and need to be watched initially. Small pets or cats may be at risk from their chase instinct.

Is puppy training easy?

With firmness, lots of patience and a slow and steady approach, Aussies achieve very high standards and are eager to please. Training regimes need to help them understand a purposeful task, not just learn by obedience, and should include plenty of praise and encouragement.

Personality Traits	Poor	Average	Good	Excellent
Attitude toward other dogs				
Quietness				
Behavior at home				
Watchdog ability				
Good with children				
Ease of training				
Obedience to owner				

Time to maturity: 3 years
Male height: 20–23 in (51–58 cm)
Female height: 18–21 in (46–53 cm)
Weight: 35–70 lb (16–32 kg)
Average lifespan: 12–15 years

Special puppy care?

Puppies and adults become destructive if not trained and kept occupied most of the time. Avoid over-exercising puppies, and grade activity so levels increase with maturity. Start training and activities early to prevent the onset of destructive behaviors.

Active, athletic, and full of energy.

Don't forget!

Buy only from reputable breeders who undertake any necessary health checks.

Possible health problems?

Aussies are healthy but can suffer from cancer, eye problems (juvenile cataracts, Collie eye anomaly, glaucoma), respiratory and skin problems, epilepsy, hypothyroidism (insufficient levels of thyroid hormone), hip and elbow dysplasia (malformation), and toxicity to certain medication chemicals. Some merle breeds suffer blindness and hearing loss.

● 10 weeks is the ideal time to start training for obedience.

What can we do together?

Ideal dogs to train for agility, flyball, frisbee, trailing, and herding (even ducks, geese, and rabbits). They also make good service and therapy dogs.

Siberian Husky *Other names: Arctic Husky*

Siberian Huskies are a working breed, originating from Spitz ancestors, and were used as sled dogs in Siberia. Bred by Chukchi tribes in northeastern Siberia, their thickly furred, double coats cope well with the harshly cold environment in the Arctic. Early in the 1900s, Huskies arrived in Canada during the gold rush, and were used for sport in sled dog racing, in which they became distinguished champions. Huskies gradually gained popularity, spreading to the U.S. by 1930, and Europe and Britain by the 1960s. With a wolf-like appearance and a howl to match, Huskies are independent and like to roam. They also have great endurance with strong hunting instincts. Huskies have excellent temperaments, great stamina, amiable personalities, and are docile and never work-shy. They easily adapt anywhere, and are becoming increasingly popular as affectionate and playful family and companion dogs, although their gentleness makes them ineffective as watchdogs.

Color choices?

Any color is acceptable; distinguishing features are beautiful coat markings and striking facial masks with a "spectacle" pattern. Puppies look attractive, but markings often change with maturity. Husky eyes are ice-blue, dark blue, amber, brown, or sometimes they have one blue eye and one brown eye.

How much grooming?

Their easy-care double coats need a thorough weekly brushing with a pin brush. The short, straight guard hair of the longer topcoat both protects them against cold weather and acts to reflect summer heat. Huskies molt heavily twice a year, and brushing daily will help to deal with this. There is minimal "doggy" smell if coat care is maintained.

Do they make good pets?

Huskies are affectionate, good-natured, and very playful, although young dogs may be too rough for small children. They need plenty of activity, walking, and training time to maintain this good nature and are

● *An adult and a 7-week-old puppy.*

not the best choice for novices. If well trained and exercised, they make great family pets.

What home suits them?

Definitely not city dogs, Huskies need large yards and very secure fencing because they can jump, dig, and chew their way out. Homes need open space close by for energetic walks, preferably away from livestock that may receive unsolicited attention.

What type of owner?

Ideal for outdoor-loving owners, Huskies benefit from experienced handling. Suitable owners are firm, patient, and confident with dog training, and should expect to participate in energetic canine activities, and enjoy long walks.

How much exercise and stimulation?

Physical and mental stimulation is essential, as Huskies are potentially destructive unless thoroughly exercised, and great escape artists when bored. They need plenty of brisk walking—around 4 miles (6 to 7 km) per day minimum. On-leash walking is best to prevent roaming and hunting. Some Huskies enjoy running beside a bicycle or participating in energetic activities for exercise and stimulation.

Friendly with other pets?

Not considered safe around any livestock, Huskies may be challenging with other household pets because of their strong hunting drive to chase moving prey. Early socialization for puppies and introductions to well-mannered dogs should prevent problems.

Personality Traits	Poor	Average	Good	Excellent
Attitude toward other dogs				
Quietness				
Behavior at home				
Watchdog ability				
Good with children				
Ease of training				
Obedience to owner				

Time to maturity: 18 months
Male height: 21–23.5 in (53–60 cm)
Female height: 20–22 in (51–56 cm)
Weight: 35–60 lb (16–27 kg)
Average lifespan: 11–13 years

Is puppy training easy?

Huskies are intelligent and independent, but not easy to train because they are not naturally obedient. They do best with positive reinforcement training. Socialization and training must start early to be successful, and patience is essential.

Special puppy care?

Carefully graded exercise is needed for puppies— gradually building up until they reach adulthood to prevent bone and joint problems.

Puppies should be introduced to coat care and formal training quite early for it to be successful.

The facial markings are characteristic of the breed.

Possible health problems?

Generally very healthy, but Huskies can suffer from eye problems and hip dysplasia (malformation of the hip sockets), as well as gastric and respiratory problems and injuries associated with high-intensity activity.

Medium dogs

What can we do together?

Huskies excel at competitive sled or cart racing, hunting, backpacking, or simply being good companions for long walks or biking expeditions.

Don't forget!

Make sure to keep Huskies on leash near livestock. Also, a securely fenced yard is essential to prevent them from escaping.

● *Alert and watchful, these 7-week-old pups are eager to investigate everything around them.*

Collie
Other names: Scotch Collie

Collies are descended from a variety of herding dogs originating in Scotland and Wales. The name Collie is thought to derive from "Colley," an early breed of Scottish black-faced sheep; other sources believe it to be an association with their beautiful thick mane or collar. Available in two coat types, either long-coated or smooth-coated, the long-coated Collies are usually more popular, and many owners will know them from the canine star *Lassie* Present-day Collies have been continually bred with the intention of improving their conformation for showing and not herding sheep, so few are now used for this purpose. Smooth Collies, particularly those with merle coats blending into different backgrounds, were used as messenger dogs during the First World War. Good-natured, reliable, energetic, friendly dogs, they are exceptionally devoted to their owners and make wonderful family dogs.

Color choices?
Available colors are sable and white, blue merle, tricolor and white. Many have white collars, legs, feet, and tail tips. In the United States, white is also accepted.

How much grooming?
Smooth coats are very low maintenance; rough long coats need more time, but are still relatively low maintenance. Brushing several times a week with a good pin brush is best. Puppies should be groomed daily with a soft brush for socialization purposes. Never shave or cut Collie coats. Neutering may cause softer coats, and so increase the necessary grooming time.

Do they make good pets?
Collies have a reliable, kind nature, which makes them ideal pets. They are quiet at home but are quick to bark an alert to strangers. They are sociable and friendly with people, and always ready to join in whatever their owners are doing. Socializing to prevent shyness is essential. Collies are normally excellent with children.

● The coat of this adult Rough Collie needs regular grooming to maintain its condition, unlike that of the Smooth Collie (top right).

What home suits them?
Collies prefer open fields, which is where they are happiest. They fit into most homes, including apartments, but must be well exercised in smaller homes.

What type of owner?
This gentle, sensitive dog needs owners who respect his good nature and friendly outlook, and sensible children who will not tease him. Collies are people-oriented dogs and do best alongside owners who give them time and enjoy having them close by.

How much exercise and stimulation?
Collies are very adaptable and will take as much exercise as they are given, but generally moderate amounts of exercise are required—about an hour daily, which should include a free run when the dog is old enough, is ideal.

Friendly with other pets?
Collies enjoy sharing their home with other pets. They are friendly, non-aggressive, and happily spend their day accompanied by other canine pals if owners are not around, although they prefer human company whenever possible.

Is puppy training easy?
Easy to train and quick to socialize Collies learn new tasks or obedience techniques quickly and efficiently, particularly if motivated with food rewards. Training should be firm, but gentle, as puppies are sensitive to an owner's mood and respond best to a positive atmosphere. Collies are sound-sensitive and can hear a whistle up to a mile

Personality Traits	Poor	Average	Good	Excellent
Attitude toward other dogs				
Quietness				
Behavior at home				
Watchdog ability				
Good with children				
Ease of training				
Obedience to owner				

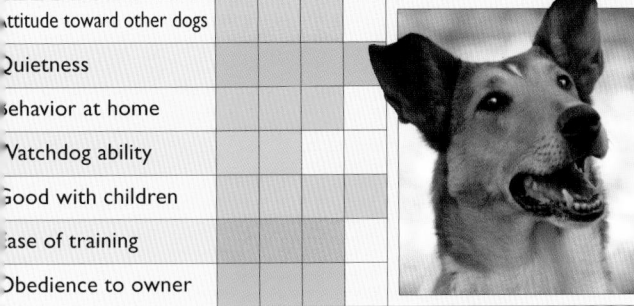

Time to maturity: 2 years
Male height: 22–24 in (56–61 cm)
Female height: 20–22 in (51–56 cm)
Weight: 60–75 lb (27–34 kg)
Average lifespan: 8–12 years

...way; training to desensitize puppies to different noises is beneficial.

Special puppy care?

Leash training should start early and socialization should begin as soon as possible, as some dogs can be a little shy and nervous as adults if they have not been socialized well in early puppyhood.

Possible health problems?

Collies have a genetic disposition to react badly to certain medications (anesthetics), pesticides, and other chemicals. They suffer from eye problems (Collie eye anomaly, which should be tested for at six to eight weeks), hip dysplasia (malformation), and a blood condition called gray Collie syndrome, which affects puppies with gray merle coloring. Collies also suffer from bloat, epilepsy, thyroid problems, and some develop allergies.

What can we do together?

Collies are ideal for agility, obedience, showing, flyball, tracking, and herding competitions, and are also used for search and rescue and as therapy and guide dogs.

● These 7-week-old puppies are ready for socialization to help them develop.

Don't forget!

Avoid choosing gray merle-colored puppies as they are known to have shorter lifespans. Puppies need eye testing prior to homing.

Medium dogs

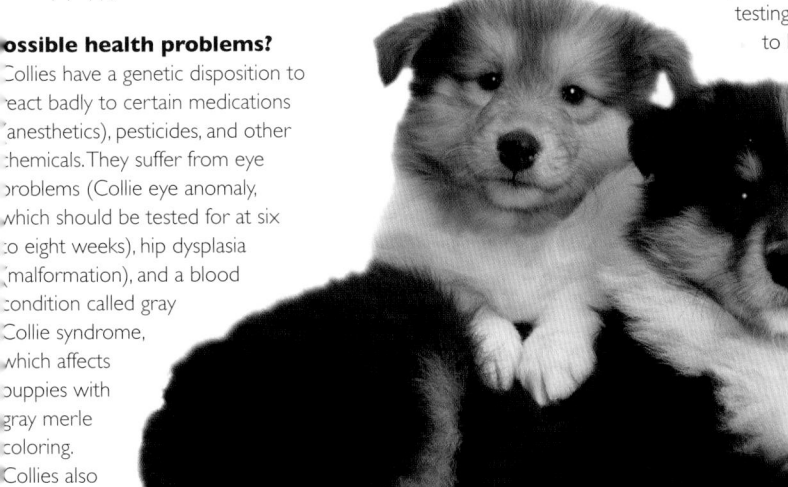

Airedale Terrier
Other names: Waterside Terrier, Bingley Terrier

Originating around 1850 in Airedale, Yorkshire, Airedales are the largest of all Terriers. They were developed as a large game Terrier suitable for country pastimes such as otter, boar, and deer hunting. Recognized as a distinct British breed in 1886, Airedales proved their worth in the First World War as messengers, ambulance dogs, and sentinels. By 1920, Airedales were one of the most popular breeds in Britain and the U.S. With legendary courage, and always alert, they are good watchdogs, but are sometimes dominant and may be aggressive toward other dogs. Airedales form close bonds with their owners, are loving and gentle with children, and make excellent family companions, provided that their need for training and plenty of exercise is recognized. Often used as working, service, and therapy dogs, they have proved their value in army and police roles and have also been trained as search and rescue dogs.

Color choices?
The usual color is black and tan, with puppies born black and gaining their tan color at about ten weeks. Adult dogs will have black (or grizzle) on the body saddle, top of the neck, and tail.

How much grooming?
Airedales have a "broken" topcoat with harsh, wiry and stiff hair (never soft) with a soft undercoat. Grooming daily is recommended plus professional hand-stripping two to three times yearly. Puppies need stripping from six months. Use a pin brush and curry comb to work through thicker parts of the coat.

Do they make good pets?
Puppies are boisterous and hard work early on, and so they are unsuitable for young families. However, they are great companions and valiantly protective of their owners. They suit active families with time for grooming, mental stimulation, and physical exercise. Strong-willed and stubborn, they

● *Strong, sturdy, alert, and active, the adult Airedale is the largest of the Terriers. He needs firm, patient training to achieve complete obedience.*

can also be noisy and destructive if left alone too long. They will always remain a puppy at heart.

What home suits them?
Airedales need space for play, exercise, and training in securely fenced yards to burn off their energy. Preferring a country or suburban life with plenty of walking and off-leash exercise, Airedales do adapt to city living but owners must be thoroughly committed to their need for high levels of exercise.

What type of owner?
This breed needs total commitment and owners who are willing to devote plenty of time and attention to their Airedale. Owners must be able to provide the right type of training. A physically strong owner is essential to handle this powerful dog—one who enjoys an active life with plenty of walking is best. A sense of humor helps, as these dogs are great characters, but likely to make mischief. They are occasionally rowdy and sometimes disruptive.

How much exercise and stimulation?
Airedales need half an hour's brisk walk twice a day, as well as free running sessions, because of their high energy levels. Regular play sessions and long walks are good, and this dog is an ideal companion for jogging, hiking, or any other active form of exercise.

Friendly with other pets?
Early socialization is essential for successful introductions to any family pets, but Airedales have a

Personality Traits	Poor	Average	Good	Excellent
Attitude toward other dogs				
Quietness				
Behavior at home				
Watchdog ability				
Good with children				
Ease of training				
Obedience to owner				

Time to maturity: 2 years
Male height: 23–24 in (58–61 cm)
Female height: 22–23 in (56–59 cm)
Weight: 44–50 lb (20–23 kg)
Average lifespan: 12–13 years

strong chase instinct and puppies may be too boisterous to be safe around smaller pets.

puppy training easy?

Firmness, time, and patience with training is essential, because Airedales are not naturally obedient. Any training should be fun and stimulating with plenty of rewards. They dislike repetitive training; owners must never be harsh, but always patient and flexible in their methods.

Special puppy care?

These energetic, powerful dogs should not be overwalked as puppies to allow bones and muscles to mature gradually. Otherwise, damage could result.

Possible health problems?

Generally a hardy breed, but they can suffer from hip malformation (dysplasia), skin allergies, cancer, and eye and cardiac problems.

What can we do together?

A lot of walking, jogging, hiking, tracking, and hunting would be great activities for the Airedale. In a working context, service training and livestock guarding is best.

Don't forget!

Airedales are a physically strong, powerful breed and they need owners who are strong in mind and body to handle them properly.

Medium dogs

Black initially, puppies gain their tan coloring as they grow.

● *Looking innocent at 3 months old, but already contemplating mischief!*

Dalmatian
Other names: Spotted Coach Dog, Carriage Dog

The origins of this breed are difficult to pin down—it possibly came from the Dalmatian coast of the Adriatic, hence the name. In the 18th century, English landowners found a role for Dalmatians as fashionable carriage dogs, energetically running miles beside horses or under the rear of carriages, ready to clear the way and guard against attacks by highwaymen. In the 1890s, Dalmatians in America accompanied horse-drawn fire engines, although with increasing mechanization, they became chiefly pets and masco[...] This breed's outgoing, friendly nature, and distinctiv[...] spotted appearance have won it popularity as an exceptional household companion. Dalmatians are sensible, dependable, intelligent, loving, courteous, a[...] playful. They are appropriately protective family pet[...] but also energetic and lively. They need the right owner who will spend time with them, and who wi[...] provide a lot of active walking to satisfy their love of exercise.

Color choices?
Born white, puppies develop spots within three weeks of birth. Show puppies must have evenly distributed coin-sized, round, black or liver (brown) spots on a white background, with spots merging on the ears. Puppies with body patches are sold as pets and are unsuitable for showing.

● This 4-year-old Dalmatian sports the "right" size spots on his body.

How much grooming?
The short, fine, dense, glossy coat benefits from regular weekly grooming with a hound glove or curry comb, because Dalmatians tend to shed all year round. With minimal coat oil, they do not smell and stay relatively clean, without the need for regular bathing.

Do they make good pets?
Temperamentally, they are perfect companion dogs. Their association with humans, horses, and other stable animals has instilled an instinct for correct behavior, and they are amenable to discipline. Dalmatians are usually well-behaved and trouble-free house dogs, naturally friendly, playful, and gentle, although young children may find puppies too boisterous for them.

What home suits them?
With plenty of energetic exercise, Dalmatians are adaptable to living in small town homes with yards. They are, however, happier with the freedom of suburban and country living and large, securely fenced yards for energetic play, with plenty of long walks available nearby.

What type of owner?
Dalmatians are unsuitable for couch potatoes. They need active owners who take regular, energetic, country walks. Better with company, on their own

Dalmatians can be destructive an[...] express their loneliness loudly an[...] vocally. They are ideal family dogs, but are unsuitable for young children or the elderly because puppies are often too boisterous.

How much exercise and stimulation?
These are tough, athletic, energet[...] dogs with loads of stamina, bred for daily cross-country running with horses, and they are at their happiest when exercised several miles daily. Without exercise they may be destructive at home, using strength and energy to wreck furniture. Stimulation is necessary for their active, intelligent minds

Friendly with other pets?
Dalmatians have an affinity for horses, and most other animals if they are well socialized. However, smaller pets and dogs may find them too bouncy and energetic.

Is puppy training easy?
Always willing to please and attentive to handlers, Dalmatians

Personality Traits	Poor	Average	Good	Excellent
Attitude toward other dogs			▧	
Quietness		▧		
Behavior at home			▧	
Watchdog ability			▧	
Good with children			▧	
Ease of training		▧		
Obedience to owner	▧	▧		

Time to maturity: 2 years
Male height: 23–24 in (58–61 cm)
Female height: 22–23 in (56–58 cm)
Weight: 50–55 lb (23–25 kg)
Average lifespan: 11–13 years

an be strong-minded and tubborn; owners need patience nd good leadership to bring out heir best. Dalmatians are not ifficult to train if handled firmly nd if obedience is started early.

pecial puppy care?
Puppies should not be overexercised o burn off their high energy, or naturing young bones and joints ould be damaged. Puppies are pouncy and boisterous, and early socialization is needed to prevent problems. Diet needs attention because Dalmatians eat anything and everything, causing problems with obesity.

ossible health problems?
Dalmatians can suffer from hyperuricemia causing kidney and bladder stones, deafness (should be tested for before purchase), hip dysplasia (malformation), and arthritic conditions.

What can we do together?
Owners may enjoy showing, jogging, agility, flyball, and horseriding companionship. Playing games with a football or a tennis ball may also appeal to many active owners.

Don't forget!
Buy puppies only from reputable sources, and request sight and hearing test certificates of the puppy's parents. Show puppies are chosen for spots, not patches, on the body.

Medium dogs

• *White at birth, at 8 weeks these puppies already have the characteristic spots emerging on their coats.*

Peaceful here, but puppies can be boisterous.

Large dogs

This group consists of breeds such as Retrievers and Setters that are ideal for training to participate in canine activities. With the right temperaments, they can make wonderful pets suitable for family homes. However, when fully grown many need larger homes and yards than other breeds. With smooth, wire, and shaggy coats to select from, there are plenty of choices for the prospective owner.

Golden Retriever

Goldens acquired recognized breed status in Britain in 1913, having descended from golden colored puppies in black retriever litters in mid 18th-century Scotland. Goldens were recognized for registration in the U.S. in 1925, and have since become hugely popular family pets. Unfortunately, their gentle disposition and ideal temperaments for families with children have also made them money spinners for puppy mills, leading to increasing health and temperament problems in recent years. Hardy, diligent, and eager, they will retrieve game even in bitterly cold weather to please their owner, and are at home on land or in water. Most common of all Retrievers as a family pet, Goldens are great all-rounders, as well as handsome, kind, and cheerful family dogs. They are often used guide, therapy, and "sniffer" dogs. They need mental and physical stimulation, have a great sense of humor, but can be exuberant.

Color choices?

Standards have changed over the years and now any shade of gold or cream is allowed.

How much grooming?

Top coats are water-resistant and wavy, some thicker than others, with a soft undercoat. They need weekly grooming with a hard brush and comb, particularly around the feathering on legs, necks, and tails to remove debris. Some shedding occurs most of the year, but also profusely twice a year. Ears need checking and cleaning weekly to prevent infections.

Do they make good pets?

A good temperament is the Golden's hallmark; they should be kind, friendly, and confident. They are ideal family pets, very patient with children, and amiable with all family members, including visitors to their home. Goldens are also prized for being calm, biddable, sociable, intelligent, eager to please, and extraordinarily willing to learn.

● *Eager to please and quick to learn, Goldens do well in training.*

What home suits them?

Too active for apartments, Goldens readily adapt to well-fenced yards in suburban or country homes, provided they have mental stimulation and plenty of exercise to burn off their excess energy.

What type of owner?

Only active, affectionate owners should purchase a Golden, as they thrive with kind, easygoing owners and well-behaved children, who respect their gentle disposition and do not mind dog hairs on the furniture. As puppies, Goldens can be exuberant and energetic, and owners should expect to spend time training them to become calm, confident, well-mannered adults.

How much exercise and stimulation?

Goldens have the high energy level typical of sporting breeds, but care is needed with puppies under nine months to limit over-exercise to prevent damage to young bones and joints. Daily exercise, in all weather, is needed for adults, and should include mental stimulation participation in events like agility, obedience, or flyball is ideal.

Friendly with other pets?

Goldens are extremely friendly with other dogs, cats, and household pets. They are so even-tempered that they can be used as surrogate mothers for other species.

Is puppy training easy?

Goldens are exceptional dogs to train. They are intelligent, eager to please, and quick to learn. They often excel at agility and obedience trials. They have a sense of humor, but are occasionally stubborn. Training should start early, and should be firm but gentle, fun, and reward-based.

Personality Traits	Poor	Average	Good	Excellent
Attitude toward other dogs				
Quietness				
Behavior at home				
Watchdog ability				
Good with children				
Ease of training				
Obedience to owner				

Time to maturity: 2 years
Male height: 22–24 in (56–61 cm)
Female height: 20–22 in (51–56 cm)
Weight: 60–80 lb (27–36 kg)
Average lifespan: 12–13 years

What can we do together?

Goldens do well in obedience, agility competitions, flyball, and field trials. They also excel as service dogs.

Don't forget!

Only buy from reputable breeders who carry out the necessary health checks on the parents of their stock.

Special puppy care?

Youngsters can be a bit of a handful, but gentle training, fun distractions, and positive reinforcement should pay dividends.

● As young puppies develop, learning starts naturally through the process of playing with their littermates.

Possible health problems?

Overbreeding in some lines has caused problems, but buying from reputable breeders helps. Generally, they suffer from cancer, hip and elbow dysplasia (malformation), dislocating kneecaps, ligament ruptures, eye problems, heart disease, epilepsy, hemophilia, gastric torsion, retinal dysplasia, and skin allergies.

Large dogs

Labrador Retriever

Labrador Retrievers are natives of Newfoundland and Labrador in Canada, the region after which they are named. They were originally used as fishermen's dogs. Imported to Poole, England in the 19th century, they proved so versatile as working dogs that kennels started breeding and training them for hunting. Labradors are one of the most popular dogs in the world, both as hunting Retrievers and as family pets. However, i[n] some countries, they are two distinct types: one us[ed] in field trials and the other as show specimens. Fiel[d] trial specimens tend to be lighter in weight, smaller, more lively, and are harder to integrate into family life, unless well trained. Labradors are active, intelligent, agile, and confident, with exceptionally good temperaments. Their delightful, warm personalities and low aggression level make them one of the best all-around dogs, ide[al] as working Retrievers or as family pets.

Color choices?

Black, chocolate, or yellow (cream to fox-red) are the only colors available.

How much grooming?

Labradors have short, dense, water-resistant, easy-care coats, which are slightly oily. They benefit from weekly grooming with a slicker or pin brush to remove dander and dead hair. As they tend to molt continuously, some owners may find that training them to stand quietly while being groomed to remove some molt is essential.

Do they make good pets?

Easygoing, kind, even-tempered, sociable dogs, Labradors need plenty of time and attention from families, because if left alone they are destructive and chew just about anything. They are very good with children, but when they are puppies they can be a little clumsy and boisterous with small children. Not the best watchdog, as they are easygoing and trusting even with strangers. They tend to "mouth" hands when playing with children, so hand washing will be essential.

● Fit, alert Labradors like this need proper nutrition to avoid risks of obesity.

What home suits them?

With sufficient levels of exercise and mental stimulation, Labradors are happiest with their owner. They are not inclined to jump over or dig under fences, but secure fencing around yards is necessary, as they may wander off with friendly strangers. Owners may find it necessary to remove items from low tables to prevent breakages from tail wagging.

What type of owner?

Owners must commit to long daily walks, in any weather, and acceptance of mischievous puppy ways as they grow into exuberant adults. Patien[ce] with training and grooming is essential, as is the realization that homes may be messy with muddy paw prints and molting hair.

How much exercise and stimulation?

Plenty of walking is needed—up to two hours daily, along with me[ntal] stimulation. Labradors can be lazy, and often overeat and become obese. But with the right levels of exercise and stimulation, these charming dogs continue to delight well into old age.

Friendly with other pets?

Early socialization and proper intro[-]ductions are necessary, but Labrad[ors] are ideal companions for other pe[ts.] They are Retrievers, and may want to carry small pets in their mouths, but they are unlikely to harm them.

Is puppy training easy?

Early leash training prevents pulling when fully grown, and Labradors a[re] easily trained, eager to please, and learn quickly, provided that session[s]

Personality Traits	Poor	Average	Good	Excellent
Attitude toward other dogs				■
Quietness	■			
Behavior at home			■	
Watchdog ability		■		
Good with children				■
Ease of training				■
Obedience to owner			■	

Time to maturity: 3 years
Male height: 22–24.5 in (56–62 cm)
Female height: 21–23.5 in (54–60 cm)
Weight: 55–75 lb (25–34 kg)
Average lifespan: 11–13 years

...are fun and reward-based to maintain interest. Frequent, daily training sessions are best, as they get restless without activity. Breaking up training time avoids the onset of boredom.

Special puppy care?

Labradors will eat anything and are persistent when demanding treats; avoid giving in to this because of the risk of obesity. Good, healthy diets that focus on different growth stages are best.

Possible health problems?

Labradors suffer from hip and elbow dysplasia (malformation), patella luxation (dislocating kneecaps), eye problems, hereditary myopathy (muscle fiber deficiency), autoimmune disease, deafness, and obesity.

● *Playful puppies, like these two at 8 weeks, have life ahead of them.*

What can we do together?

Labradors are ideal companions for playing ball (obsessively!), agility, frisbee, and flyball. They are also good at search and rescue and are great therapy dogs.

Don't forget!

All breeding stock should be hip and eye tested.

Boxer
Other names: German Boxer

The original ancestors of Boxers came from dogs used for fighting and defending their owners' herds from wild animals. Later versions developed from crossing that original version, the German Bullenbeisser (now extinct), with English Bulldogs. The resulting Boxers developed from these strains in the 1880s. Their high intelligence meant they were ideal for training as service dogs, and they were used by German forces during the First World War as messengers, pack carriers, attack, and guard dogs. Proving also to be ideal family dogs, Boxers have become one of the most popular breeds in the United States in recent years. These are fun dogs, loveable clowns who are very affectionate. They are energetic and likely to be playful well into old age. Owners must commit to give them enough exercise, have patience to cope with their exuberance, and offer plenty of training. This is not a breed for someone seeking a peaceful life.

Color choices?

Boxers are fawn or brindle (black stripes on fawn background) with or without white markings, which should not exceed one third of the base colors. They have black muzzles and white markings ("flash" marks), and usually white underbody and feet. White Boxers occur, but can suffer from deafness.

● *Adult Boxers still have plenty of "bounce" and need firm training.*

How much grooming?

A Boxer's short, dense coat is low maintenance, needing only occasional brushing with a hound glove to remove dead hair.

Do they make good pets?

Energetic, impetuous, and dominant, Boxers make good pets if trained early, but they should not live in rowdy households, as they can be unmanageable. If well trained, Boxers are loyal, loving, humorous, and playful with older, sensible children. They are too boisterous for small children and the elderly.

What home suits them?

Adapting to both suburban or country dwelling, Boxers need space and plenty of exercise, and so are unsuitable for apartments. Secure high fencing around large yards is best, as puppies are excellent escapologists. Boxers are sensitive to extremes of temperature, so provide shade to prevent overheating in summer and keep homes warm in winter.

What type of owner?

Unsuitable for novices, Boxers prefer experienced, active owners who appreciate dogs that are extremely affectionate and loyal. Owners need a sense of fun and the commitment to provide energetic walking and training. Kindness is essential because Boxers are sensitive dogs, and firmness is needed to control the occasional whirlwind of activity.

How much exercise and stimulation?

Boxers are high-energy dogs—they need plenty of walking, up to two hours daily. Activity should be fun for both dogs and owners, and it should provide essential mental stimulation.

Friendly with other pets?

Early socialization is best, as Boxers can be dominant with other dogs of the same gender. Smaller pets find them too boisterous for comfort. Generally, they are good-natured and friendly.

Is puppy training easy?

Training should start very early and needs to be firm, kind, consistent, and patient. Boxers can be challenging because they are strong-minded and stubborn. Kindness is essential, and mutual respect between dog and owner should develop for successful results. Training must be fun-based, as this loveable clown tends to make a game of obedience and avoids serious learning.

Personality Traits	Poor	Average	Good	Excellent
Attitude toward other dogs				
Quietness				
Behavior at home				
Watchdog ability				
Good with children				
Ease of training				
Obedience to owner				

Time to maturity: 2–3 years
Male height: 22.5–25 in (57–63.5 cm)
Female height: 21–23 in (53–59 cm)
Weight: 55–70 lb (25–32 kg)
Average lifespan: 9–12 years

Special puppy care?

Puppies often mirror their owners' moods and their attention span is short. They endear themselves to owners, who may not be as firm as they should be. Do not overwalk puppies—doing so can injure young bones and joints.

● *This row of obedient 8-week-old puppies are making a good start with training to "Sit."*

Possible health problems?

They are sensitive to certain medications so always check with your veterinarian. Other health issues are eye and heart problems, cancer, hip dysplasia (malformation), epilepsy, gastric and intestinal problems including gastric torsion, and allergies (related to dietary intolerance). White puppies may suffer from deafness.

What can we do together?

Great companions for jogging or running, Boxers also enjoy agility, obedience, and flyball. They train well as service and therapy dogs.

Don't forget!

Buy from reputable breeders who perform health checks to ensure healthy stock.

Large dogs

Vizsla
Other names: Hungarian Pointer

Vizslas are Hungary's national dog, with a long history as an ancient Magyar hunting breed and favored sporting dog of Hungarian nobility. There are two modern varieties: a short-haired version and a wire-haired strain (now a separate breed), which dates from around 1930. The Short-haired Vizsla became better known, and with rising popularity in France, was first registered in Europe in 1938. These are lively, adaptable dogs with an excellent scenting ability. They tend to stay close to their owner, and are famed for their ability as upland bird dogs, very skilled over rough terrain in pointing and retrieving game. Over the years, these beautiful dogs have gained popularity as a companion breed. Their even temper, outgoing personality, friendliness, and sociable attitude make them ideal family pets, provided that their needs are met—plenty of exercise, stimulation, human contact, and a lo of company. They don't like being left alone

Color choices?
Vizslas are solid golden/russet in different shades. Small white patches on the chest and neck are allowed, but not desired in show puppies.

How much grooming?
Weekly brushing of the short, smooth coat will suffice. Ears need checking regularly, and skin needs to be checked for cuts and thorns after hunting or rambling in scrub and brambles. Vizslas rarely have any doggy smell.

Do they make good pets?
These high-energy puppies can be demanding, but are gentle, caring, and loving. They bond well with owners, are good with children, and are often called "velcro" dogs because they are so loyal, affectionate, and owner-oriented. Vizslas often cry if neglected or lonely, and are not happy if left home alone.

What home suits them?
Vizslas put their owners first, so home is most important; while life in the country is preferred, they can

● *Vizslas' gentle nature and kind disposition make them easy to live with.*

adapt to town living. Country or suburban homes with space for regular exercise and well-fenced, secure yards are best. They do jump fences if bored.

What type of owner?
These are not part-time dogs, and meeting their demands for exercise and stimulation is a lifetime commitment. Good owners and

families are involved with their Vizsla daily, and spend weekends doing canine activities. They shoul expect full-time companionship and interaction with their puppy.

How much exercise and stimulation?
Vizslas need plenty of exercise and stimulation daily, with time to gallop and run in open space. Staying healthy and happy require high levels of exercise and stimulation. Vizslas thrive on attention, exercise, and interaction Puppies need limited short walks and play when very young.

Friendly with other pets?
Vizslas are hunting dogs, so expec family pets to be at some risk, unless they have been well socialized with good introductions as puppies. There may be an inclination to chase cats, although these are usually friendly dogs.

Is puppy training easy?
A sensible approach to training puppies is necessary; their natural

Personality Traits	Poor	Average	Good	Excellent
Attitude toward other dogs				
Quietness				
Behavior at home				
Watchdog ability				
Good with children				
Ease of training				
Obedience to owner				

Time to maturity: 2 years
Male height: 22.5–25 in (57–63.5 cm)
Female height: 21–23.5 in (53–60 cm)
Weight: 44–66 lb (20–30 kg)
Average lifespan: 12–14 years

Instinct is pointing and retrieving, which can be utilized for involvement in activities that contribute to good training. They can be willful and easily distracted, but are eager to please, responding well to firm, patient handling.

Special puppy care?

These are sad puppies if left home alone, and will cry and become very destructive if they are lonely. Some puppies may mouth

- *12 weeks old, but take care not to let them over-exercise.*

owners' arms or legs, and can be clingy; training puppies while young to accept being left on their own for short periods is essential.

Possible health problems?

Vizslas can suffer from hip malformation (rarely), epilepsy, cancer, sebaceous adenitis (a skin disease), hypothyroidism (lack of thyroid hormone), heart and eye problems, skin and certain food allergies.

Large dogs

What can we do together?

Owners can choose from many activities, but they have a special talent for competitive obedience, tracking, and agility.

Don't forget!

Buy from responsible breeders and avoid overexercising energetic youngsters to prevent damage to young bones and joints.

Flat-Coated Retriever

Originating in Great Britain in the 19th century as land and water Retrievers, Flat-Coats are strong swimmers and natural water dogs, who mark, retrieve, and deliver game with admirable style. They are often considered more elegant and stylish than other Retrievers. They were not recognized as a separate breed until around 1860. They later achieved popularity in the United States, although numbers dwindled between the wars, but the efforts of enthusiasts rescued them, and by 1960 they were again popula as excellent companion and family dogs. These live intelligent sporting dogs love attention and companionship, but they are not couch potatoes, preferring to be active and gainfully employed in plenty of activity and walking. Flat-Coats continue be youthful, playful, and mischievous well into old a which accounts for their popularity as fam pets. Owners must be prepared to me their needs for plenty of exercise.

● The black gleaming shine of the adult Flat-Coat's mantle is a joy to groom because it oozes health and condition.

Color choices?

Flat-Coats are available in solid black or liver (brown).

How much grooming?

Flat-Coats have easy-care, medium-length, weatherproof coats that need brushing and combing two or three times weekly right down to the skin. Feathering on the head, under the body, and tail needs combing to remove tangles. More frequent combing is needed during seasonal molting.

Do they make good pets?

These puppies enjoy being the center of attention and being around their families most of the time. They love children, although they may be too boisterous for toddlers or hurt them with their wagging tails. Flat-Coats are exuberant, outgoing, and confident, with a strong desire to please. They make excellent companion dogs for active families.

What home suits them?

Flat-Coats are unsuitable for city life and definitely unsuitable for apartment living; they prefer space and activity in the suburbs or the country. Well-fenced large yards and long walks suit them best.

What type of owner?

Owners should be firm and sensitive to this active dog's need for exercise, and should be able to appreciate their sense of humor. Flat-Coats are unsuitable for working families planning to leave them home alone, as they can be destructive and noisy if bored.

How much exercise and stimulation?

Adult Flat-Coats need either one good long walk daily or several moderate walks to satisfy their need for exercise. They also need off-leash running and will enjoy regular swim. They prefer to stay near their owner when out walking, and so are unlikely to disappear on their own private pursuits.

Friendly with other pets?

They have a very friendly disposition to other dogs and household pets, but they need to be socialized early and introduced correctly for the relationship to develop properly. Be careful with boisterous puppies though, as they may be too rough for other small pets, and unknown cats may be considered fair game for chasing.

Is puppy training easy?

Eager and quick to learn, the Flat-Coats should be treated with firmness and consistency or they are inclined to play the fool and clown around. Short sessions with

Personality Traits	Poor	Average	Good	Excellent
Attitude toward other dogs				
Quietness				
Behavior at home				
Watchdog ability				
Good with children				
Ease of training				
Obedience to owner				

Time to maturity: 3 years
Male height: 23–24 in (58–61 cm)
Female height: 22–23 in (56–58 cm)
Weight: 55–80 lb (25–36 kg)
Average lifespan: 12–14 years

plenty of variety and little repetition are best. This puppy has a sensitive nature, and so any overbearing treatment during training will simply be counter-productive.

Special puppy care?

Overexercising exuberant, immature youngsters must be avoided, as there is a risk of injury to young bones and joints. Gradually increase exercise duration to allow for growth without risk of damage.

Possible health problems?

This breed has a higher risk of cancer than average. Other conditions that Flat-Coats may

suffer from are hip dysplasia (malformation), dislocating kneecaps, eye problems, and epilepsy. Eye testing and hip scoring are recommended for this breed.

What can we do together?

Flat-Coats are great family dogs and good companions, but can also be used for hunting. Some are used as therapy companions and in the services as "sniffer" dogs.

Don't forget!

Always buy from reputable breeders who complete necessary health checks on their breeding stock.

Large dogs

Even at 6 weeks, these puppies benefit from patient handling and socialization to help them develop into friendly family dogs.

German Shorthaired Pointer

Developed in Germany between the 17th and 19th centuries, Pointers are noted for their powerful fast gallop, great endurance, hunting ability over any terrain, and tolerance of cold. They are excellent working dogs for hunting, pointing, and retrieving game, and they boast a stylish appearance. Believed to descend from similar species as other pointers, they were popular at one time with German, French, and Spanish nobility. The curr breed has existed since 1880, and today, GSPs are recognized worldwide for their versatility and their virtues as excellent family dogs. Energetic, sociable, and even-tempered, they are attached to their owners, love children, are good watchdogs, and exc as companion pets. GSPs can be stubborn and stror willed, and need their physical and mental needs satisfied or they can be destructive. Plenty of exercise and time spent grooming and training will be needed

Color choices?

Coat colors are solid black or liver, black and white, liver and white. Bicolors are ticked, spotted, or both.

How much grooming?

The short, flat, dense coat, protected by guard hairs, is water-resistant and low maintenance, despite shedding constantly. Occasional brushing removes dead hair. Bathe only when needed. The floppy ears need regular checking and cleaning.

Do they make good pets?

Intelligent, bold, and affectionate, even slightly eccentric, they are cooperative and easily trained dogs. Puppies are boisterous and demanding, so they may not suit young family members, but active families who keep them busy with suitable energetic activities should have no problem with them.

What home suits them?

Unsuitable for small homes and apartments, GSPs are happier in country or suburban homes with high-fenced, large yards. They enjoy

● These 3-year-old GSPs will be good company for one another if their owner decides to go out for a while.

digging! They are athletic, and benefit from open space nearby for plenty of daily exercise.

What type of owner?

Inactive, inexperienced, or working owners are unsuitable, as GSPs form strong bonds with their owners and dislike being left alone for too long. They can be destructive and make mischief if bored or lonely. An active owner, who enjoys walking, whatever the weather, will suit them best. The high energy levels will not suit elderly, frail owners or families with young children.

How much exercise and stimulation?

GSPs need plenty of vigorous exercise, around two hours daily with off-leash running, plus other suitably stimulating canine activitie such as agility. Unused energy can be channeled into undesirable destructive behaviors.

Friendly with other pets?

GSPs get along well with other dogs, although there may be som gender disagreements between dominant males, or females in season. With their hunting back-ground, smaller pet animals may b at risk, and early socialization is essential to prevent problems. During exercise, owners should b cautious if their GSP shows intere in prey or a neighbor's small anim

Is puppy training easy?

GSPs are easy to train as biddabl and well-behaved family members They need firm training, and agilit

Personality Traits	Poor	Average	Good	Excellent
ttitude toward other dogs				
Quietness				
ehavior at home				
Vatchdog ability				
Good with children				
ase of training				
Obedience to owner				

Time to maturity: 2 years
Male height: 23–25 in (58–63.5 cm)
Female height: 21–23 in (53–58 cm)
Weight: 60–70 lb (27–32 kg)
Average lifespan: 12–14 years

What can we do together?

Owners may enjoy GSPs as running companions and for hunting, carting, showing, agility, and obedience competitions.

Don't forget!

GSPs can suffer from separation anxiety and are high maintenance in terms of exercise and training needs.

r obedience competitions are deal for making the most of their uperb ability to learn and eagerness to please, as well as for timulating their intelligent minds.

ecial puppy care?

e careful with puppies under nine months—don't exercise them too ard or you will risk injuring young oints. Fresh water must always be vailable—these active puppies ften drink copious amounts.

ossible health problems?

GSPs can suffer from hip dysplasia malformation), eye problems, pilepsy, cancer, lymphedema, astric torsion (bloat), and skin roblems. Damage (cuts and brasions) to skin while out unting is also a risk.

● Even at 10 weeks, this puppy's large pendulous ears will need attention to keep them clean and free from infection.

Large dogs

Standard Poodle

The early 15th century version of the Standard Poodle was bred for hunting, but they are now known for their companionship and classy looks. Fashionable French ladies in Louis XIV's court loved their elegant and refined charm. Today there are four popular coat clips: Lion, Dutch, Lamb, and Puppy clip. The original style was created to protect large joints from the cold when retrieving game from water.

Highly intelligent dogs, and with a great sense of humor, Poodles make a popular choice for owners wanting to participate in obedience, agility, and sledding, as well as providing support for the disab In recent generations, smaller sizes have been bred (Miniature and Toy), which some pet owners may f are better accommodated to apartment living. Virtually identical except in size, all make excellent family dogs. Apart from the extensive coat care required, Poodles are great companions and ideal for novices because they are easy to train.

Color choices?

Usually available in solid colors: black, blue, white, brown, café-au-lait, gray, silver, and apricot. Less common colors are particolors (solid colors and white), phantom (black and tan markings), and tuxedo (solid color tuxedo markings and white).

How much grooming?

Poodles have single coats of fine, soft, thick hair that require extensive grooming and clipping; a slicker brush and wide-toothed comb are best on this coat. Most pet owners find that Lamb or Puppy clips, done every six weeks, are the easiest to maintain. The coat is moisture-resistant and produces little molt, so it needs daily grooming to remove dead hair. Bathing is needed regularly.

Do they make good pets?

Poodles are very popular because of their outgoing and good-natured approach to life, and they make excellent pets. They are loyal and intelligent, but can be possessive. They make obedient pets if trained

● Adult Poodles can be trimmed in different coat clips to suit their owners.

well. Puppies need supervision by adults, because they can be vulnerable to young or boisterous family members.

What home suits them?

Although Poodles are very adaptable, Standards may be a little too large for apartment living and will suit a larger house and yard better. Very companionable by nature, Poodles prefer homes with plenty to do and interesting company.

What type of owner?

A Poodle owner must be committed to grooming and providing company. Puppies should be treated as proper dogs, not as

a fashion accessory or toy. They need affection, training, and quite a lot of attention, without being pampered or overindulged.

How much exercise and stimulation?

Energetic and intelligent, they hav a great sense of fun, but as a large active breed they need to be walked regularly and provided with adequate levels of mental stimulation. Short outings as puppies building up to longer walks as adults are best.

Friendly with other pets?

They are very accepting of other household pets, but mischievous puppies must be discouraged fron becoming an irritant to older pet Small pets are at less risk at hom if early socialization is practiced.

Is puppy training easy?

Highly intelligent, Poodles are an ideal breed for training by anyone in the family. Puppies will be quick to learn and can be trained to do tricks, as well as obedience.

Personality Traits	Poor	Average	Good	Excellent
Attitude toward other dogs				
Quietness				
Behavior at home				
Watchdog ability				
Good with children				
Ease of training				
Obedience to owner				

Time to maturity: 2 years
Male height: 23–26 in (58–66 cm)
Female height: 21–24 in (53–61 cm)
Weight: 45–70 lb (20–32 kg)
Average lifespan: 13–15 years

Special puppy care?

It is most important that puppies are groomed daily to prevent hair from becoming matted and painful to remove, even if they are clipped. Early training and mental stimulation is particularly recommended, as they will become mischievous if bored. Noisy households with young children may cause stress to puppies.

Possible health problems?

There are various inherited health problems, although Standard Poodles are usually recommended as the most healthy of all the sizes, so only buy from reputable breeders who do regular health checks on their breeding stock. The most common problems are eye, heart, thyroid and joint conditions, Addison's disease (failure of the adrenal glands), Cushing's disease (a hormonal disorder), sebaceous adenitis, gastric torsion, and epilepsy.

What can we do together?

This breed does particularly well in agility, obedience, tracking, and herding. Some owners may also enjoy showing their Poodle, although the latter involves a lot of grooming time.

Large dogs

Don't forget!

Buy only from reputable breeders.

● *Puppies can be trained at 2 months to perform simple tricks.*

● *This shaggy, 2-month-old apricot-colored Poodle already has a thick coat that will soon need to be trimmed.*

Chesapeake Bay Retriever

Although rare in Europe, the Chesapeake Bay Retriever is an old American breed that derived from two Newfoundland puppies that were rescued from a shipwreck off the coast of Maryland in 1807. Used for hunting wildfowl in swampland, they are hardy, with webbed feet and powerful chests that can break ice when swimming to retrieve fowl in water. First recognized as a breed in the United States in 1878, Chesapeakes were declared the official state dog of Maryland in 1964. These are good all-around dogs, tireless when working, superb when hunting, reliable watchdogs, ideal as "sniffer" or therapy dogs, and great companions. Chesapeakes are devoted to their owner and family, but they do need their working drive satisfied to be happy. Exercise, socialization, and training will be an important part of their development in early life, or they may become excessively shy or sometimes aggressive with strangers.

Color choices?

Three basic colors are available: brown, from light to dark, deadgrass color (straw to bracken), or sedge (red gold to strawberry blond). Small amounts of white—under body, on the chest, toes, and back of the feet—are allowed.

How much grooming?

Chessies have double, wavy outer coats and soft woolly undercoats. The coat feels slightly oily which makes it waterproof, and it often gives off a slight musky odor. This low-maintenance coat needs brushing weekly with a rubber or short-toothed brush. Grooming too often damages its waterproof properties. Bathe every three to four months with a mild shampoo.

Do they make good pets?

Chessies are intelligent, alert, intensely loyal, with affectionate, protective natures and bright, happy dispositions. Some can be vocal or may "smile" by grinning with their teeth bared to express their pleasure.

● This 9-week-old puppy will need to spend time socializing with adults (right) and learning manners in preparation for later training and habituation.

What home suits them?

A country home suits this energetic working dog best, with a well-fenced-in, large yard. Suburban life is possible provided that plenty of long walks are given, and they have enough space for exercise. They are definitely not suited to apartment living.

What type of owner?

Owners need to be strong-natured as this breed has a powerful working instinct, and is not ideal for novices. Owners need to be active and enjoy plenty of exercise in any weather. They should also have experience working and training dogs with strong personalities. Not a part-time breed, this puppy needs company and work to keep him happy.

How much exercise and stimulation?

Chessies need plenty of exercise and stimulation involving activities that appeal to their working instincts. Exercise should be athletic, energetic, and interesting for mental stimulation, preferably with some swimming included.

Friendly with other pets?

As a working, hunting breed, they may see small animals, and sometimes cats, as ideal for chasing. Chessies can be dominant and males particularly may be territorially aggressive, so plenty of early socialization is essential.

Is puppy training easy?

This is an intelligent and attentive breed that learns skills quickly. Consistent, daily, obedience training with a firm approach, without

Personality Traits	Poor	Average	Good	Excellent
Attitude toward other dogs				
Quietness				
Behavior at home				
Watchdog ability				
Good with children				
Ease of training				
Obedience to owner				

Time to maturity: 2 years
Male height: 23–26 in (58–66 cm)
Female height: 21–24 in (53–61 cm)
Weight: 55–80 lb (25–36 kg)
Average lifespan: 10–13 years

allowing the puppy's independent nature to take over, is best. Playtime before, during, and after may be necessary to maintain interest. Rules for obedience should be established for puppies, but they will not respond to harsh discipline.

Special puppy care?

Some puppies can be boisterous and have a tendency to mouth hands, so encourage children to wash their hands after playing with them.

Possible health problems?

Chessies are a hardy breed but may suffer eye problems, hip dysplasia (malformation), von Willebrand's disease (a blood disorder), gastric torsion, and alopecia (hair loss).

What can we do together?

As an active and very versatile dog, Chessies will do well in field trial competitions, hunt tests, tracking, showing, obedience, and agility.

● *Learning a "Down" should be one of the first training tasks.*

Don't forget!

Chessies will be unhappy unless kept well occupied, and they need to be effectively socialized and trained, or they may become dominant.

Spinone Italiano
Other names: Italian Spinone, Italian Wire-haired Pointer, Italian Griffon

One of the most popular show dogs in its native Italy, the Spinone is the oldest griffon-type pointer. Its exact origins are unknown, but it is thought to have developed in the Piedmont area of Italy around 500 years ago. The name Spinone is derived from the Italian for "thorn" which denotes the thick, thorny undergrowth that game hides in. The Spinone, protected by its thick skin and coarse hair, is an excellent hunting companion in harsh terrains, and also in water, and is a versatile hunter, pointer, and retriever. Spinones almost became extinct during the Second World War, but were nursed back to popularity by small groups of enthusiasts, and are now well-loved and very individual members of many families. Spinones are inclined to drool, and have a particular "doggy" smell. They also need substantial amounts of exercise. Their calm, friendly, playful nature delights many families.

Color choices?

Color variations are solid white, white with orange or brown markings, and roan (white with flecked color—either orange or brown with or without markings). Skin coloring on nose, lips, and paw pads varies with different coat colors. Shades or combinations of black markings are undesirable.

● *Well protected from thorny undergrowth, this adult Spinone's coat will need regular brushing after walks.*

How much grooming?

Coats are tough, wiry, oily, weatherproof, and close-fitting, without an undercoat. Grooming twice a week is sufficient to remove dander and shed, with some stripping of dead hair needed during periods of molt. Spinones should not be overgroomed, as the coat is likely to become long, soft, and silky, which is undesirable.

Do they make good pets?

Spinones are docile, affectionate dogs with an easygoing nature. They are gentle, patient, playful, and dependable with children, but puppies can be boisterous and may overwhelm small children. A very loyal family dog, as adults they display little aggression to strangers or other pets, but they do need early socialization and a lot of exercise or they may be destructive. They are inclined to scavenge for food. They can also be highly vocal and "talkative."

What home suits them?

Unsuitable for apartment living, Spinones prefer to be country or suburban dwellers with space to run around. Small, well-fenced yards are acceptable, provided that regular long walks are available.

What type of owner?

Spinones need patient, gentle owners willing to be fully involved with their care. Owners should be committed to constant companionship with plenty of active walking.

How much exercise and stimulation?

They need plenty of physical activity and mental stimulation. Adults need one to two hours minimum of walking and galloping daily. Length of walks for puppies should be built up gradually until at least nine months old to prevent damage to developing joints and bones.

Friendly with other pets?

These are sociable dogs, and with early socialization and proper introductions they get along well with other dogs and household pets. They are hunters with strong chase instincts, however, and need educating not to give chase to neighbors' cats.

Personality Traits	Poor	Average	Good	Excellent
Attitude toward other dogs				
Quietness				
Behavior at home				
Watchdog ability				
Good with children				
Ease of training				
Obedience to owner				

Time to maturity: 2.5 years
Male height: 23.5–27.5 in (60–70 cm)
Female height: 23–25.5 in (58–65 cm)
Weight: 64–86 lb (29–39 kg)
Average lifespan: 12–14 years

Is puppy training easy?

These loyal, intelligent, sensitive puppies have had working roles for centuries, and are easily trained and very biddable, but can be stubborn. They need firm training and are slow to mature, so training sessions should be short and often. Treat them sensitively—their feelings are easily hurt. Motivational training with positive reinforcement is best.

Special puppy care?

Puppies under nine months should not be overexercised to prevent risk of damage to young bones and joints. These are demanding puppies and very destructive if bored.

Possible health problems?

Spinones are relatively healthy, but suffer from hip dysplasia (malformation), arthritis, eye problems (ectropion and entropion), and cerebellar ataxia (affects control of the limbs). Parents should be tested for this before breeding, as puppies die under a year old.

Large dogs

What can we do together?

These are perfect companions for running or jogging, and good hunting dogs.

Don't forget!

Spinones can be demanding and will be destructive if bored; they are also scavengers and food-stealers.

● *This puppy is just the right age at 12 weeks to start training to an acceptable standard using food rewards or clicker training. If properly trained, he will make a super family pet.*

German Shepherd Dog *Other names: Alsatian*

Developed more than 100 years ago from ancestral working and herding dogs, these fine dogs originated in the Bavarian hills of Germany. They successfully proved their worth during the First World War as guard dogs, and as search and rescue specialists. Their versatility continues to this day: German Shepherds perform valuable roles in police and military work, alongside security guards, in search and rescue, and as therapy dogs. German Shepherd are now one of the world's most popular dogs, although they were previously vilified in some area for their German origins. Introduced into the U.K. and U.S. after the First World War, German Shepherds became popular family dogs, valued for their even-tempered nature, unfailing loyalty, and devotion. They are proud, courageous, intelligent companions and enjoy the company of their human friends. They must have plenty of exercise, stimulation, and training.

Color choices?
Colors are solid black, sable, bicolored (tan with black saddles) or tricolored (black with combinations of reddish brown, tan, or light gray). White, blue, or liver colors are unacceptable for the breed standard, and so are not registered by Kennel Clubs.

● *A 7-week-old puppy with an adult GSD.*

How much grooming?
Outer coats are weatherproof, straight, and harsh, lying over a softer, thick undercoat. The coat needs brushing twice weekly to maintain condition, with extra attention paid to thicker areas. Long-coated Shepherds need daily grooming, but this type of coat is unacceptable for showing.

Do they make good pets?
Shepherds need the right owner to turn them into ideal family dogs. Properly trained, they are loyal, obedient, and protective of their family. Early socialization prevents any tendency to nervousness or dominance, but having active owners helps. They are unsuitable for frail, elderly owners.

What home suits them?
Unsuitable for apartments or small homes, German Shepherds appreciate country homes but adapt well to suburban homes with space for walking. They dislike being confined within four walls, and need stimulation, activity, and human company to thrive.

What type of owner?
This highly intelligent dog needs owners who are willing to commit time to training, walking, grooming, and companionship. They are unsuitable for owners who work full-time. Shepherds need physical and mental activity daily; solitude leading to boredom is unkind to such intelligent, active dogs.

How much exercise and stimulation?
Adult dogs need up to two hour of exercise daily, which should include time off-leash for running. Youngsters should not be overexercised to prevent damage to young bones and joints. Puppies benefit from several short walks daily, gradually building up to longer, less frequent walks.

Friendly with other pets?
Generally, with appropriate socialization and supervised introductions, German Shepherds do well with other household pets but they are boisterous.

Is puppy training easy?
Shepherds are supremely willing to learn, eager for purpose, and with an excellent working ability. They are very intelligent dogs, responsive to training, and enjoy

Personality Traits	Poor	Average	Good	Excellent
Attitude toward other dogs				
Quietness				
Behavior at home				
Watchdog ability				
Good with children				
Ease of training				
Obedience to owner				

Time to maturity: 2 years
Male height: 24–26 in (61–66 cm)
Female height: 22–24 in (56–61 cm)
Weight: 75–95 lb (34–43 kg)
Average lifespan: 10–13 years

spending time learning obedience skills to perfection. Many are able to participate in advanced training classes, and have potential for competition success.

Special puppy care?

Be careful that puppies do not upset other pets, as this could cause friction later as they mature. Start training early—dominant German Shepherds can become quite pushy if untrained, or can become nervous through poor socialization.

Possible health problems?

Earlier inbreeding did these lovely dogs no favors; they suffer from hip and elbow dysplasia (malformation), arthritis, ear infections, gastric torsion (bloat), von Willebrand's disease (a blood disorder), anal furunculosis (ulcerated anal tissue), and skin problems. The inbred sloping toplines of some show specimens may

result in impairment of hind leg action and poor gait.

What can we do together?

GSDs excel at agility, competitive obedience, as companion

● Cute, intelligent puppies at 8 weeks, destined to be loyal to the right owner.

dogs for walking and hiking, guide dogs, tracking, service dogs, and as loyal, affectionate pets.

Don't forget!

These are bright dogs that need training and plenty of exercise.

Large dogs

Old English Sheepdog *Other names: Bobtail*

This is a large breed, and one of England's most ancient herding dogs. They originated as tough shepherd's and cattle drover's dogs in southwest England. Appearing in British show rings from 1873, the breed was recognized in the U.S. in the 1880s. They subsequently gained popularity worldwide when the rich and famous began to take an interest in them. Some are naturally bobbed (tailless); others will be found with full-length tails as docking is now banned in many countries. Friendly, faithful, intelligent, even-tempered dogs, with a boisterous nature, these ultimate shaggy dogs love children and are an ideal choice for many families. They are high maintenance, and need physical and mental stimulation and a lot of grooming. In the right family they make super pets and great companions. Like many working breeds, they need a lot of company to prevent them from becoming bored and destructive.

Color choices?
The OES is available in shades of gray, grizzle, black, blue, or blue merle on the body and hindquarters. Head, neck, forequarters, underbody, and paws are white. Puppies have black and white coats; true color develops as the puppy coat sheds as the dog grows.

How much grooming?
The OES requires plenty of grooming (three or four hours a week for pets); owners may prefer trimming professionally to a short, neat outline. Coats are hard-textured, shaggy, curl-free, profuse, with water resistant undercoats. Tangles need to be gently teased out by hand, and groomed with a stiff brush and comb. Dead hair needs to be brushed out to prevent mats. Show puppies need training for grooming sessions (around 15 hours weekly) to maintain show condition.

Do they make good pets?
Playful, quiet, dignified, but never bois-terous, they make good children's

● *Full adult coats like these (3 years) is impractical for the average family. Owners may prefer their pet to be trimmed neat and short.*

companions and playmates. They are intelligent, sociable, and adapt to most situations, but some have clownish energy and are clumsy with small children. They may try herding people together, but their intentions are always friendly.

What home suits them?
These dogs have amiable, home-loving natures; they adapt and fit best in farm and countryside locations with open spaces. With proper exercise and training they can be accommodated to a sub-urban lifestyle, if owners meet their needs appropriately.

What type of owner?
Old English Sheepdogs are unsuitable for owners who are out all day, as they are gregarious and could become bored and destructive if left alone. They need active owners who enjoy long walks, and who will spend time on exercise and training. Commitment to regular grooming is essential.

How much exercise and stimulation?
These dogs need daily exercise (two hours a day), plus active play to reduce their energy levels adequately. Never overwalk puppies to avoid damaging young bones and joints; energy is better channeled into play activities.

Friendly with other pets?
Good with other pets, the OES will need early socialization and super-vised introductions for the correct

Personality Traits	Poor	Average	Good	Excellent
Attitude toward other dogs				
Quietness				
Behavior at home				
Watchdog ability				
Good with children				
Ease of training				
Obedience to owner				

Time to maturity: 2 years
Male height: 24–26 in (61–66 cm)
Female height: 22–24 in (56–61 cm)
Weight: 60–90 lb (27–41 kg)
Average lifespan: 10–12 years

dynamics. They are unlikely to chase family cats, but the neighbors' cats may be fair game. Smaller animals may feel threatened by their size and the risk of being squashed.

Is puppy training easy?
Moderately easy to train, this puppy is eager to please and a quick learner with a great thirst for new and varied activities. Training should be firm with positive reinforcement, or they can be stubborn, self-willed, and uncooperative.

Special puppy care?
Early training is essential, but never overwalk young dogs. Make sure to prevent them from over heating.

Possible health problems?
Cancer can be a problem. They can also suffer hip dysplasia (malformation), eye problems, thyroid and heart disorders, hemophilia, deafness, diabetes, allergies, and skin problems. Their thick, heavy coat may cause overheating in hot weather.

What can we do together?
These dogs are successful at sledding, tracking, and herding, and are ideal for agility, obedience, rallying, flyball, and competition showing.

Large dogs

Don't forget!
Buy only from reputable breeders who complete health checks.

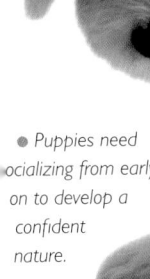

● Puppies need socializing from early on to develop a confident nature.

At 4 months, the coat is growing and needs gentle brushing daily.

Weimaraner

Other names: Weimar Pointer

One of the most striking of all the sporting breeds, Weimaraners spring from various hunting dogs of the 17th century. In the 19th century, the German court of Weimar specifically bred and refined Weimaraners from carefully chosen native working dogs for hunting purposes. Good all-arounders, Weimaraners were employed to hunt large forest animals (deer, bear, wild boar) and also used for pointing and retrieving game birds. After their introduction into the U.S. in 1929, they became popular hunting dogs, and subsequently found their way to Britain in 1952. Intelligent, powerful, rangy dogs, they need extensive socialization, but in the right hands they are relatively easy to train. They need experienced handlers and are unsuitable for novices, but for experienced, strong-minded handlers, and with suitable outlets for their abundant energy, they make marvelous family dogs.

Color choices?

Nicknamed the "gray ghost," the only color is metallic gray, with shades from charcoal blue to mouse gray, silver gray, and blue gray. Some have a darker gray stripe ("eel stripe") along their spine. Puppies are born striped, but this soon disappears. Eyes are amber or blue gray.

● *Intelligent and powerful, this 2-year-old bitch should be well trained, obedient, and loyal to her owner.*

How much grooming?

Brushing with a hound glove twice weekly removes dead hair and buffs the natural, glossy coat to a shine. Long-haired Weimaraners (a variety that appeared in 1973) need brushing and combing daily.

Do they make good pets?

Weimaraners are responsive to handling, happy to protect their family, and are usually gregarious and devoted to their owners. They prefer being with their family most of the time and are gentle and reliable with children. Properly exercised, they are good companions, but sometimes they can prove too boisterous for small children or frail elderly.

What home suits them?

Weimaraners are unsuitable for small homes or apartments, and do better in large country or suburban homes with high, well-fenced yards, and access to open areas for running, galloping, or supervised hunting.

What type of owner?

They are powerful dogs, and only suitable for physically strong and mentally tough-minded owners. Firm, kind leadership is needed, and owners should expect working companions, not placid lapdogs. Owners must be prepared to spend time in the open, whatever the weather, and to keep them gainfully employed, perhaps also participating in canine activities. Bored or dominant Weimaraners are destructive, possessive, over-protective, and noisy.

How much exercise and stimulation?

From adolescence, Weimaraners need extensive exercise to satisfy their physical endurance and stamina. Long walks, play, and games are appreciated in abundance. Ideal jogging companions, owners may struggle to provide enough exercise for this energetic dog.

Friendly with other pets?

These puppies have a strong instinctive drive to hunt. They may tolerate family cats if introduced and socialized early, but most cats are seen as fair game, and they will not hesitate to chase deer or livestock if an opportunity occurs.

Is puppy training easy?

A consistent, firm, patient approach is best, keeping sessions short and interesting, particularly

Personality Traits	Poor	Average	Good	Excellent
Attitude toward other dogs				
Quietness				
Behavior at home				
Watchdog ability				
Good with children				
Ease of training				
Obedience to owner				

Time to maturity: 18–24 months
Male height: 24–27 in (61–69 cm)
Female height: 22–25 in (56–63.5 cm)
Weight: 70–86 lb (32–39 kg)
Average lifespan: 10–12 years

during the first year. Teaching "Sit" using positive reinforcement is important to prevent jumping later on. Weimaraners are stubborn and can be boisterous, but when trained properly, they are obedient and they stay close to their owners.

Special puppy care?

Weimaraners lack undercoat, and puppies feel the chill in cold weather. Puppies may suffer from separation anxiety; training to reduce this problem is necessary. Destructive puppies are best contained in pens or crates when left alone, as they chew and eat anything.

Possible health problems?

Weimaraners are reasonably healthy, but can suffer hip and elbow dysplasia (malformation), eye problems, hypothyroidism (lack of thyroid hormone), gastric torsion, heart defects, von Willebrand's disease (a blood disorder), dwarfism, and hernia. Rapid growth in puppies also poses problems.

Large dogs

● Slight color variations are evident in 5-week-old puppies until their coats mature.

A cozy bed keeps young puppies warm.

What can we do together?

Hunting, working, jogging, walking, and hiking are all great activities for this breed.

Don't forget!

These are strong, powerful dogs and unsuitable for novice owners.

Gordon Setter

Other names: Scottish Setter, Black and Tan Setter

These intelligent, noble, and dignified dogs were originally bred in 17th-century Scotland for hunting game birds that preferred concealment in undergrowth, instead of taking flight. Partridge, grouse, ptarmigan, and woodcock were popular hunting targets, usually on open moors. Then, British farming methods changed and limited opportunities for this type of hunting—it is now mainly confined to Scottish moorland. Gordons first appeared in the U.S. in 1842, and were officially recognized in 1892. Considered a good choice for active families, these are calm, docile, affectionate pets. They need sensitive, firm handling, as they enjoy roaming after a scent. They can be boisterous and slow to mature, but they particularly enjoy being members of a family household. Owners must be prepared to spend time on exercise, grooming, and patient and gentle training to develop this dog to his true potential.

Color choices?

Rich, glossy coal-black with distinctive glossy tan markings (two spots over the eyes, on the muzzle, chest, and inside the legs) is the only color available. A small patch of white on the chest is allowed for showing.

How much grooming?

The hair is silky and fine on the back, head, and front of legs, with longer feathering elsewhere. Time must be spent grooming to remove any undergrowth debris after walks. Brushing and combing daily is needed to keep coats in good condition. Ears need to be checked and cleaned regularly.

Do they make good pets?

Gordons thrive in attentive, loving environments, as they are intensely loyal. They make excellent family pets because they love to please, and are patient and protective of their family—sometimes to the point of jealousy. Training may need to continue for longer than with other dogs, as they are

● *No longer used primarily for hunting birds, this breed has now become popular as loving and devoted family pets. They make an enthusiastic addition to any family who can cope with their large size.*

slower to mature, retaining their puppy ways well into old age. They may be too boisterous for elderly owners, or families with young children.

What home suits them?

Unsuitable for apartments, this puppy will really appreciate country or suburban homes with large, well-fenced yards, and open areas nearby for walking.

What type of owner?

Owners will love the Gordon's empathy, and their enjoyment of "talking" in response. Time and commitment are needed for training, as well as regular coat care. Gordons enjoy sniffing in undergrowth and may bring mud and debris into the home.

How much exercise and stimulation?

A Gordon's working instinct mean that they appreciate vigorous daily exercise, preferably two hours plus each day, which can include swimming. Walking needs to be graded for puppies, with several shorter walks throughout the day, increasing to fewer longer walks with maturity. These are intelligent dogs, and socialization and obedience training are important.

Friendly with other pets?

Their calm, docile nature ensures they are friendly with other pets, although some may find them too boisterous. Small household pets

Personality Traits	Poor	Average	Good	Excellent
ttitude toward other dogs				
Quietness				
ehavior at home				
Vatchdog ability				
iood with children				
ase of training				
Obedience to owner				

Time to maturity: 3–4 years
Male height: 24–27 in (61–69 cm)
Female height: 23–26 in (58–66 cm)
Weight: 45–80 lb (20–36 kg)
Average lifespan: 10–12 years

nay be overwhelmed, and some iordons can be jealous of other ets around their family. With good arly socialization and supervised ntroductions, these problems can e overcome.

puppy training easy?

Gordons are quick to learn and ager to please, but they need firm, atient, and gentle handling because hey can be sensitive. Agility raining, ideal for adult xercise, should not tart until at least 8 months of age o prevent damage o young joints.

Special puppy care?

Avoid overwalking puppies to reduce any possible damage to young bones and joints.

Possible health problems?

Gordons are fairly hardy but can suffer from hip dysplasia (malformation), hypothyroidism (lack of thyroid hormone), gastric torsion (bloat), and eye problems.

What can we do together?

Gordons will enjoy hunting, walking, and a lot of fun and games with their family.

Don't forget!

Make sure puppies are walked away from busy roads, as they like to roam ahead of owners following scents. Keep them on a leash when near the road or in open areas.

Large dogs

● Calm and docile at 16 weeks.

Rhodesian Ridgeback

Other names: Lion Dog, African Lion Hound

In the 1860s, settlers in Africa brought their own hunting dogs, which were crossed with the indigenous Hottentot dogs of the Khoikhoi people of Rhodesia. These hunting dogs were distinguished by the ridges of hair on their spine, growing in reverse directions to the rest of the coat. They were fierce, courageous hunting dogs able to track and hold lions at bay, and to hunt wild pigs or baboons. Ridgebacks achieved recognition in Africa 1922, and in Britain not long after, although they d not reach America until the 1950s. The handsome dogs of today are protective and strong-willed, and make excellent watchdogs, but they are also loyal devoted companions. Very much a "people's dog," Ridgebacks need strong-minded, experienced, confident owners who will spend time and effort early socialization, and appropriate training and exercise for this powerful, independent dog.

Color choices?

Available colors are light to red wheaten, with dark muzzles and ears; a small white patch on the chest is allowed. White on paws is undesirable for show puppies.

How much grooming?

The short, sleek, glossy coat can be maintained by a once-weekly brush with a hound glove.

Do they make good pets?

With good socialization, Ridgebacks make excellent pets. They are calm, affectionate, rarely bark, and are good with respectful, older children. But these dogs are unsuitable for novices, and are best owned by experienced dog handlers who provide the right level of training and socialization. Their guarding instinct should not be over-encouraged, as they can become aggressive. They can be mischievous, but are loving and intelligent and with the right owner, they do really well as companion dogs.

● *Ridgebacks have a distinctive ridge of hair down the spine. They were bred to hunt big game and to guard property.*

What home suits them?

Country or suburban homes are best for these puppies, unless plenty of walking is available for city dwellers. Ridgebacks are athletic dogs, and need sturdy high fencing, as they are quite likely to jump clear over fences if bored.

What type of owner?

These strong-willed dogs are very demanding—they need confident, experienced owners. Training and socialization will be successful if the owner is able to gain an appropriate level of leadership over them.

How much exercise and stimulation?

Ridgebacks need several brisk daily walks, up to 2 miles (3 km) each time, interspersed with free running and play. Owners will nee to make sure that they do not chase joggers, livestock, or other dogs for their enjoyment.

Friendly with other pets?

Ridgebacks have a high prey drive and small family pets will definitel be at risk. They may be fine if raised with family cats, but other cats in the neighborhood should beware. This is a dominant breed, and is quite likely to be aggressive with other dogs of the same gender, unless well socialized and trained to accept them.

Is puppy training easy?

Ridgebacks need rigorous training Owners should be fair, firm, consistent, but not harsh or training will be counterproductive It is particularly important that training starts early and puppies view their owner as their leader,

Personality Traits	Poor	Average	Good	Excellent
Attitude toward other dogs				
Quietness				
Behavior at home				
Watchdog ability				
Good with children				
Ease of training				
Obedience to owner				

Time to maturity: 2 years
Male height: 25–27 in (63.5–68.5 cm)
Female height: 24–26 in (61–66 cm)
Weight: 65–75 lb (29–34 kg)
Average lifespan: 10–12 years

● From this age (weeks), puppies develop their natural behaviors. Training is necessary to prevent unwanted habits.

otherwise they can be strong-willed and stubborn. Reward-based training will add motivation and works best.

Special puppy care?

Puppies under six months should not be over-exercised because of the risks of damage to young bones and joints.

Possible health problems?

In America, breeders are expected to perform health screening for hips, elbows, thyroid, and eyes, with cardiac and hearing tests optional. Ridgebacks are also known to suffer from dermoid sinus (abnormal tissue on the neck), degenerative

myelopathy (a spinal cord disease affecting the legs), hypothyroidism (lack of thyroid hormone), and gastric torsion (bloat).

What can we do together?

Lure coursing and agility are fun, and appreciated by both owners and Ridgebacks. They are also excellent walking companions.

Don't forget!

Buy from reputable breeders who perform necessary health checks.

Large dogs

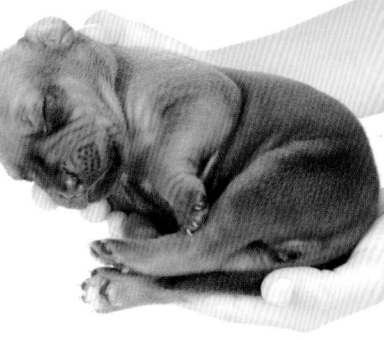

● This tiny puppy's eyes and ears will not open for several more days.

Bullmastiff

Bred from crossing Mastiffs and Bulldogs, Bullmastiffs combine qualities of being fast, active, large, and heavy. These impressive, powerful dogs were bred in the 19th century, and used for guarding property. Sometimes dubbed the "Gamekeeper's Night Dog," they were used in Victorian Britain to tackle problems with violent intruders and poaching on large estates.

These agile, solid, courageous, and fearless dogs certainly have the looks to deter criminals. They were recognized in Britain by the Kennel Club in 1924 and in the U.S. in 1933. Despite their fierce appearance, they are well liked because they are excellent family dogs and watchdogs. Today's Bullmastiff, were it not for its size, would enjoy life as a lapdog! This breed is dignified, loyal, and affectionate and makes a gentle member of the right family. However, they need firm training and are not a good choice for novices.

Color choices?

Fawn, red or brindle solid colors are available. White is undesirable, although a small white mark on the chest is acceptable.

How much grooming?

Regular brushing of their short, coarse hair with a firm brush, ten minutes twice a week, removes dead hair and dander. Cleaning and drying face folds prevents skin infection. Check feet for damage weekly, as these are heavy dogs. Some Bullmastiffs slobber, so wiping the mouth regularly is necessary.

Do they make good pets?

This big, powerful dog has strong protective instincts, so is not a good choice for families with younger children. Some may be overly protective, placing visiting children at risk, and may misinterpret rough play from strangers. They can be excellent, companionable family pets if well trained by the right owner and in the right home environment. If left alone they will be unhappy, but are more likely to sleep than become destructive.

● *Bullmastiffs are natural guardians of the home.*

What home suits them?

Large country and suburban homes with strongly fenced yards are best, as Bullmastiffs can barge their way through flimsy fences and hedges. Shady trees are good because they do not tolerate hot weather. They are quiet dogs who seldom bark, so they are not likely to upset neighbors.

What type of owner?

Bullmastiffs need strong, experienced owners to prevent this puppy from becoming a real liability. Their fearless guarding instinct needs early socialization, and firm direction from an owner prepared to put in the time and effort to make sure that

aggressive tendencies are not encouraged.

How much exercise and stimulation?

While their exercise needs are moderate, they do need regular daily walking to prevent laziness and health-threatening obesity. Puppies should have gentle walks gradually increasing in distance as they get older.

Friendly with other pets?

Bullmastiffs will be friendly but their size alone places small animals at risk. Early socialization will be necessary to encourage family relations; closely supervise when introducing puppies to prevent any adult dominance and aggression, which may occur with other dogs of the same gender.

Is puppy training easy?

Bullmastiffs are strong and can be stubborn, so training may be moderately difficult. Training must start early and owners must be firm, patient, and consistent, providing short, non-repetitive

Personality Traits	Poor	Average	Good	Excellent
Attitude toward other dogs		■		
Quietness			■	
Behavior at home			■	
Watchdog ability				■
Good with children			■	
Ease of training		■		
Obedience to owner			■	

Time to maturity: 3.5 years
Male height: 25–27 in (63.5–69 cm)
Female height: 24–26 in (61–66 cm)
Weight: 100–133 lb (45–60 kg)
Average lifespan: 8–10 years

...essions and using treats for motivation. Harsh training or bullying simply will not work.

Special puppy care?

Puppies should not be subjected to long walks until at least two years old to prevent damage to young bones and joints. Early socialization is a must for Bullmastiffs.

Possible health problems?

Their size makes bone and joint conditions a serious

● *Only 12 weeks old, this puppy is already large and active.*

problem. Other conditions they suffer from are hip dysplasia (malformation), eye problems, cancer, gastric torsion (bloat), and hypothyroidism (lack of thyroid hormone). This dog has a relatively short lifespan.

What can we do together?

Obedience, agility, tracking, and carting are ideal activities for this breed.

Don't forget!

This breed is unsuitable for novice owners. Bullmastiffs need careful, early socializing and training to make good family dogs.

Large dogs

Bullmastiffs are powerful, and will demand a lot of time and commitment from the right owner.

Rottweiler

Rotties earned their name as the "butcher's dog of Rottweil" from tradesmen in this thriving market town in southern Germany. This powerful breed was developed as a droving dog, to herd cattle from farms to market, and to bring their master's cash (tied securely around their necks) safely home. Rotties have fearsome looks, and for their size, are one of the strongest breeds of dog in the world. They have a powerful sense of duty, a natural watchdog ability within their territory, and make excellent dogs for service work in military and police use, as therapy and guide dogs, and for search and rescue. Despite this, they have developed a bad reputation because of irresponsible ownership by unsuitable people.

However, with good socializing and training they can be trained to an excellent standard. With proper discipline, love, and attention, they are excellent companions and family dogs.

Color choices?

Rotties are black with tan markings above the eyes, on muzzles, cheeks, chest, under their necks, on legs, and at the base of the tail.

How much grooming?

The low-maintenance coat needs brushing twice weekly to keep its healthy shine and to remove dead hair. Female Rotties shed prior to being in heat, males usually have a yearly seasonal molt.

Do they make good pets?

Happy, well-balanced Rotties are fabulous family dogs, but they need an experienced owner to train them to be well disciplined. This is not a suitable dog to let children take responsibility for, or for novice owners. They need a strong, confident owner, who knows how to handle them with assurance. In the wrong hands, Rotties can be aggressive and dangerous, and sometimes a liability.

What home suits them?

This is a versatile breed, but big dogs need space, and Rotties are no

● *These two 7-week-old puppies still need time for weaning, socializing, and learning some manners through play before they leave for a new home.*

exception. They are unsuitable as apartment dogs. Securely fenced yards will be essential, whether in the suburbs or the country, and access to plenty of space for walking will be needed daily, in all types of weather.

What type of owner?

Rotties need firm, consistent leadership from a calm, assertive owner, plus plenty of affection. Time has to be devoted to training and exercise. Owners will need experience in dog handling to take on this big breed, and to provide sufficient physical and mental stimulation. Rotties are unsuitable for novices and child handlers.

How much exercise and stimulation?

Modern owners are unlikely to be able to offer the many miles of exercise that Rotties' ancestors would have enjoyed (anything up to around 40 miles/65 km); however, several miles of walking daily to maintain good health is ideal.

Friendly with other pets?

The dominant nature of the Rottie is likely to place other family pets at some risk, particularly same-gender dogs, even with excellent socializing and training. More docile Rotties, if introduced early enough, may do well with supervision.

Is puppy training easy?

Formal training must be started early because Rotties are strong-willed, but training is extremely rewarding for conscientious owners who are calm and confident. Training will be easiest if it is non-confrontational, and owners earn respect by being firm and sympathetic using reward-based incentives.

Personality Traits	Poor	Average	Good	Excellent
Attitude toward other dogs				
Quietness				
Behavior at home				
Watchdog ability				
Good with children				
Ease of training				
Obedience to owner				

Time to maturity: 2 years
Male height: 25–27 in (63.5–69 cm)
Female height: 23–25 in (58–63.5 cm)
Weight: 85–135 lb (39–61 kg)
Average lifespan: 9–11 years

What can we do together?

Well-trained Rotties are successful in obedience competitions and herding trials, and they make good walking or jogging companions.

Don't forget!

In some European countries, Rotties have developed bad reputations, are placed on dangerous dog lists, and may be banned or unavailable.

Special puppy care?

Puppies should not be over-exercised to reduce their energy levels. It is essential that training starts as early as possible with puppies to prevent dominance issues later. Bad habits learned as puppies will grow with them into adulthood.

Possible health problems?

Rotties can suffer from hip and elbow dysplasia (malformation), cruciate ligament problems, eye problems, and cancer. Obesity caused by a poor diet can lead to heart failure, arthritis, respiratory problems, diabetes, and skin disease.

Just 8 weeks old and no bad habits yet!

Large dogs

● *A puppy's paw size is often an indicator of its future size when fully grown.*

Bloodhound

Other names: Ardennes Hound, Flanders Hound

One of the greatest tracking dogs, Bloodhounds are second to none as scent hounds.

These dogs were developed in the 9th century from St. Hubert Hounds in the Ardennes region of Belgium. The presence of Bloodhounds in Britain in 1066 is attributed to William the Conqueror. The Bloodhound's name alludes to its noble breeding, as great care was taken with maintaining pure bloodlines. Later specimens formed hunting packs for French kings indulging their love of sporting pursuits. Present-day Bloodhounds look very similar to their ancestors, and are generally good-natured dogs and very affectionate. Though they are kind, gentle, and pleasant companions, Bloodhounds are powerful dogs, ruled by their noses, and are difficult to walk off-leash as they follow any interesting scent and are often stubborn to recall. They eat vast amounts, are destructive when bored, slobber copiously, and bay loudly when lonely.

Color choices?

Colors are black, liver, or red, all with tan. Some have small white markings on the chest, feet, or tail tip.

How much grooming?

The short coat is low-maintenance, requiring brushing with a hound glove once weekly to remove dead hair and dander. Regular grooming reduces unpleasant "doggy" smells. Their pendulous ears hang down into food bowls and collect mouth slobber and need cleaning daily. Expect slobber to reach the corners of the room when a Bloodhound shakes his huge head.

Do they make good pets?

These affectionate, calm, even-tempered, gentle puppies are companionable family dogs, although stubborn and difficult to train. However, size and a clumsy gait may accidentally bowl over or trample small children or frail elderly, so they are not ideal for all families. Bloodhounds tend to be one-person dogs, and may not bond with everyone. Some are food-possessive.

● *Powerfully built for hunting, Bloodhounds are well known for their tracking abilities and will enjoy being out and about detecting scents to follow.*

What home suits them?

Unsuitable for small apartments or houses, Bloodhounds need country or suburban dwellings with large yards and long daily walks. Secure fencing will prevent them from escaping to follow every new smell. Neighbors are unlikely to appreciate their magnificent, melodious voice.

What type of owner?

Bloodhounds are best for owners who can harness their natural ability in tracking activities, and devote time to exercise and training. This puppy needs considerate owners who are not rough or insensitive.

How much exercise and stimulation?

Never overexercise puppies, and make sure to grade exercise levels to prevent damaging bones and joints. Adult Bloodhounds require extensive walking. They feel compelled to follow interesting scents, so they must be kept on long leashes to prevent them from disappearing, or they must be walked in safe and secure areas.

Friendly with other pets?

Very good-natured dogs, Bloodhounds get along well with most pets, although they can be clumsy and their sheer size may put small animals at risk.

Is puppy training easy?

Expect difficulty in training—they are stubborn and willful, and complete obedience is unlikely. Owners should be firm, kind, and incredibly patient in training—Bloodhounds are gentle and sensitive to every kindness or correction. Puppies and

Personality Traits	Poor	Average	Good	Excellent
Attitude toward other dogs				
Quietness				
Behavior at home				
Watchdog ability				
Good with children				
Ease of training				
Obedience to owner				

Time to maturity: 2.5 years
Male height: 25–27 in (63.5–69 cm)
Female height: 23–25 in (58–63.5 cm)
Weight: 80–110 lb (36–50 kg)
Average lifespan: 9–10 years

adolescents may be more unpre-dictable until mature, and need consistent, sensible guidance.

Special puppy care?
Ensure that puppies learn a recall to prevent them straying too far following scents, and never over-exercise to burn off their abundant energy. When choosing, avoid puppies with

A Bloodhound's large nose is excellent for scent detection when hunting.

excessive skin folds and runny eyes. Adolescents need firm, kind leadership.

Possible health problems?
Bloodhounds suffer from eye problems, ear infections, hip dysplasia (malformation), skin allergies, and gastro-intestinal problems (bloat). Not walking them within an hour of feeding can help prevent bloat. Bloodhounds also suffer from overheating.

Large dogs

What can we do together?
Single Bloodhounds are used for hunting. Problem solving or tracking activities are great for satisfying their need for mental stimulation.

Don't forget!
Never use harsh treatment in training, as this ruins their gentle temperament.

● *This 6-week-old puppy already has head folds and large ears that will need attention.*

Bernese Mountain Dog
Other names: Bernese Cattle Dog

This ancient breed, which dates back to Roman times, developed in the canton of Bern in Switzerland. Bernese are one of a small group of Swiss national dogs, and are the best known and most popular outside Switzerland. They were bred to accompany Alpine herders and dairymen called Senn. Mainly farm dogs, Bernese were draft animals used to pull carts and to drive cattle from farms to Alpine pastures, and to haul small carts of goods to market for the weavers of Bern. Rescued from near extinction in the 19th century, Bernese gained recognition in the U.S. and Britain in the 1930s, and have now achieve worldwide popularity. Noted as appealing family dogs, they are people-oriented, gentle, tolerant, and loving companions, but these big, powerful, intellige dogs can be demanding. Bernese need to be kept occupied, can be strong-willed, and ar unsuitable for inexperienced owners.

Color choices?
The distinctive tricolored coat is black with a white facial blaze and white on the chest, at the sides of the mouth, on the front feet, and tail tip. A white "Swiss cross" marks the chest with a kiss of white on the neck. Tan marks appear above the eyes, on the sides of the mouth, paws, and chest.

● *Adult and a 14-month-old juvenile.*

How much grooming?
Bernese need brushing twice weekly. They shed all year with seasonal changes causing the heaviest molt. During heavy shedding, daily brushing to reduce hair fall helps. Bathing is usually done bimonthly, sometimes more frequently if needed.

Do they make good pets?
Bernese make excellent pets. They are very tolerant of children climbing over them during play, although puppies may be too boisterous for young children. Generally, Bernese make ideal family pets because they are placid, docile, good-natured, self-confident, affectionate, and stranger-friendly.

What home suits them?
Unsuitable for small homes or apartments, Bernese need space outdoors. Very warm houses and yards without shady trees are not good because the heavy coat makes overheating a problem.

What type of owner?
These strong-minded, powerful dogs need experienced owners prepared to spend time on training them and keeping them occupied. They are unsuitable for novices or those without the time to devote to the relationship.

How much exercise and stimulation?
Outdoor dogs at heart, Bernese need activity and exercise. When motivated, they move quickly, but they have little endurance and tend to stay near their owner. Bernese are used to working and need stimulation in the form of activities such as hiking or herding. An hour's walk or a long hike will be appreciated by adults.

Friendly with other pets?
Bernese are boisterous puppies and need socializing sensibly, but otherwise they are mostly compatible with other pets and ge along just fine. Some males can be dominant and may need corrective training to curb this tendency.

Is puppy training easy?
Training varies according to individual dogs, but usually moderate difficulty may be experienced. Owners must be firm patient, gentle, and consistent. Plan to train employing regular interesting, but short, sessions.

Personality Traits	Poor	Average	Good	Excellent
Attitude toward other dogs				
Quietness				
Behavior at home				
Watchdog ability				
Good with children				
Ease of training				
Obedience to owner				

Time to maturity: 18–24 months
Male height: 25–27.5 in (63.5–70 cm)
Female height: 23–26 in (58–66 cm)
Weight: 90–120 lb (41–54 kg)
Average lifespan: 7–9 years

...eady large,
...n at 12
...eks old.

Bernese do have minds of their own, but they also have a willingness to please, and a good sense of humor.

Special puppy care?
As puppies grow they need to be well socialized and owners must appreciate that they will grow into large, powerful dogs. Young puppies should not

● *Left alone, puppies may become destructive if bored. It is best to train them early to stay home alone or temporarily contained in a crate.*

be overwalked and exercise should be graded to avoid problems with developing bones and joints, particularly as young dogs in this breed can be prone to musculoskeletal problems.

Possible health problems?
Bernese have a high incidence of cancer. They also have eye problems, hip dysplasia (malformation), hypoadrenocorti-cism (lack of a particular hormone), arthritis and musculoskeletal problems (cruciate ligament rupture is fairly common), and elbow dysplasia.

Large dogs

What can we do together?
Owners may enjoy non-competitive herding trials, cart pulling, agility, and hiking. Some are used as therapy dogs and for police work.

Don't forget!
Buy only from reputable breeders or sources.

Alaskan Malamute

One of the oldest dog breeds, Malamutes are the official state dog of Alaska. Bred as utilitarian dogs, they were used for hunting bears, guarding caribou herds, finding seal blow holes, hauling heavily loaded sledges, and for companionship. Life was varied and their human keepers—an Inuit tribe called Mahlemuts for whom they were named—reputedly kept them for centuries. Arctic exploration increased interest in Malamutes because of their incredible ability to withstand impossible weather frozen snow and icy blizzards. Today, Malamutes are primarily used for sled racing or hunting. Although not originally intended as family pets, they are affectionate, playful, gentle with children, and attached to people. This is a powerful dog, who may be stubborn at times, and needs firm training. Their dignified nature and friendly demeanor make them excellent companions for sensible families.

Color choices?

Colors are either solid white, or gray shades through to black, or shadings of sable to red, with white markings on underbody, face, legs, and feet. Face markings form a cap or mask, and coat shading is either mantled or splash coated.

How much grooming?

Brushing this dense coat twice weekly using a curry comb will usually suffice. Daily grooming during the annual seasonal shedding is necessary, as hair comes out in clumps. These dogs seldom have a doggy smell.

Do they make good pets?

Not good watchdogs, Malamutes rarely bark, are not aggressive, and are generally very sociable dogs. Size puts small children at a disadvantage because they may get injured accidentally, although Malamutes are patient and gentle. They need to be active and are likely to be destructive unless gainfully employed in active tasks such as sledding.

● *Malamutes are unsuitable for novices or owners who do not like an active life.*

What home suits them?

Malamutes dislike being shut in small spaces, and apartments or city life is unsuitable for them. Larger country or suburban homes with space to run and walk are best. Close neighbors may not appreciate their enjoyment of a good howl, so isolated or detached properties are a better proposition.

What type of owner?

Malamutes are ideal for owners who enjoy being active, out in all types of weather and involved in backpacking, sled racing, and hunting; this is not a dog for stay-at-home people. Owners need to be strong-willed and ready to enjoy a Malamute's company full-time.

How much exercise and stimulation?

Adult Malamutes will need at least 5 miles (8 km) of walking daily, and would be happy for more. Walks near livestock should definitely be avoided—remember, these dogs enjoy hunting and have strong prey drives.

Friendly with other pets?

Not ideal for keeping with other pets or even other dogs, because Malamutes have natural hunting instincts and are likely to chase smaller animals. Even those happy around other pets should be supervised carefully.

Is puppy training easy?

Malamutes are highly intelligent dogs, but can be difficult to train. Owners who understand their independence, resourcefulness, natural behaviors, and can keep them motivated will be successful,

Personality Traits	Poor	Average	Good	Excellent
Attitude toward other dogs				
Quietness				
Behavior at home				
Watchdog ability				
Good with children				
Ease of training				
Obedience to owner				

Time to maturity: 18–24 months
Male height: 25 in (64 cm)
Female height: 23 in (58 cm)
Weight: Up to 95 lb (43 kg)
Average lifespan: 12–15 years

...ut natural obedience will be hard to achieve. Trainers should start early, show plenty of patience, and no harshness. Definitely not a dog for owners with no experience of training strong-willed dogs.

● *Puppies will be ready for training from 8 weeks.*

Special puppy care?

Build up walking activities gradually until puppies are fully developed at 18 to 24 months old, or young bones and joints could be permanently damaged. Early careful socialization should help to control natural hunting behaviors. Signs of illness in puppies should be checked out immediately, as some conditions in this breed affect young dogs.

Possible health problems?

Malamutes suffer from hip dysplasia (malformation), eye problems, epilepsy, kidney problems, congenital heart problems, and skin disorders.

What can we do together?

Owners will enjoy recreational sledding (known as mushing), skijoring, bikejoring, carting, and canicross with their dogs. Malamutes also enjoy weight pulling and agility.

Don't forget!

This is not a novice's dog and he needs plenty of time devoted to training and vigorous activity.

● *Not easy pets to train, but this puppy has strength, brains, and beauty.*

English Setter

Other names: Laverack Setter (show specimens), Llewellin Setter (working)

The oldest of English-bred setters, this breed was used in the 16th century for hunting game birds in wetlands and swamps. At a time when falconry hunting was popular, they approached game (usually woodcock) quietly, and crouched down to mark the position of the prey in a similar way to how they "point" when working as sporting dogs today. The best known and most common of modern setters, they typify idyllic English country scenes with their quiet, elegant, and handsome appearance. More popular as companion dogs, they have friendly temperament, sociable natures, and are calm, gentle, and fun-loving. English Setters radiate grace and intelligence from within a beautiful white and flecked coat. Given their hunting background, they can be energetic as youngsters. They are highly intelligent, need plenty of exercise and companionship, and are unsuitable for owners who are unable to cope with mud and mess or who want a quiet life.

Color choices?
Setters have white coats with ticked or flecked coloring (known as "belton"), without heavy patches. Coloring is black and white (blue belton), orange and white (orange belton), lemon and white (lemon belton), brown and white (liver belton), or tricolor (black, tan, or brown and white). Puppies are born white; color develops later.

How much grooming?
Regular grooming removes dead hair, tangles, and debris from their long, silky hair. Neutered pets need more grooming because coats become thicker and woollier. Ears need checking and cleaning regularly.

Do they make good pets?
They make great pets and willing participants in family activities, but small children may be overwhelmed by their exuberance. However, with careful training and exercise they will suit most families. Some are one-person dogs, and have a habit of wheedling food and privileges from owners, which should be resisted.

● *An orange belton adult, showing the smooth, silky coat of a mature dog, that will need regular grooming to keep it looking good.*

Smaller working specimens are usually more active than those specifically bred for show purposes.

What home suits them?
English Setters dislike being confined, preferring the outdoors where they can express their exuberance and vivacious nature, so country or suburban homes are better. They do adapt to city living provided that enough time is allowed for walking and periods of running free.

What type of owner?
These are dogs for active owners, who enjoy walking reasonable distances in any weather. Owners must be firm, patient, and provide plenty of company for these sociable dogs. Confidence and consistency is needed, as they sense an owner's weakness.

How much exercise and stimulation?
Easily covering a lot of ground—many miles when out running free—and dependable in any terrain, exercise is important for this dog. Space to run is essential, but a good recall is necessary to prevent them from tearing off on an interesting solo expedition. Highly intelligent, they need mental stimulation to maintain happiness.

Friendly with other pets?
English Setters are very sociable and friendly with other pets, but early socialization will teach them manners, such as not chasing the family cat or being too bouncy with small household pets.

Is puppy training easy?
Meek owners may find them rather willful and stubborn in

Personality Traits	Poor	Average	Good	Excellent
Attitude toward other dogs			●	
Quietness		●		
Behavior at home			●	
Watchdog ability		●		
Good with children				●
Ease of training			●	
Obedience to owner			●	

Time to maturity: 2.5–3 years
Male height: 25.5–27 in (65–69 cm)
Female height: 24–25.5 in (61–65 cm)
Weight: 55–66 lb (25–30 kg)
Average lifespan: 10–14 years

...raining; a firm, patient, gentle approach with handling is the best method. Reward-based, patient, and repetitive training will normally pay dividends.

Special puppy care?

Puppies can be very demanding and are slow to mature, so training may continue for longer than for an average breed.

Lack of exercise, attention, or stimulation are likely to trigger their potential for being destructive.

This puppy's watchful eyes are always on his owner.

Large dogs

Possible health problems?

English Setters can suffer from hip dysplasia (malformation), eye problems, hypothyroidism (lack of thyroid hormone), and skin allergies. Some puppies are born deaf.

What can we do together?

These very sociable dogs are ideal as walking, jogging, and hiking companions, as well as being great all-around family dogs for playing.

Don't forget!

This is a boisterous, exuberant breed that needs plenty of walking and firm, authoritative training.

Blue belton puppy at 16 weeks showing early signs of flecks and ticking as his coat matures.

Giant and Standard Schnauzer

Standard Schnauzers originated around 500 years ago in the German provinces of Württemburg and Bavaria. Crossed with other breeds at different times during the early years of their development, both larger and smaller sizes were produced, although both conform to similar standards. They were used for vermin hunting or guarding farms, factories, or homes. Schnauzers were not popular outside Germany until the 1950s, with little interest show in Britain until 1960, although American owners t to them much earlier. Giant Schnauzers are more popular in Europe than the Standard. The versatil of Schnauzers is a bonus because owners can cho between sizes according to their circumstances. Schnauzers, particularly Giants, are strong-minded and benefit from experienced owners. Both sizes make excellent family pets when well train but need experienced, strong-minded owners, not novices.

Color choices?

Colors are black, salt and pepper, or black and silver, with a dark mask. There are no white markings; pure white and particolor Schnauzers are bred, but not recognized as standard.

● Bred for working, Giant Schnauzers, and the smaller Standards, are energetic and high-spirited dogs.

How much grooming?

Coats are high maintenance and need hand-stripping, not trimming, to retain the wiry top coat over a softer undercoat. Puppy owners may prefer trimming. A stiff brush through the coat daily, starting when a puppy, and combing the whiskers and legs and washing the beard after meals is best.

Do they make good pets?

Schnauzers are powerful, high-spirited, strong-willed, energetic, and quite dominant; inexperienced owners or those with young children may find the larger Schnauzers a handful. Schnauzers are loyal and obedient, and make excellent family dogs, but the Giant's size and dominant nature make them unsuitable for novice families or as first dogs.

What home suits them?

Giant Schnauzers need a large yard and plenty of walking as they grow up to satisfy their exercise needs. Standard Schnauzers suit smaller homes and yards better, but still need plenty of exercise. Giants, particularly, are unsuitable for apartment living.

What type of owner?

Schnauzers' strong will and dominant nature demand owners who give firm discipline from the start, allowing plenty of time for socialization and training to command loyalty and obedience.

How much exercise and stimulation?

Puppies need gently increasing amounts of exercise; Giant Schnauzers, particularly, should no be overexercised as their bigger s and greater weight can cause bon growth problems. In adult life one two hours a day of exercise may needed, with a little less for the Standard. Schnauzers do not appreciate being confined indoor and need regular vigorous exercis to stay fit, as well as extensive socialization and stimulation for their mental well-being.

Friendly with other pets?

Schnauzers can be dominant, so in ductions to other family pets nee supervision, and socialization must accomplished early on. Male dogs can be overly dominant with othe male dogs, so problems can occu

Is puppy training easy?

Giant Schnauzers are powerful an strong-minded but learn quickly v the right training. Firm handling is essential to prevent them from ch

Personality Traits	Poor	Average	Good	Excellent
Attitude toward other dogs				
Quietness				
Behavior at home				
Watchdog ability				
Good with children				
Ease of training				
Obedience to owner				

Time to maturity: 2.5 years
Male height: Giant 25.5–27.5 in (65–70 cm) Standard 18–20 in (45–50 cm)
Weight: Giant 66–88 lb (30–40 kg) Standard around 40–45 lb (18–20 kg)
Average lifespan: Giant 10–12 years Standard 13–14 years

enging their owners for leadership. Training should be fun with some rewards, and without excessive repetition to prevent boredom. Calm, confident owners will be well rewarded. Plenty of puppy training through games and play is essential.

pecial puppy care?

Puppies up to 12 months need less walking and more play to learn obedience. Plan exercise regimes with care to prevent damage to growing bones. Schnauzers are excellent watchdogs, but can bark a lot, so conditioning acceptable behavior early on can help to prevent problems later.

Possible health problems?

Usually healthy, the Giant's size can cause hip dysplasia; other conditions include hypothyroidism, cataracts, epilepsy, skin problems, and digestive disorders.

● *At 10 weeks old, these puppies are in need of regular stimulation, and will benefit from early socialization and training.*

What can we do together?

Schnauzers are devoted, loyal companions, and ideal watchdogs. Well-trained dogs have been known to achieve success in obedience trials.

Don't forget!

This breed (particularly Giants) are dominant, territorial, and very protective dogs, so you must start socialization early.

Large dogs

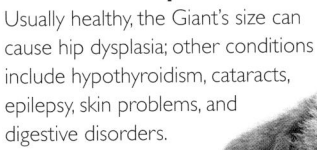

Coat color will change as these puppies grow.

Doberman Pinscher

Other names: Dobermann

This very elegant, fast, fearless dog was developed by the German Louis Dobermann in the late 19th century as a vigilant guard dog to accompany him on his rounds when he collected taxes.

As working dogs, Dobermans have been used for farm activities such as herding, tracking, retrieving, and as police dogs. During the Second World War, the U.S. Marines made the "devil dog" its official war dog, although this fierce reputation belies their loyalty to their owner, trained obedience, and trustworthiness with children. At heart, Dobermans dislike conflict and c be emotionally sensitive. In the wrong hands, if bad trained or abused, they can be a dangerous liability. They are capable of being strong-minded, dominant and compulsive and are not for inexperienced or novice owners. Well trained Dobermans are stable, composed, and sociable, performing to high standar of obedience with experienced handling.

Color choices?

Choices are black and tan, blue and tan, brown and tan, isabella (fawn), and tan. Other colors may be available, but are not recognized for registration.

How much grooming?

The short coat is low maintenance and needs only a once-weekly wipe with a hound glove or stiff brush to keep it glossy, in good condition, and free of loose hair. Bathing is only needed occasionally.

Do they make good pets?

When well trained, Dobermans make excellent family pets, but be aware—training needs a lot of time, patience, and dedication. They enjoy being part of a family group, but need to be well supervised through their adolescent phase when they can be very rowdy with children, so Dobermans are not recommended for homes with young children.

What home suits them?

Due to their size and active nature, Dobermans need a fair amount of

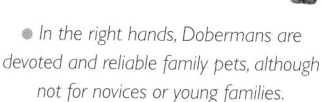

● *In the right hands, Dobermans are devoted and reliable family pets, although not for novices or young families.*

space and would not be suitable for small homes or apartments. They will need a well-fenced yard with plenty of space for playing and running free, with good walks nearby to release high energy levels.

What type of owner?

Dobermans need experienced owners who are fair, patient, strong-willed, and confident leaders, and very committed to spending time on training. This is not a dog to leave alone for long periods of time, and some may become territorial if left

to their own devices for too long. Novices and inexperienced dog owners would be well advised no to consider this dog as a choice for a companion.

How much exercise and stimulation?

They are very active, energetic dogs, and will need at least two hours of exercise daily, plus time fe running free. They need daily training sessions, and a variety of challenges to stimulate their highly intelligent minds.

Friendly with other pets?

Dogs reared from puppies should tolerate other household pets we but they need to be well socialize and introductions must be made when they are still puppies. Males can be dominant, and may be aggressive with other males.

Is puppy training easy?

A Doberman is very intelligent an strong-willed, but also highly trainable in the right hands; owner must maintain calm, confident

Personality Traits	Poor	Average	Good	Excellent
Attitude toward other dogs		■		
Quietness	■			
Behavior at home			■	
Watchdog ability				■
Good with children			■	
Ease of training				■
Obedience to owner				■

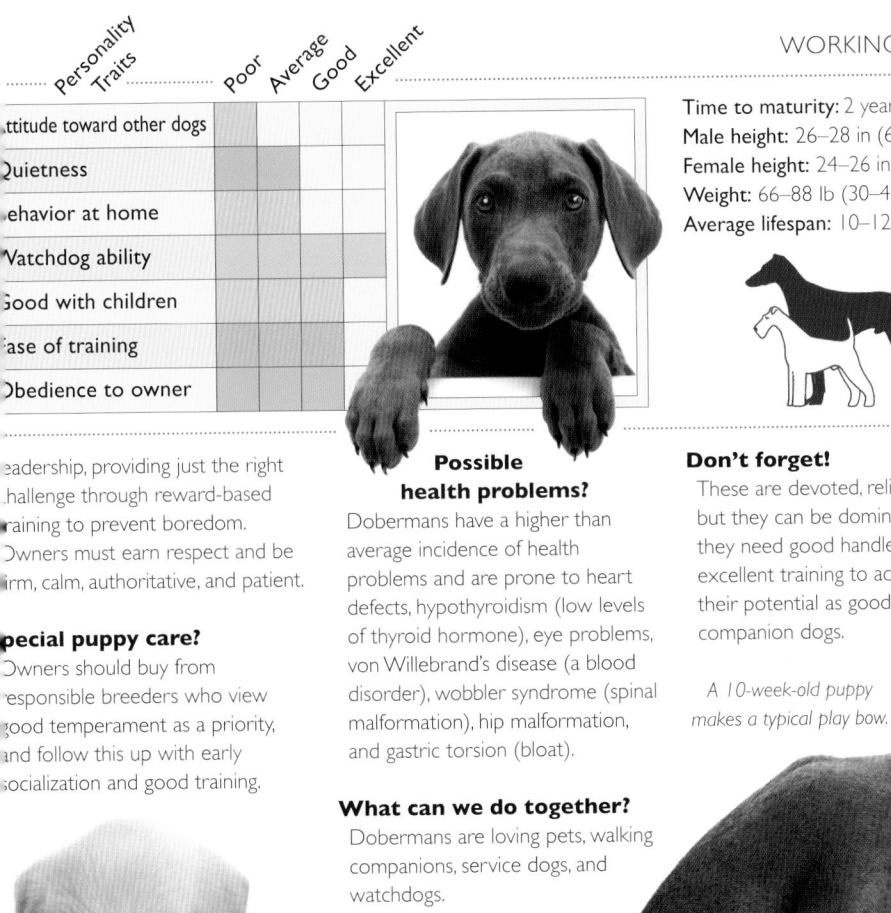

Time to maturity: 2 years
Male height: 26–28 in (66–71 cm)
Female height: 24–26 in (61–66 cm)
Weight: 66–88 lb (30–40 kg)
Average lifespan: 10–12 years

...eadership, providing just the right ...hallenge through reward-based ...raining to prevent boredom. Owners must earn respect and be ...irm, calm, authoritative, and patient.

...pecial puppy care?
Owners should buy from ...responsible breeders who view ...ood temperament as a priority, ...nd follow this up with early ...socialization and good training.

Possible health problems?
Dobermans have a higher than average incidence of health problems and are prone to heart defects, hypothyroidism (low levels of thyroid hormone), eye problems, von Willebrand's disease (a blood disorder), wobbler syndrome (spinal malformation), hip malformation, and gastric torsion (bloat).

What can we do together?
Dobermans are loving pets, walking companions, service dogs, and watchdogs.

● *Playing with other dogs will boost confidence.*

Don't forget!
These are devoted, reliable dogs, but they can be dominant, so they need good handlers and excellent training to achieve their potential as good companion dogs.

A 10-week-old puppy makes a typical play bow.

Irish Setter Other names: Red Setter

This breed was developed in 18th-century Ireland by crossing Spaniels, Setters, and Retrievers for use as working dogs. Originally red and white, the beautiful coat developed into its present chestnut red during the 19th century. Irish Setter popularity grew with their introduction to the U.S. and as their capabilities as hunting dogs, with tireless staying power, became evident. Early use in falconry for marking game birds later evolved into modern hunting practices, and they were trained as sporting dogs. Irish Setters a fun-loving and good tempered. Their racy lines and glamorous silky coats have ensured their popularity as beautiful dogs that fit well into family life. Puppi can be excitable, and in the wrong hands, this big a boisterous personality may cause problems. Well trained, and with their boundless energy firmly focused through obedience, they have eye-catching beauty, are great companion dogs a ideal family pets.

Color choices?

The color is chestnut to mahogany red, with white on chest, throat, chin or toes allowed.

How much grooming?

The long, silky coat needs moderate care. The undercoat is thicker in winter with a fine top coat, and feathers on ears, chest, legs, and tail. Brushing daily is best, while thicker parts of feathering need combing. Tying the ears back, or providing raised food bowls, helps to prevent them getting soiled with food.

● A Setter's beautiful feathered tail wags constantly.

Do they make good pets?

Slower maturing than other breeds, puppies can be too boisterous for small children. They make super pets for families prepared to spend time and effort developing their potential, but they can be exuberant. Well trained with plentiful exercise, they are great family dogs for active families.

What home suits them?

Best in country or suburban homes, Irish Setters need space, away from traffic, for off-leash running. Well-fenced, large yards are essential. They adapt to city environments, but only if they are well exercised regularly.

What type of owner?

Owners need to be patient with these slow-maturing, exuberant dogs, as they are not particularly obedient. Firmness, lots of exercise, and consistent training are necessary to cope with their clown-like personalities. Irish Setters need constant company or they can become neurotic and destructive. They should not be left at home alone—they thrive on company.

How much exercise and stimulation?

An active breed, puppies are a re handful, needing plenty of exercise with long daily walks, and off-leash running. Working-stock Irish Setters can be more active than show-bred stock. Lack of activity and mental stimulation causes boredom, which may lead to high levels of destructive behavior.

Friendly with other pets?

Wonderful family dogs, when socialized and trained, they get along well with children, other dog and pets, and are happy greeting visitors to their home. The only problem may be their energy and enthusiasm for play, which is too boisterous for children and may overwhelm small household pets.

Is puppy training easy?

Irish Setters have a reputation for being difficult in training. They

Personality Traits	Poor	Average	Good	Excellent
Attitude toward other dogs			■	
Quietness		■		
Behavior at home		■		
Watchdog ability		■		
Good with children			■	
Ease of training		■		
Obedience to owner	■			

Time to maturity: 2.5–3 years
Male height: 26–28 in (66–71 cm)
Female height: 24–26 in (61–66 cm)
Weight: 55–75 lb (25–34 kg)
Average lifespan: 12–14 years

...naturally work ahead of owners as working retrievers, and often play "deaf"; positive reinforcement with good recalls works best. Eager to please and highly intelligent, they thrive on stimulation derived from walking and companionship. Giving them "jobs" to do works well and makes training fun.

Special puppy care?

Puppies demand a lot of commit-ment, as they need com-pany and patient training. Successful training may take longer than with other breeds. Walking reduces energy levels, but build up exercise gradually to avoid damaging young bones and joints.

Possible health problems?

Generally healthy, but Irish Setters can suffer from hip dysplasia (malformation), eye problems, epilepsy, cancer, hypothyroidism (lack of thyroid hormone), gastric torsion (bloat), von Willebrand's disease (a blood-clotting disorder), and intestinal problems.

Large dogs

What can we do together?

These dogs enjoy hunting, and companionable walking and hiking.

Don't forget!

Not for owners wanting instantly obedient puppies, as training takes time and patience. Expect to find mud and leaves brought indoors on their paws and coats.

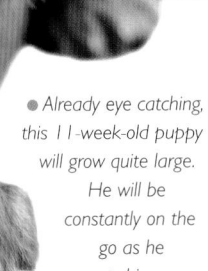

● Already eye catching, this 11-week-old puppy will grow quite large. He will be constantly on the go as he gets bigger.

Akita
Other names: Japanese Akita, Akita Inu

Akitas are the largest of three Japanese spitz breeds developed in the Akita prefecture on the island of Honshu. Their ancestors were medium-sized hunting dogs; later they were used for dog fighting and this dominant strain remains in their character. Facing near extinction during the First World War, interest in Akitas increased in recognition of their significance as part of Japan's national heritage, and was spurred by the introduction of new gene pools to America. American and Japanese Akita bloodlines have now diverged so much that they are recognized as two different breeds in Europe (Akita and Japanese Akita-Inu). Akitas are impressively powerful, magnificent, and dignified animals with strong characters and a natural watchdog ability. They make excellent pets for people who enjoy close relationships with powerful dogs, but owners must be very experienced and confident in handling them.

Color choices?
American Akitas are usually white, red, black, silver, gray, pinto (white and another color) or brindle, with or without black masks. Japanese Akitas must be red, fawn, sesame, brindle or white, without black masks on the face.

● Powerful and independent, Akitas are great dogs when trained well, but they are not the right choice for a first-time owner.

How much grooming?
The thick, coarse coat needs thorough brushing twice weekly. The twice-yearly heavy seasonal molt needs daily grooming to remove dead hair from the coat.

Do they make good pets?
Akitas are strong, independent, dominant, and powerful, usually aloof with strangers, but affectionate in a family context. Akitas are not ideal around children, because their low tolerance of teasing or rough handling makes the risks too great.

What home suits them?
These puppies are better in country or suburban homes because they require space and a secure yard. Close supervision is needed near livestock.

What type of owner?
Owners need to be very experienced with handling large, dominant, powerful dogs. They need dedication to own dogs as challenging as this, and must spend plenty of time socializing, training, and exercising their Akita. Owners must be committed to companionship with them, and prevent them from becoming bored or they will be destructive.

How much exercise and stimulation?
Akitas need a minimum of two to three hours of daily exercise, preferably much more. Off-leash walking is definitely risky near livestock, and challenges from other dogs met by chance may cause Akitas to respond aggressively.

Friendly with other pets?
Akitas are highly dominant unless they are with the opposite sex of their own breed; same gender rivalry can be dangerous. They were originally bred to live and work alone or in pairs. Other small pets will definitely be at risk from the Akita's strong prey drive.

Is puppy training easy?
This breed has natural dominance and is very strong-minded, so training will be very difficult. It must start early, and socialization even earlier. Bullying will not work— owners must be very patient and firm, using reward-based guidance to motivate these puppies to respond well. Badly trained Akitas are a liability and may cause legal problems, as some countries list them as a dangerous breed.

Special puppy care?
Start training early, and make sure this puppy responds well and does

Personality Traits	Poor	Average	Good	Excellent
Attitude toward other dogs				
Quietness				
Behavior at home				
Watchdog ability				
Good with children				
Ease of training				
Obedience to owner				

Time to maturity: 2.5 years
Male height: 26–28 in (66–71 cm)
Female height: 24–26 in (61–66 cm)
Weight: 80–130 lb (36–59 kg)
Average lifespan: 10–12 years

not get bored. Good discipline may only be possible through constant supervision, consistency, and unwavering attention.

Possible health problems?

Akitas suffer from a wide range of health problems, but two significant ones are pseudohyperkalemia (a rise in potassium levels) and immune sensitivity to chemicals in vaccinations, drugs, anesthetics, and insecticides. Owners contemplating this breed should question breeders closely and research the literature on other conditions that affect Akitas.

● *Docile-looking teddy bears at just 7 weeks. These dogs are described in Japan as "tender in heart and mighty in strength."*

What can we do together?

Today, Akitas participate in obedience trials, good citizen programs, tracking trials, agility competitions, weight pulling, hunting, and showing. Some have also been used as therapy dogs.

Don't forget!

Unsuitable for novices, Akitas should only be considered by experienced owners.

Large dogs

Greater Swiss Mountain Dog

Greater Swiss Mountain Dogs are the oldest and largest of all mountain dogs. They are thought to have developed from breeding indigenous dogs with imported Mastiffs. Large and heavy boned, their physical strength made them ideal dogs for Alpine farmers, and they were used for cattle herding, hunting, and as heavy-duty draft dogs by farmers who needed a substitute for horses to pull carts and wagons.

They were believed to have died out in the 19th century when mechanization increasingly made the redundant, but sufficient stock was found in 1900 t resurrect the breed and rescue it from extinction. GSMDs are versatile, outgoing, eager to please, eas trained, and good watchdogs—although not territorial. Loyal, gentle, and exceptionally good wit children, they are relatively healthy compared to other large breeds. They make great family dogs, bu size and exercise needs render them unsuitable for many family homes.

Color choices?

There is only one color combination: tricolor coats of black, with symmetrical markings of tan/rust and white.

These gentle giants enjoy being at the heart of a loving family.

How much grooming?

The short, double, waterproof coat, which comes in varying degrees of thickness, is less oily than other breeds, and smells less. GSMDs molt all year, with copious seasonal shedding twice a year. They require regular brushing using a rubber curry comb and a heavy-duty brush, with more grooming during heavier shedding.

Do they make good pets?

These are happy dogs with an enthusiastic nature. They are sociable, active, calm, and dignified. They love people and are particularly good with children. They enjoy being part of a family provided that the family is active and enjoys exercise as much as the dog does.

What home suits them?

This breed will not suit many modern homes because they are simply too big. They need suburban homes or farms with space for plenty of exercise, or working pastimes, to keep them happy.

What type of owner?

GSMDs are attentive, alert, and active, and need owners who respect these qualities, and keep them gainfully employed in stimulating activities.

How much exercise and stimulation?

Plenty of exercise and stimulation is needed, usually 3–6 miles (5–10 km) daily spread over two or thre walks. These are natural working dogs that enjoy the stimulation of performing farm or carting tasks.

Friendly with other pets?

With very low aggression and a reluctance to bite, GSMDs are usually very accepting of other do and household pets. However, as with any breed, early socializing and sensible introductions to othe animals will be necessary.

Is puppy training easy?

Training should use patient, reliabl training techniques to teach manners and physical self-control. Owners must build trust through positive reinforcement, and avoid harsh methods. GSMDs can be stubborn and determined, and ma be boisterous as youngsters; they should be socialized early, and provided with suitable activities as part of training.

Special puppy care?

Some female puppies (but occasionally males, too) are

Personality Traits	Poor	Average	Good	Excellent
Attitude toward other dogs				
Quietness				
Behavior at home				
Watchdog ability				
Good with children				
Ease of training				
Obedience to owner				

Time to maturity: 2–3 years
Male height: 25.5–28.5 in (65–72 cm)
Female height: 23.5–27 in (60–69 cm)
Weight: 105–140 lb (48–64 kg)
Average lifespan: 10–12 years

difficult to housetrain, and lack bladder control until six months, or older. They tend to eat or lick anything, even if inedible, and need supervising to prevent them eating something harmful.

Possible health problems?

Longer living than some larger breeds, GSMDs can suffer from hip and elbow dysplasia (malformation), gastric torsion (bloat), spleen disorders, epilepsy, eye problems, and osteochondrosis (degenerative joint disease).

What can we do together?

This puppy prefers a job to do, and most owners will enjoy participating with them in agility, carting, tracking, herding trials, obedience, weight-pulling, walking, hiking and backpacking. They are also used as drovers, draft, and rescue dogs.

Don't forget!

With a limited gene pool due to low breeding numbers, potential owners should buy from reputable breeders who check for health problems.

● *Looking forward to a future as a loyal family companion, this 6-month-old puppy is already learning some basic skills in a "Down."*

Large dogs

Newfoundland

Newfies were originally bred by working fisherman in Newfoundland, Canada. Their exact origin is unknown, but they are thought to descend from Scandinavian "bear dogs" imported into Canada by immigrants. Exceptional and powerful water dogs, braving rough ocean waves and storm tides, their importance for carrying ship's lines and fishing nets ashore was exceptional, as was their legendary ability to save human lives at sea. They were valuable working dogs on ships, and so their popularity spread. In England, their fame was bolstered by Sir Edwin Landseer, who featured them in his paintings. Sweet-tempered, gentle, friendly, and very loyal family pets, these huge dogs are expensive to feed, tend to drool, need a lot of space, and shed copiously everywhere. They are unsuitable for many families as their size alone poses a problem. These puppies need space, constant company and loving, easygoing owners.

Color choices?

Available colors are black or brown, with white splashes on chest, toes, and tail tip. The only bicolor choice (recognized as a separate breed in Europe) is "Landseer"—white with black markings, the black head has a narrow white blaze, saddle, rump, and upper tail.

How much grooming?

Newfies have flat, coarse, oily, water-resistant coats, with dense undercoats. Regular (twice weekly) brushing and grooming right down to the skin is needed, removing accumulations of mats in undercoats. Extra grooming is needed during times of extreme molting twice a year.

Do they make good pets?

The Newfie's temperament is near perfect, and his mellow disposition makes him one of the kindest dogs. Very affectionate, deeply attached to families, they adore children and capable of keeping them safe, but not territorial. Children must not

● These two fine specimens at 9 years (left) and 19 months are examples of the only bicolor choice available. The Landseer was named after Sir Edwin Landseer, a fashionable London painter.

take advantage of their gentle nature or be allowed to ride on this puppy, as it causes back problems.

What home suits them?

These are huge dogs and are only suitable for larger homes with well-fenced yards. Puppies need space to accommodate their giant size when fully grown and, because of the heavy, hot coat, cool areas to rest, even in winter.

What type of owner?

Newfies want to be part of the family, and owners must commit to spending time and attention on exercise and grooming. Ideal for including in family activities and trustworthy with children, they do need supervising with toddlers to prevent accidental injury. Unsuitable for owners who can't tolerate a mess indoors. Conscientious owners who groom regularly and provide suitable accommodations are best.

How much exercise and stimulation?

Moderate exercise is needed. Newfies are not active and an hour's walk a day is ideal, with opportunities for swimming. Puppies under 12 months should not be overexercised to avoid damage to young bones and joints.

Friendly with other pets?

Pleasant and docile, with early socialization and proper introductions Newfies live successfully with other household

Personality Traits	Poor	Average	Good	Excellent
Attitude toward other dogs				
Quietness				
Behavior at home				
Watchdog ability				
Good with children				
Ease of training				
Obedience to owner				

Time to maturity: 2.5 years
Male height: 27–29 in (69–73.5 cm)
Female height: 25–27 in (63.5–69 cm)
Weight: 110–150 lb (50–68 kg)
Average lifespan: 8–10 years

pets. Be careful with small pets to avoid the risk of this gentle giant treading on them.

puppy training easy?

Newfies reach emotional maturity around the age of two, and are sensitive and gentle. Training must start early because of their size, but is very easy. Firmness, patience, and positive reinforcement and encouragement work best.

pecial puppy care?

Puppies should be trained early to learn good behaviors and obedience in readiness for maturity.

Owners who lack physical strength, should leash-train them early to avoid being dragged along by an unruly adult.

Possible health problems?

Due to their size, the risk of hip, elbow, and other joint problems is higher. Newfies also suffer from heart disease, lip fold infections, pulmonic stenosis, gastric torsion, and eye problems.

What can we do together?

Loyal, devoted, and playful companions, they also enjoy carting (pulling a wheeled carriage) and swimming.

Don't forget!

Owners must give careful thought to how this puppy will be housed when fully grown.

● *Already quite large at 12 weeks, these three will need kind, patient owners who will provide the space they need to grow and develop.*

Large dogs

Greyhound
Other names: English Greyhound

Considered the oldest breed in the world, Greyhounds are sighthounds and they were used for royal sports as early as ancient Egyptian times. Brought to Britain by the Phoenicians, their name is probably derived from "Greek hound." Greyhounds were popular with the aristocracy, and frequently appear on the crests of many noble families. Used for competitive sports such as hare coursing and speed running, they achieve a top speed of 45 mph (72 km/h). Greyhound racing, popular since 1920, continues today, although mechanical hares are used now. Despite their aptitude for running and their sporting pedigree, Greyhounds enjoy a relatively sedentary life, preferring to be curled up on the so rather than actively running around. Their gentle, affectionate nature and adaptability make them ide family dogs. It is often possible to rehom 3- to 5-year-olds who have been retire from track life.

Color choices?

There are around 30 recognized colors, all variations of white, black, fawn, red, brindle, and blue, either as solid colors or combinations.

How much grooming?

The single, fine coat needs regular brushing with a hound glove to remove dead hair. After grooming, the coat should look clean, smell fresh, and lie flat against the body.

Do they make good pets?

Greyhounds are loving, quiet, and loyal, enjoying their owners' or other dogs' company. Gentle and loving with children, they appreciate respect and prefer quiet lives. Children must learn to treat them kindly, although Greyhounds can be boisterous as youngsters. Greyhounds suffer from separation anxiety, and may be happier with another dog to share their days.

What home suits them?

Suburban or country homes suit Greyhounds equally well, with space to run off-leash daily. They are

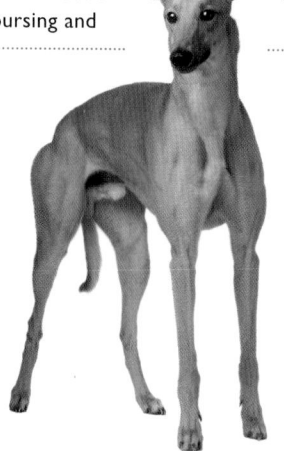

● *Well-muscled and powerful, this young dog is approaching maturity.*

happiest lying in the warm weather, sleeping up to 18 hours, and don't need much space, often adapting to apartment living, provided that they have daily exercise. High, secure fencing is necessary to prevent them escaping.

What type of owner?

Gentle, sensitive owners who appreciate quiet, friendly, and extremely loyal dogs will find these puppies calm, good-natured companions. Giving retired racing Greyhounds a second chance brings a sense of reward and pleasure. Owners who are patien sensitive, and firm with training ar best suited to Greyhounds.

How much exercise and stimulation?

Greyhounds do not need miles of walking; they need short, sharp sprints rather than endurance running. They need to expend their energy, and youngsters need mental stimulation because they can be hyperactive and destructive. Leash-walking and fre running in enclosed spaces is ideal

Friendly with other pets?

Some Greyhounds have high prey drives, and wear muzzles when out, as they may chase small animals and cats, but this depends on the individual dog. Others live happily with other family pets, but all need socializing and introducing properly to prevent problems. Greyhound rescues will advise owners on this.

Personality Traits	Poor	Average	Good	Excellent
Attitude toward other dogs				
Quietness				
Behavior at home				
Watchdog ability				
Good with children				
Ease of training				
Obedience to owner				

Time to maturity: 2 years
Male height: 28–30 in (71–76 cm)
Female height: 27–28 in (69–71 cm)
Weight: 60–70 lb (27–32 kg)
Average lifespan: 10–13 years

nding his feet at 6 weeks.

Is puppy training easy?

Greyhounds are moderately easy to train, but need firm, gentle, and sensitive training, as they are not naturally obedient. Teaching a good recall is essential for off-leash running, but with patience and time they are ready learners and eager to please.

Special puppy care?

Puppies feel the cold because their coat/skin is thin, with lean body fat, and they should wear coats in cold weather. Be cautious around small animals, as they sometimes chase them. Puppy hyperactivity needs careful management to prevent injuries to skin or bones from jumping and running.

Possible health problems?

Hereditary illness is a low risk, and they may suffer from gastric torsion (bloat), eye problems,

● *A family favorite and a gentle, dependable companion.*

skin sores from lying on hard bedding or floors, and inability to metabolize anesthetics or chemical products used to treat parasites. Fractures and injuries from running can also be a potential risk.

What can we do together?

Greyhounds are gentle, loyal companions and enjoy racing and hunting, or just sitting with you.

Large dogs

● *Play will be important for young puppies like this.*

Don't forget!

Consider giving a home to a retired Greyhound—they can make delightful pets. Teaching a good recall will be important.

Mastiff *Other names: English Mastiff*

Historically, "Mastiff" was a name given to any large heavy dog, but this breed is thought to be of Old English origin from pre-Medieval times. Julius Caesar describes them as fighting against his Roman legions when he invaded Britain in 55 BC. Later they served as guard dogs on the estates of the noble class. The breed almost disappeared in the early 20th century, but American enthusiasts managed to restore them as popular family dogs. Today's Mastiff is one of the heaviest breeds, but is most definitely a gentle giant. Although still retaining their territorial instinct for protecting the home and family, Mastiffs are calm, dignified, and very loving. Tending to be big "softies" most of the time, they love to please and to spend time with their owner. With good training and socialization, Mastiffs are peaceful, gentle, and affectionate. Their size, however, may work against them, as they need plenty of living space to be comfortable.

Color choices?
Color choices are apricot/fawn, silver/fawn, dark fawn/brindle, with black mask on ears, nose, and around eyes.

How much grooming?
This short and close-lying coat needs brushing once or twice weekly to remove dead hair, but is otherwise low maintenance.

Do they make good pets?
Good natured, calm, and loving, while also courageous and protective, Mastiffs are docile and affectionate with their families and are prized for their patience. However, their physical size alone makes them unsuitable for young children, who may be unintentionally knocked over or injured by a wag of their powerful tail.

What home suits them?
This huge dog needs space and is best suited to country or suburban life; this is not a dog for small homes or apartments. Well-fenced yards and spacious homes are suitable.

● *Adults will happily sit around enjoying company, but they need to regular exercise to keep fit.*

Don't keep this dog outside for long periods, as they prefer being near their family.

What type of owner?
Mastiffs need tolerant owners who accept that their size means more mess in the home. They are sensitive puppies, and owners must accept that companionship is a full-time commitment. This breed should be handled by physically fit and strong owners with experience handling such breeds, as dogs can easily pull their handlers over.

How much exercise and stimulation?
Too much exercise and running is not recommended while puppies are young, as this causes damage to bones and joints. Mastiffs would like to lead a couch potato life, but moderate exercise is necessary to maintain good health and to prevent laziness or obesity. Socialization is of great importance with a dog of this size.

Friendly with other pets?
These very good-natured puppies get along well with most other pets, provided that early socialization and good introductions take place. Size is a concern, as other pets could be injured in play, unintentionally knocked over. Some males can be aggressive with other males, so firm training is necessary to prevent this from occurring.

Is puppy training easy?
Mastiffs are stubborn, but sensitive and effective training of such a large dog is essential. Owners must be rigorous and firm, using short fun-filled sessions. Negative associations are likely to upset them, so plenty of praise and rewards for good behavior work best.

Personality Traits	Poor	Average	Good	Excellent
Attitude toward other dogs				
Quietness				
Behavior at home				
Watchdog ability				
Good with children				
Ease of training				
Obedience to owner				

Time to maturity: 2.5 years
Male height: 29.5–32 in (75–82 cm)
Female height: 27.5–30 in (70–76 cm)
Weight: 175–198 lb (79–90 kg)
Average lifespan: 8–10 years

Special puppy care?

Mastiffs are prone to calluses, arthritis, and hygroma (inflammatory swellings on joints), so soft surfaces for sleeping should be provided. Special diets are needed for puppies to ensure they maintain the correct growth rate, and do not become obese.

Possible health problems?

Not the hardiest or longest living breed, Mastiffs can suffer from hip dysplasia (malformation), gastric problems (bloat), heart disease, ligament ruptures, arthritis, hypothyroidism (low thyroid hormone levels), eye problems, obesity, and allergies.

● *Encouraging activity using suitable toys and providing a healthy diet will prevent puppies from becoming overweight.*

What can we do together?

Mastiffs are ideal as loving companions and vigilant watchdogs.

Don't forget!

Given the size of this puppy, veterinary and food bills will all be high to maintain good health. Mastiffs are unsuitable dogs for owners who cannot cope with drooling, snoring, and flatulence, which all comes on a large scale because of their size.

St. Bernard
Other names: Alpine Mastiff

In the Great St. Bernard Pass that links Switzerland and Italy, St. Bernards became famous for saving the lives of people trapped in snow high in the mountains. Resident at St. Bernard's Hospice in the Swiss Alps from the 17th century, they trained as pack dogs and guide dogs, rescuing lost travelers and finding avalanche victims. Originally, Saints were smooth-coated, but rough coats developed with the introduction of Newfoundland crossing to reduce inbreeding problems. The rough-coated variety is the most common today. Saints are devoted companions, but owners must realize that they are taking on one of the heaviest and strongest dogs in the world. This peace-loving, calm, gentle, and friendly dog is sociable, devoted to his family, and adores children but his size and the quantity of good-quality food he needs is enough to put off the average family owner. However, they make fantastic pets in the right home.

Color choices?

Available colors are red and white. Red ranges through shades of orange, mahogany brindle, and red brindle, with white markings on muzzle, head, collar, chest, legs, and tail tip. Black shading appears on face and ears, with ticking and spots.

How much grooming?

Rough-haired varieties have dense, flat-lying coats that need energetic daily brushing through to the skin. Poor brushing leaves dead hair underneath the top coat that is liable to form mats. Smooth-coats need brushing weekly. Saints shed copiously and extra grooming is needed during molting.

Do they make good pets?

Fantastic dogs, despite their huge size, Saints are extremely gentle and friendly, and are exceptionally tolerant of and careful with children. They make ideal family pets, provided that they are cared for with correct feeding and exercise. They are devoted to their owners, and become distressed and

● *Growing completed, this gentle giant is a beautiful specimen of a mature dog.*

destructive if left alone for long periods.

What home suits them?

Not recommended for apartment living, they need open space. They must be allowed sufficient room to move and lie down. When they settle down indoors, they rarely move far from their master's feet. Saints are happiest in larger homes, with well-fenced yards to keep them secure.

What type of owner?

Owners need to give time and attention and include Saints in family activities, and must be tolerant of drooling and copious hair shed during molting. Saints are happiest in family company and are trustworthy with children.

How much exercise and stimulation?

Due to their huge size and fast growth rate, it is important that they receive the right amount of exercise and proper food or they could suffer bone deterioration. Adults are satisfied with a 2 mile (3 km) walk daily, but puppy exercise should be limited to frequent short walks until the age of two.

Friendly with other pets?

Saints need socializing with other pets and visitors to their home to prevent any aggressive tendencies. Generally, they get along well with other pets provided that proper introductions are made, but care is needed to prevent them from treading on smaller pets.

Personality Traits	Poor	Average	Good	Excellent
Attitude toward other dogs				
Quietness				
Behavior at home				
Watchdog ability				
Good with children				
Ease of training				
Obedience to owner				

Time to maturity: 2–3 years
Male height: 28–36 in (71–91 cm)
Female height: 26–36 in (66–91 cm)
Weight: 110–200 lb (50–91 kg)
Average lifespan: 8–10 years

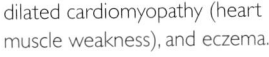

puppy training easy?

Their enormous adult size, and the need to keep adults under control, demands proper training, which must start early. Control must be asserted from the start. Owners should be firm, patient, and consistent, as puppies are willing to learn but are slow to respond.

special puppy care?

Limit the length of walks for a puppy to prevent damage to young bones and joints.

possible health problems?

Due to fast growth and heavy weight, Saints need correct feeding or health can suffer. Major health concerns are hip and elbow dysplasia (malformation), gastric torsion, cancer, eye problems, epilepsy, dilated cardiomyopathy (heart muscle weakness), and eczema.

What can we do together?

Saints are excellent companion dogs, devoted to their family, but not a great deal else!

Don't forget!

They are expensive to keep, should never be left alone, but are still amazing companion dogs.

Large dogs

At 9 weeks, this puppy will be happiest being at the heart of family life.

● *The circumference of puppies' necks will need regular monthly checking since they will need a bigger collar as they grow and put on weight..*

Scottish Deerhound

Deerhounds, even in early Celtic times, were highly prized by Scottish chieftains who exploited their power, speed, and stamina for coursing or tracking red deer. Deerhounds have been used in Australia for hunting kangaroo and wild boar, and in North America for hunting wolves. Their ancestors were sporting dogs, used by both landowners and poachers, who appreciated their fast, silent hunting skills. As Scottish clans broke up and hunting practices changed, there was less need for the Deerhound's skills, but enthusiasts of the breed helped ensure their survival by developing an interest in showing them. The Deerhound's powerful body can cover rough terrain at tremendous speed, and they need plenty of space to exercise for their health and well being. Although too big for the average home, these dogs are gentle, calm, dignified, well-mannered (maybe not as puppies), and devoted to their owners.

Color choices?
Historically, Deerhounds were available in blue, brindle, fawn, gray, red, and yellow. Modern dogs are now usually found in varying shades of gray, with a little white on the chest, toes, and tail tip.

How much grooming?
The harsh, wiry coat is relatively easy to care for, but it still needs to be brushed regularly, using a slicker brush and metal comb to remove tangles and dead hair. Underbody and facial hair is best tended gently with a comb. Bathing is needed infrequently.

Do they make good pets?
This is an attractive dog temperamentally: obedient, biddable, rarely boisterous, quiet, and trustworthy. Deerhounds tend to attach themselves to one person and are extremely faithful to them. They are very trusting, never aggressive, and love children—although puppies may be too boisterous for toddlers. Time commitments in maintaining regular exercise for this active dog

● Most owners today would agree with Sir Walter Scott, who said about his own Deerhound, Maida, that they are "the most perfect creature of heaven."

may need to be a consideration for parents with young children.

What home suits them?
Deerhounds should have access to well-fenced (fencing at least 6 ft/2 m high), large yards for free play and running, with plenty of exercise space available close by for longer off-leash runs. Puppies may be destructive if energy levels are high and their exercise needs are not met. They do not tolerate heat well, so keep this in mind during warmer months.

What type of owner?
This breed suits owners who want a devoted companion, are prepared to walk long distances, and are happy to sacrifice their sofa for rests in between. These are gentle dogs, happiest with patient, gentle, easy-going owners who can expect unswerving loyalty and the close scrutiny of a warm, honest gaze in return.

How much exercise and stimulation?
Long walks of at least an hour, preferably over several miles, which should include off-leash running. Regional clubs organize lure coursing, which provides opportunities for exercising Deerhounds to satisfy their need to run free and fast.

Friendly with other pets?
Deerhounds are very friendly, especially with other sighthounds and most household pets, if well socialized as a puppy. However, supervision may be needed with unknown pets as they have a

Personality Traits	Poor	Average	Good	Excellent
Attitude toward other dogs				
Quietness				
Behavior at home				
Watchdog ability				
Good with children				
Ease of training				
Obedience to owner				

Time to maturity: 2.5 years
Male height: 30–32 in (76–81 cm)
Female height: 28–30 in (71–76 cm)
Weight: 80–120 lb (36–54 kg)
Average lifespan: 8–11 years

strong chase instinct and are very fast. The neighbor's cat may be seen as fair game for a chase.

puppy training easy?

Training should be calm, consistent, and gentle to achieve the best from Deerhounds; they are the most trainable of sighthounds, although the degree of trainablilty may not satisfy owners with an interest in obedience competitions. Their eagerness to please and quickness to learn are a pleasure for owners wanting a sweet-natured companion.

Special puppy care?

Young puppies should not be overexercised too early, as their young bones and joints may be susceptible to injury. Starting to teach a recall early is essential, as these dogs love to run and may need to be reminded how far they can venture away from their owner when out and about.

Possible health problems?

The most serious problems this breed experiences are heart disease, osteosarcoma (bone cancer), gastric torsion (bloat), liver shunt (insufficient blood supply), hip dysplasia (malformation), and eye problems.

What can we do together?

Deerhounds are mainly ideal as companion pets, but owners may enjoy lure coursing or long walks with them.

Don't forget!

Buy from a reputable breeder who has completed any necessary health checks on their stock, especially in relation to heart disease. Be careful when exercising puppies, as immature bones are at risk of injury if they are overexercised.

● *Patient and loyal, these puppies want to be close to their owner, and are unhappy if left alone.*

Great Dane
Other names: Danish Hound, German Mastiff

These magnificent, noble dogs are German in origin, and are often called the "Apollo of dogs" because of their huge size and majestic bearing. One of several large Mastiff-type hunting dogs, Danes were bred to run down and fight wild boar. English nobility later appreciated their abilities and elegant style, and they became popular carriage dogs. Subsequently, they were also found useful for guarding South African gold mines, which they did admirably. Today's Great Dane continues to display a superior but gentle, countenance and is probably the most peace-loving of Mastiff breeds, with a kind, affectionate, sensitive nature. They are good with children, but their size—some can weigh as much as a person does—does make the risk of injury to toddlers a possibility. If owners commit time to training and exercising them, however, and have sufficient home and yard space, these sociable family dogs will thrive on human company.

Color choices?
Acceptable show colors are fawn with black mask, brindle, blue, black, harlequin (irregular patches of black and gray on white), and Boston (black or blue specific body patterns with white shirt front and socks). Merle or other advertised "rare" coloring is unacceptable, and sometimes occurs in conjunction with deafness.

How much grooming?
Danes have easy-care coats, requiring occasional brushing with a hound glove or firm brush over their smooth, short coat to remove any hair shed.

Do they make good pets?
Not all families appreciate Danes, because youngsters under three years old are boisterous and clumsy, and small children or frail elderly may be knocked over or accidentally trodden on. However, with good early socialization, Danes make sensitive, affectionate, and peace-loving companions for appreciative families.

● *The color of this magnificent Great Dane is called harlequin.*

What home suits them?
Large and spacious homes with high-fenced, large yards will meet a Dane's needs. Apartments or small homes are definitely unsuitable, because these dogs need space.

What type of owner?
Owners need physical strength and reasonable experience to deal with Danes, who can be stubborn and strong-willed. They are, however, sensitive, gentle, and kind and owners must spend time with these puppies, and be patient and confident in handling them.

How much exercise and stimulation?
Moderate exercise is needed, and for owners with sufficient land, Danes may exercise themselves. Some walking should be off-leash for free running, and exercise and stimulation can include agility training. Puppies under 18 months should have limited exercise because their immature bones and joints are at risk of damage.

Friendly with other pets?
Danes are friendly with other household pets, provided that early socialization occurs, and that introductions are done properly. Their size and strength are a drawback, because of the risk that they may knock over other pets, or tread on them unintentionally. They are not usually aggressive, unless another pet irritates them.

Is puppy training easy?
These puppies are remarkably tractable, and responsive to commands, but early training is best. Danes should be firmly

Personality Traits	Poor	Average	Good	Excellent
Attitude toward other dogs				
Quietness				
Behavior at home				
Watchdog ability				
Good with children				
Ease of training				
Obedience to owner				

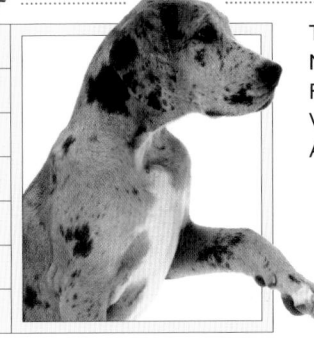

Time to maturity: 2.5 years
Male height: 30–34 in (76–86 cm)
Female height: 28–32 in (71–81 cm)
Weight: 100–132 lb (45–60 kg)
Average lifespan: 6–8 years

handled, and treated with patience, kindness, and positive reinforcement. Encouragement and praise work best; harsh, overbearing methods do not. It is important to prevent puppies from jumping up or sitting on people's laps—they may still expect it when fully grown!

Special puppy care?
Puppies grow fast and get large; do not overexercise them because of risks to their growing joints. They need correct feeding at every stage, taking account of their eventual

size and correct development. Soft bedding prevents painful sores from occurring on joints.

Possible health problems?
Danes are not long-lived dogs, and may suffer from gastric torsion (bloat), hip/elbow dysplasia (dislocation), tumors, hypothyroidism (lack of thyroid hormone), von Willebrand's disease (a blood disorder), heart disease (breeders can check this prior to homing), and sometimes damaged tails from knocks. Merle-colored Danes can suffer from deafness and blindness.

What can we do together?
Danes and their owners may enjoy agility and flyball, and they make good walking companions.

Don't forget!
Buy from reputable breeders with longer-living stock, and choose recognized colors, not merle colors which carry health risks.

● *This litter of 5-week-old puppies shows the range of colors available for owners to choose from.*

Large dogs

Designer dogs

Designer dogs have pure-breed ancestry from two pedigree parents, but they are cross breeds and cannot be registered with Kennel Clubs. Many owners find them loveable, but determining adult form in terms of eventual size, health, and coat quality can be difficult when choosing puppies. Both parent breeds should appeal to prospective owners before a choice is made.

Yorkiepoo

Other names: Yo-Yopoo, Yorkapoo, Yoodle

Time to maturity: 18 months
Male height: 7–15 in (18–38 cm)
Female height: 7–15 in (18–38 cm)
Weight: 4–14 lb (2–6 kg)
Average lifespan: 10–15 years

A recent addition to designer selections, Yorkshire Terrier/Poodle mixes appeared in the early 2000s. They have affectionate dispositions and hypoallergenic coats.

Personality Traits	Poor	Average	Good	E
Attitude toward other dogs				
Quietness				
Behavior at home				
Watchdog ability				
Good with children				
Ease of training				
Obedience to owner				

Color choices?

Colors vary from tan to black to white and brown.

How much grooming?

Yorkiepoos have smooth, fine coats of silky, wavy hair that requires brushing daily to keep it free of mats and tangles. Most coats are hypoallergenic, but not all.

Do they make good pets?

They are very confident, they love people, and are generally fun-loving and willing to play. Not suitable for young children, Yorkiepoos make excellent companions for older children or the elderly. Barking is a favorite hobby, but can be stopped with training.

What home suits them?

The small size lends itself to apartments and small homes.

How much exercise and stimulation?

Short daily walks and play sessions suffice, but they can go longer as they have plenty of energy.

Is puppy training easy?

Yorkiepoos are highly intelligent, quick learners so they need early training. They excel in agility, obedience, therapy dog training, and enjoy performing tricks. Training must be sensitive and use positive reinforcement, as strict methods only make them stubborn.

Possible health problems?

Epilepsy, patellar luxation (kneecap dislocation), liver shunt, Legg-Perthes syndrome (hip deformity), hypothyroidism (low thyroid levels), Addison's disease (an endocrine disorder), and atopic dermatitis (skin allergy) are all possible.

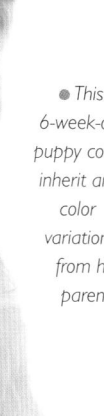

● This 6-week-c puppy co inherit ar color variation from h paren

Morkie
Other names: Yorktese, Malkie

Time to maturity: 2 years
Male height: 8–12 in (20–30 cm)
Female height: 8–12 in (20–30 cm)
Weight: 3–10 lb (1.5–4.5 kg)
Average lifespan: 12–15 years

Personality Traits	Poor	Average	Good	Excellent
Attitude toward other dogs				
Quietness				
Behavior at home				
Watchdog ability				
Good with children				
Ease of training				
Obedience to owner				

This Maltese/Yorkie mix can exhibit a wide variety of looks and personality traits. Early training develops their potential as delightful and obedient companions.

Color choices?

Most are black and tan but apricot, white, brown, and Maltese coloring are also seen.

How much grooming?

Coats are long, very soft, and straight. They need brushing two or three times weekly, and hair around the eyes should be cleaned. Ears are dropped or erect, and need cleaning weekly.

Do they make good pets?

Loyal and loving, but sometimes bossy, this mix of two breed personalities can be difficult to predict. They should not be spoiled or overindulged. They often crave attention and may suffer from separation anxiety. They are usually ideal for the elderly, provided that they can be exercised adequately.

What home suits them?

Morkies usually adapt well to apartment living.

● *Be careful with young puppies, as they are vulnerable to injury if dropped.*

How much exercise and stimulation?

Highly energetic, Morkies love playing, running, and some walking, and need exercise to prevent boredom, obesity, and poor health. Socialization brings out their best, encouraging friendliness to strangers and other pets.

Is puppy training easy?

These puppies are intelligent and fearless, and are easy to train. But they can be stubborn, so patience is needed.

Possible health problems?

Hydrocephalus (water on the brain), patellar luxation (dislocating kneecaps), tracheal collapse (obstruction of the airway), eye problems, and heart disease can occur. Avoid obesity by correct feeding.

Looking cute and cuddly, and easy to spoil!

Cavapoo *Other names: Cavadoodle*

Time to maturity: 2 years
Male height: 8–14 in (20–36 cm)
Female height: 8–14 in (20–36 cm)
Weight: 10–18 lb (4.5–8 kg)
Average lifespan: 10–14 years

Cavapoos originated in the U.S. in 1950 by mixing Cavalier King Charles Spaniels and Poodles. Cavapoos have a gentle nature and luxurious coats.

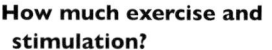

Personality Traits	Poor	Average	Good	
Attitude toward other dogs				
Quietness				
Behavior at home				
Watchdog ability				
Good with children				
Ease of training				
Obedience to owner				

Color choices?

They are usually multi-colored, but mostly light/red-brown, black, or white.

How much grooming?

The most distinctive feature is their low-shed, hypoallergenic, luxurious coat, which can be either curly or feathered. Brushing and combing is a daily commitment to remove tangles and mats, and to prevent skin problems. Professional trimming several times a year is best, as coats can form dreadlocks.

Do they make good pets?

Cavapoos are good-natured, gentle, loving, and playful with children and other pets.

They frequently demand attention, are unhappy if left on their own, but make poor watchdogs.

What home suits them?

Ideally sized for small homes with backyards or apartments, but they still need exercise. Their natural curiosity encourages jumping onto furniture.

● A puppy at 8 weeks with his mother.

How much exercise and stimulation?

Cavapoos enjoy, but do not crave exercise. They need stimulation through activity and play.

Is puppy training easy?

Highly intelligent, Cavapoos will excel at obedience if started earl[y]

Possible health problems?

Parent breeds have sever[al] health issues. Cavapoo problems include ear, e[ye] and heart disorders, hypothyroidism (low thyroid levels), syringomyelia (fluid in the spinal cord), epileps[y] hip dysplasia (malformatio[n] and von Willebrand's disease (a blo[od] disorder).

Shihpoo

Other names: Pooshih

Time to maturity: 2 years
Male height: 8–15 in (20–38 cm)
Female height: 8–15 in (20–38 cm)
Weight: 7–10 lb (3–4.5 kg)
Average lifespan: 14–17 years

This Shih Tzu/Poodle mix was bred for its companionable quality, cute looks, low-shedding coat, and small size. It is ideal as a loving domestic pet.

Personality Traits	Poor	Average	Good	Excellent
Attitude toward other dogs				
Quietness				
Behavior at home				
Watchdog ability				
Good with children				
Ease of training				
Obedience to owner				

Color choices?

Any color or combination of colors are usually available.

How much grooming?

Shihpoos' coats are long, wavy, and low-shedding. They need daily brushing and trimming as necessary. Bathing is needed only occasionally. Clean ears and eyes regularly.

Do they make good pets?

Intelligent, alert, playful, friendly, and affectionate lapdogs, they are always ready to love someone. Not ideal for small children, but they are good family companions, friendly with other pets, and courageous watchdogs, although they can be rather yappy.

What home suits them?

These small dogs will suit apartment living or homes in suburbs or the country, as long as they have company to keep them happy.

How much exercise and stimulation?

Shihpoos need moderate exercise and usually adapt well to their owners' lifestyle. They enjoy a stroll and playtime daily.

Is puppy training easy?

Very easy to train, Shihpoos are quick to learn and enjoy showing off their tricks; some do well in agility and obedience. Training to stop them from barking may be needed.

Designer dogs

Possible health problems?

Ear and breathing problems can occur, and poor tolerance to extremes of heat and cold.

● *The coats of these 8-week-old puppies will need daily attention.*

Cavachon

Time to maturity: 2 years
Male height: 10–12.5 in (25–32 cm)
Female height: 10–12.5 in (25–32 cm)
Weight: 12–18 lb (5.5–8 kg)
Average lifespan: 10–12 years

Originating in the U.S., these Cavalier King Charles Spaniels and Bichon Frise mixes are popular for their intelligent, loving nature and cute, teddy bear looks.

Personality Traits	Poor	Average	Good	E
Attitude toward other dogs				
Quietness				
Behavior at home				
Watchdog ability				
Good with children				
Ease of training				
Obedience to owner				

Color choices?

White and/or shades of brown, with mixed patches, spotting, and flecking of these colors are available.

How much grooming?

Cavachons shed their puppy coats as the adult coat grows in. It is best to groom early, removing tangles with a comb. Adults may be non-shedding, although some have seasonal changes. This luxurious, long, curly coat needs daily attention, with regular baths once or twice a month. Professional trimming is occasionally required, although some puppy owners learn to do this themselves.

Do they make good pets?

Cavachons are great family dogs, and are good with children and other pets. Loving, affectionate, and sociable, but they may not be the best watchdog.

What home suits them?

Their size makes them ideal for most homes and apartments, and they can be trained to stay within property boundaries.

How much exercise and stimulation?

Active and alert, Cavachons enjoy daily walks with playtime, and owners who enjoy teaching them tricks.

Is puppy training easy?

Training is easy, as they are intelligent and biddable, and often good at obedience activities.

Possible health problems?

Both parent breeds have health issues, so ear, eye, and heart problems are possible, as are syringomyelia (fluid filled cavities within the spinal cord) and hypothyroidism (lack of thyroid hormone).

● This charming little dog (12 weeks) may not always have a non-shedding coat, and will need grooming daily with some trimming as necessary.

Make training fun for this puppy, as he will respond best to stimulating methods of learning.

Cockapoo

Other names: Cockerpoo, Spoodle

Time to maturity: 2.5 years
Male height: 10–15 in (25–38 cm)
Female height: 10–15 in (25–38 cm)
Weight: 12–24 lb (5.5–11 kg)
Average lifespan: 14–15 years

Cockapoos result from mixing American or English Cocker Spaniels with Poodles. Bred in the U.S. since 1950, they even have their own species clubs.

Personality Traits	Poor	Average	Good	Excellent
Attitude toward other dogs				
Quietness				
Behavior at home				
Watchdog ability				
Good with children				
Ease of training				
Obedience to owner				

Color choices?

Solid colors of black, tan/buff, red, brown, brindle, sable, silver, cream, white, and occasionally merle are available. Some are white with patches of color, other spots, or ticking (freckles).

How much grooming?

Most have coats somewhere between Poodle and Cocker type, although they may be similar to either parent. All coats need daily grooming using brushes and wide-toothed combs, and monthly bathing.

Do they make good pets?

Popular as family pets, they combine the Cocker's outgoing personality with a Poodles' reduced coat shedding. They can inherit their personality from either parent breed, and generally are intelligent, friendly, playful, and loving pets.

What home suits them?

Active and versatile, Cockapoos prefer homes with yards, but will adapt quite readily to apartment living.

How much exercise and stimulation?

Cockapoos do best with regular daily exercise, and intelligent puppies need stimulation through play, walks, training, flyball, or agility.

Is puppy training easy?

These puppies love to please, and with early training should do well.

Possible health problems?

They are robust and healthy, but they can have luxating patellas (dislocating kneecaps), eye problems, and are susceptible to ear infections.

● *These two 7-week-old puppies are just growing their longer coats, but it will be some time before it becomes clear if they have inherited hypoallergenic coats.*

Puggle

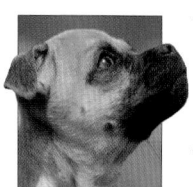

Time to maturity: 2 years
Male height: 13–15 in (33–38 cm)
Female height: 13–15 in (33–38 cm)
Weight: 18–30 lb (8–14 kg)
Average lifespan: 10–15 years

One of the three most popular designer dogs, Puggles are Beagles crossed with Pugs. They were developed in 2000 for owners wanting a distinctive type of dog.

Personality Traits	Poor	Average	Good	E
Attitude toward other dogs				
Quietness				
Behavior at home				
Watchdog ability				
Good with children				
Ease of training				
Obedience to owner				

Color choices?

Fawn, red, tan, lemon, black, or various particolors are available.

How much grooming?

The short, dense undercoat and longer top coat shed, and so they need weekly grooming. Cleaning and drying eyes and skin folds daily prevents the onset of infections; bathe only when needed.

Do they make good pets?

Good-natured, sociable, intelligent puppies, Puggles are playful, cuddly, love people, and are friendly with other pets. Their hunting instincts may put smaller pets at risk.

What home suits them?

They adapt to most homes, or apartments if well-exercised, but Puggles bark or howl a lot, and are unsuitable for working owners.

● *Puggles have a tendency to beg for food leading to overeating. This puppy should not be overindulged or obesity may result.*

How much exercise and stimulation?

Puggles need good daily walks with play time; exercise and agility preve them from becoming unruly. Walk them on a leash, because Beagle instincts may ignore recalls in preference to interesting smells. Good stimulation and socialization produce well-rounded dogs.

Is puppy training easy?

Neither parent breed is easy to train. Intelligent but stubborn, Puggles respond to positive reinforcement training using rewards, play, and a lot of praise. Patience will be essential in traini a Puggle to achieve good and consistent results.

Possible health problems

Breathing problems (if mostly Pug-like), eye problems (cherr eye), hypothyroidism (low thyroid levels), patella luxation (dislocating kneecaps), hip dysplasia (malformation) epilepsy, and allergies can occ

Schnoodle

Time to maturity: 2 years
Standard height: 15–26 in (38–66 cm)
Standard weight: 20–75 lb (9–34 kg)
Miniature height: 10–12 in (25–30 cm)
Miniature weight: 6–10 lb (3–4.5 kg)
Average lifespan: 10–15 years
Based on largest and smallest parent sizes

Currently rising to canine stardom, this Schnauzer/Poodle mix is a popular family dog in three sizes, with a low shed coat, and endearing personality.

Personality Traits	Poor	Average	Good	Excellent
Attitude toward other dogs			●	
Quietness		●		
Behavior at home			●	
Watchdog ability				●
Good with children				●
Ease of training				●
Obedience to owner			●	

Color choices?

Colors are black, gray, silver, brown, apricot, sable, black with white or tan, and particolors.

How much grooming?

The non-shedding coats are either soft and silky, needing daily brushing, or wiry, needing less brushing; both need trimming bimonthly. Clean the ears weekly.

Do they make good pets?

Schnoodles are good watchdogs, love car rides, and are clever, friendly, fun-loving, good with children, and great family pets.

At 8 weeks old, this little Schnoodle is developing a thicker coat that will need daily brushing.

Devoted and affectionate to owners, and friendly toward other pets, they can suffer separation anxiety if left on their own.

What home suits them?

Schnoodles adapt to most locations, but eventual size matters, as small dogs suit apartment living, while larger dogs prefer homes with yards or countryside locations, and the opportunity for plenty of activity.

How much exercise and stimulation?

Schnoodles need daily exercise, activity, and stimulation.

Is puppy training easy?

Schnoodles are naturally protective, strong-willed, excitable and active, not unlike their parent breeds. Easily trained, they excel at obedience, agility, and flyball, and make ideal therapy dogs.

Designer dogs

Possible health problems?

Addison's disease (an endocrine disorder), gastric torsion, diabetes, epilepsy, Legg-Perthes syndrome (hip deformity), kneecap dislocation, eye disease, and ear and anal gland infections can occur.

● *Smaller puppies at this age are likely to be miniatures, but buyers should check the parents' heights.*

Labradoodle

Time to maturity: 2 years
Standard height: 21–25 in (53–63.5 cm)
Standard weight: 50–66 lb (23–30 kg)
Miniature height: 14–16.5 in (36–42 cm)
Miniature weight: 15.5–28 lb (7–13 kg)
Average lifespan: 12–14 years
Based on largest and smallest parent sizes

The Labradoodle is a Labrador Retriever and Standard or Miniature Poodle mix that was first bred in 1955 as a guide/therapy dog. They are now popular as family pets.

Personality Traits	Poor	Average	Good	E
Attitude toward other dogs				
Quietness				
Behavior at home				
Watchdog ability				
Good with children				
Ease of training				
Obedience to owner				

Color choices?

Colors are black, chocolate, cafe, gold, apricot, red, silver, chalk, cream, and various particolors.

How much grooming?

Labradoodle coats vary between wiry to soft, and can be straight, wavy, or curly. Grooming daily is best, using brushes and combs that are suitable for the coat texture. They may have hypoallergenic, non-shedding coats, but not always. They simply shed less, and have less odor. Professional grooming may be necessary.

Do they make good pets?

These are friendly, energetic, enthusiastic, good-natured puppies, and ideal family dogs. Often too rough for small children, their good natured boisterousness is usually fine with other pets.

What home suits them?

Labradoodles are unsuitable for apartment living; homes with yards are preferable.

How much exercise and stimulation?

Exercise needs are dependent on size, but around one hour daily, and stimulation levels need to be high. Puppies are destructive if bored.

Is puppy training easy?

Sensible, patient, and consistent reward-based training is the best approach with this eager-to-please, easy-to-train, intelligent puppy.

Possible health problems?

Addison's disease (an endocrine disorder), hip dysplasia (malformation), and eye problems (research indicates higher incidences in Labradoodles than in their parents can occur. Ear infections may be frequent.

● *At 9 weeks these puppies are ready to go home with new owners*

Goldendoodle

Time to maturity: 2 years
Male height: 24–26 in (61–66 cm)
Female height: 22–23 in (56–58.5 cm)
Weight: 45–70 lb (20–32 kg)
Average lifespan: 12–14 years

Goldendoodles were developed in Australia and North America as guide dogs for owners prone to allergies by mixing Poodles with Golden Retrievers.

Personality Traits	Poor	Average	Good	Excellent
Attitude toward other dogs				
Quietness				
Behavior at home				
Watchdog ability				
Good with children				
Ease of training				
Obedience to owner				

Color choices?

Goldendoodles are black, sandy, gold, red, apricot, cream, or white.

How much grooming?

They have similar coats to either parent, and some in-between. Low- or non-shedding coats require daily grooming with slicker brushes and wide-toothed combs. Use slicker or pin brushes on shedding coats. Ears need regular cleaning.

Do they make good pets?

Person-oriented and affectionate with owners and other pets, Goldendoodles are calm and good natured and great with children. They are used as therapy/assistance dogs, and are suitable for allergy sufferers, although this quality depends on coat type.

What home suits them?

Goldendoodles are usually mixed with standard-height parents (occasionally with Miniature Poodles), but all usually suit larger homes with yards and walking close by.

How much exercise and stimulation?

These active dogs require daily walks, with stimulation through play and activities such as agility, obedience, and bird hunting.

Is puppy training easy?

Highly intelligent, these dogs are very trainable.

● *Puppies like this 7-week-old have coats more like their Poodle parent.*

Possible health problems?

Hip dysplasia (malformation), inherited eye problems, von Willebrand's disease (a blood disorder), and ear infections can occur.

Index

Picture Credits

The publisher wishes to thank the individual photographers and picture libraries who have contributed photographs reproduced in this book. Their pictures are here credited by page number. Note: t = top, c = centre, b = bottom, l = left, r = right.

David Dalton: 162tl.

John Daniels: 87t, 128c, 06tl.

Dreamstime.com
kellyphoto: 197t.
elfreth: 180tl.
Jupco Smokovski: 4.

Fotolia
glama: 108c.
Hallaloo Twisty: 207t, 207b.
purmalet06: 128tl.
ottelhund: 133b.

ll's Pet Nutrition:
7 (based on a growth
art first published in *Hill's*

Atlas of Growth, 1998.
Reprinted with permission by the copyright owner, Hill's Pet Nutrition, Inc.)

Interpet Archive: 2, 12 (teeth cleaning), 13 (diagram), 19t, 19b, 22t, 45t.

iStockphoto.com
101cats: 191t, 191b.
Aldra: 13t.
Vyacheslav Anyakin: 11 (meat).
BrandyTaylor: 171t.
craftvision: 164c.
DaydreamsGirl: 163t.
hnijjar007: 176c.
Eric Isselée: 223.
Erik Lam: 14c (puppy).
Stacey Gamez: 23cl.
icelandr: 169t.
LivingImages: 160tl.
LockieCurrie: 169b.
Valentin Mosichev: 11 (tomatoes).
Xseon: 200tl.
Zts: 11 (carrots).

Alun John: 113t.

The Kennel Club, London:
55t (Diane Pearce), 111t (Farlap), 129b (Alice van Kempen), 133t (Alice van Kempen), 181b (Farlap), 206c.

Pictures of Pets/ GotPetsOnline: 129t (Meghan).

Geoff Rogers (for Interpet): 12 (puppy handling).

Shutterstock.com
Africa Studio: 12 (puppy and chew).
Stefan Petru Andronache: 192c.
AnetaPics: 193t, 218t.
Anneka: 142tl.
Yuri Arcurs: 102c.
Art_man: 104b.
Inna Astakhova: 177t, 177b.
Denis Babenko: 112tl.
Baevskiy Dmitry: 158tl.
Gualberto Becerra: 171.
blanche: 44cr, 45b.
Anthony Bolan: 176tl.

Scott Bolster: 219b.
Dan Breckwoldt: 145t.
Joy Brown: 216tl.
Katrina Brown: 43t.
Tony Campbell: 166tl.
Paul Cotney: 20t.
cristovao: 153t.
Linn Currie: 50tl, 51c, 76c, 179cl.
cynoclub: 8 (carrier), 124c, 125t, 132tl, 186tl.
Frantisek Czanner: 175t.
Waldemar Dabrowski: 130tl, 135t, 141t, 199t, 204tl.
Dennis Dore: 93b.
eAlisa: 58tl.
Ermolaev Alexander: 3 (puppy eating), 10cl, 10br (puppy).
Ewa Studio: 134c.
exposurefantasy: 152tl.
Falcona: 32tl.
filmfoto: 46tl.
Galen D.: 205b.
gillmar: 139t.
Glenkar: 173t, 173b.
Warren Goldswain: 21br.
Antonio Guillem: 123t.
Hannahmariah: 92tl, 221t.